Transaction Costs, Markets and Hierarchies

Transaction Costs, Markets and Hierarchies

Edited by
Christos Pitelis

BLACKWELL
Oxford UK & Cambridge USA

Copyright © Basil Blackwell Ltd 1993

First published 1993

Blackwell Publishers
108 Cowley Road
Oxford OX4 1JF
UK

238 Main Street, Suite 501
Cambridge, Massachusetts 02142
USA

British Library Cataloguing in Publication Data

A CIP catalogue record for this book is available from the British Library.

Library of Congress Cataloging-in-Publication Data

Transaction costs, markets and hierarchies/edited by
Christos Pitelis.
p.   cm.
Includes bibliographical references and index.
ISBN 0-631-18371-X.—ISBN 0-631-18898-3 (pbk.)
1. Transaction costs. 2. Institutional economics.   I. Pitelis,
Christos.
HB846.3.S87   1993
658.4′063—dc20   92-30554   CIP

Typeset in 10 on 12 pt Times
by Best-set Typesetter Ltd., Hong Kong
Printed in Great Britain by T.J. Press Ltd., Padstow, Cornwall

This book is printed on acid-free paper

Contents

List of Contributors

Keith Cowling, Professor of Economics, University of Warwick, Coventry

Michael Dietrich, Lecturer in Economics, University of Sheffield

Gregory K. Dow, Professor of Economics, University of Alberta, Edmonton

William M. Dugger, Professor of Economics, DePaul University, Chicago

Frederick C. v. N. Fourie, Professor of Economics, University of the Orange Free State, Bloemfontein

Geoffrey M. Hodgson, University Lecturer in Economics, Judge Institute of Management Studies, University of Cambridge

Neil M. Kay, Professor of Economics, University of Strathclyde, Glasgow

Paul Marginson, Lecturer in Industrial Relations, Business School, University of Warwick, Coventry

Christos Pitelis, Barclays Bank Lecturer in Industrial Organization and Corporate Strategy, Judge Institute of Management Studies, and Fellow in Economics, Queens' College, University of Cambridge

Malcolm C. Sawyer, Professor of Economics, University of Leeds

Roger Sugden, Director of the Research Centre for Industrial Strategy, The Birmingham Business School, University of Birmingham

Steve Thompson, Senior Lecturer in Economics, University of Manchester Institute of Science and Technology

Mike Wright, Professor of Financial Studies, University of Nottingham

Introduction

This introduction contains slightly amended versions of summaries of the chapters in the volume, written by the authors themselves.

The first chapter, 'Transaction costs, markets and hierarchies: the issues', by Christos Pitelis, aims to provide an introduction and overall perspective to the volume. Following a brief account of the transaction costs, markets and hierarchies perspective, there is a discussion of the reasons for the recent recognition of its importance. This is followed by a summary account of some of the existing and potential conceptual criticisms of the perspective and a short guide to other books and articles where more can be learnt about the theory. Next there is a short account of the individual contributions to the volume, including the reasons for their inclusion and their logical sequence. Some potential limitations and criticisms of the book are also stressed.

Chapter 2, 'The nature and role of the market', by Malcolm Sawyer, begins by discussing the ways in which markets and market forces have been conceptualized in economic analysis. It is argued that the conceptualization in general equilibrium analysis is unsatisfactory, with all transactions between people reduced to exchange relations. Arguments that a 'pure' market would not be sustainable are then reviewed. The idea that firms and markets are alternative modes of coordination is then discussed and viewed as inadequate in that it overlooks the quite different functions performed by firms and by markets. It is then argued that prices considered as signals do not convey sufficient information and that prices have a range of non-allocative roles.

In chapter 3, 'In the beginning there were markets?', Frederick Fourie argues that the transaction and contract approaches have definite limitations in analysing the nature of, and relation between, firms and markets. These limitations flow from the exclusive focus on the role of *transactions* and the inter-*individual* nature of these exchanges.

It is demonstrated that the generic firm, the firm *as such*, cannot be distinctively characterized exclusively in terms of market transactions. Therefore the distinguishing mark of the firm as such (as against markets and as against other organizations) cannot be the supersession of the price mechanism. More particularly the existence of the firm as such cannot be explained by transaction cost arguments. The employment decision of a firm cannot be explained by transaction cost considerations either. Finally, not only transactions (exchanges) but also rivalry relations within markets are relevant in the determination of the boundary of the firm.

An alternative approach has as starting points: (a) the intrinsic, generic dissimilarity between the firm and the market, and (b) the real existence of the firm as a cohesive, durable institution. This is shown to provide consistent characterizations of the differences between firms and markets, between internal and external relations, and between employment, integration and subcontracting. More basically the author warns against trying to explain everything in terms of market relations, and argues that exclusively individualistic explanations that disregard the existence of real societal structures encounter debilitating problems.

Chapter 4, 'Control, markets and firms', provides some foundations for an alternative theory of the firm. Keith Cowling and Roger Sugden use a critique of Coase's 1937 *Economica* paper as a basis for defining a firm as the means of coordinating production from one centre of strategic decision-making. This rejects Coase's focus on market versus non-market transactions in favour of a concern with the essential qualities of trans-actions. The authors then explore ideas in Williamson's 1975 volume, *Markets and Hierarchies*. This volume is said to pose two basic questions, both answered with a focus on transactions costs and efficiency. The first is: why markets versus hierarchies? Cowling and Sugden see this question as fundamentally flawed and instead suggest: why are some transactions performed inside a firm and other performed outside a firm? It is argued that the answer to this does not concentrate on transactions costs. The second question is: what organizational form within a hierarchy? This question is seen as relevant but as raising issues and requiring answers different from and, to some extent, at odds with those in *Markets and Hierarchies*. For instance, the authors emphasize the importance of distributional considerations. They also comment on the central features of Japanese firms. It is argued that adaptations towards 'J-mode struc-tures' currently being made in Western 'H-mode' firms do not undermine the central thesis.

After clarifying both the concept of the firm and the concept of trans-action costs, Geoffrey Hodgson claims in chapter 5, 'Transaction costs and the evolution of the firm', that the transaction costs concept must refer in the main to problems of radical uncertainty and lack of knowledge. In addition, it cannot be simultaneously combined with both the notion of omniscient calculation and Herbert Simon's idea of bounded rationality. However, rejecting the idea of omniscient calculation means that we are in want of an explanation as to why a governance structure associated with lower transaction costs should predominate over another. The main viable alternative mode of transaction cost analysis would seem to be an evolutionary one. But an evolutionary analysis poses a problem as to whether the individual or the firm is the unit of selection, and this is related to the 'appropriability critique' of Gregory Dow (see chapter 6). To protect against the appropriability critique, the firm itself must be regarded as a unit of selection, rather than the individuals within it. As a result, the most viable arguments for regarding the firm as such a collective entity bring us closer to the propositions of the 'old' rather than the 'new' institutionalism. Furthermore, the evolutionary framework of analysis does not give support to some key propositions concerning hierarchy and efficiency advanced by Williamson.

In chapter 6, 'The appropriability critique of transaction cost economics', Gregory Dow examines the claim, made by transaction cost economics, that governance structures maximize the aggregate surplus derived from production and exchange. This claim presumes that utility can be costlessly transferred among the individual input suppliers who constitute a production coalition. But in fact there are good theoretical and empirical reasons to doubt the feasibility of such side payments, especially in the labour market. If *ex ante* side payments cannot be arranged, the *ex post* distribution of quasi-rents matters. In this case, viable governance structures must obey appropriability constraints, which are independent of social efficiency criteria.

Transactions costs economics has tried to demonstrate that the evolution of the firm from the putting-out system to the large modern corporation has taken place primarily for efficiency reasons. In contrast, radical economics has stressed the search for superior means of management control over labour in its account of the evolution of the firm. In chapter 7, 'Power and efficiency in the firm: understanding the employment relationship', Paul Marginson develops a critique of the transactions costs analysis of the employment relationship as an efficient institution. Drawing on logical and empirical lines of argument, he shows that: hierarchy may be used in the interests of one party rather than both; workers' bargaining power need not rest on their possession of firm-specific skills; the peculiarities of the labour contract are not reducible to the problem of opportunism; and efficiency considerations cannot account for the firm's evolution. Considerations of power, it is argued, are essential to an adequate theorization of the firm. Existing work from a power perspective is, however, criticized for its preoccupation with the exercise of coercive means of labour control by employers. Greater attention needs to be paid to the potential of non-coercive forms of labour management for securing commensurate as distinct from perfunctory performance on the part of the workforce.

Orthodox transaction cost economics suggests that the rationale for firms may be understood in terms of minimization of transaction costs given exogenously specified technologically separable activities. In chapter 8, 'Transaction costs . . . and revenues', Michael Dietrich suggests an alternative rationale: different organizational configurations facilitate changes in the activities themselves, characterized as governance structure benefits, based on revenue generating ability. Consideration of governance structure benefits implies the endogenization of transaction (product-market) characteristics. Transaction cost economics must assume these characteristics unchanged when comparing governance structures to avoid analytical incoherence.

A general framework is developed that recognizes both governance structure benefits and costs. Using this framework it is shown that orthodox transaction cost economics is organizational general equilibrium comparative statics. The introduction of governance structure benefits allows a dynamic analysis based on idiosyncratic organizational advantage and differential economic power. In dynamic circumstances idiosyncratic advantage is arguably more important than governance structure costs for understanding the rationale for the firm. Differential economic power is endemic in a non-zero sum world, an argument that is applied to the development of factory organization and multinational corporation operations. The partial and constrained nature of transaction cost economics, which ignores useful avenues of investigation, is therefore shown to be based on implicit *ceteris paribus* assumptions, which are unnecessary in a more general framework.

Several important implications for the role of the state in the economy flow from transaction cost economics. Yet these implications have been largely ignored in the transaction cost literature. William Dugger in chapter 9, 'Transaction cost economics and the state', identifies the resulting gap in the literature and makes a small contribution towards filling it. Investigating the gap leads to several decidedly non-*laissez-faire* conclusions. The state plays a determining role in the institutionalization of exchange transactions. The state's definitions and protections of property rights are essential to exchange. Furthermore, the state helps to establish, interpret and enforce a whole series of rules and procedures governing specific exchange processes. Principles of transaction cost analysis raise serious doubts about the efficiency of contracting out or privatizing public goods and services. In conceptualization of the role of the state, instead of being seen as intervening in the exchange process, the state should be seen as an important participant in the exchange process. The state is best seen as a transaction cost minimizer, not as an inefficient intervener. Furthermore, two kinds of states serve the role of transaction cost minimizer: the traditional nation state and the rising corporate state. The choice of which state to rely upon as a transaction cost minimizer in different situations is exceedingly important and is fraught with efficiency and equity implications.

Much of the literature concerning corporate governance and internal organization has focused upon the appropriate degree of decentralization within the given boundaries of the firm. There has been relatively little attention devoted to the dismantling of hierarchies. In chapter 10, 'Markets, hierarchies and markets again', Steve Thompson and Mike Wright analyse the problems of internalization, and consider the conditions under which divestment (externalization) might occur and the factors that influence whether or not it will occur. The chapter examines conditions relating to both conglomerate divestiture and divestment involving trading relationships (vertical or horizontal). It is argued that a key element in the optimal location of asset ownership is where individuals have the greatest incentive to maximize value. Where it is not possible to achieve the appropriate level of incentives inside the firm, divestment may be appropriate. Moreover, new organizational forms and financing instruments make divestment an increasingly feasible option.

Neil Kay in chapter 11, 'Markets, false hierarchies and the role of asset specificity', conducts a reappraisal of the transaction cost approach in the light of Oliver Williamson's contribution to the subject. It is argued that there are difficulties with Williamson's approach in view of the restrictions he has imposed on what he considers to be the essential foundations of transaction cost analysis. In particular the reliance on asset specificity is especially problematic and creates critical limitations on the ability of the framework to deal with internalization problems beyond the case of vertical integration. It is argued in chapter 11 that asset *non*-specificities in the form of economics of scope and public goods are likely to encourage internalization such as corporate diversification and multinational strategies. Consideration is also given to other difficulties associated with Williamson's interpretation of transaction cost economics, especially the analysis of the evolution of the M-form corporation and conglomerateness. The implications of the absence of a satisfactory evolutionary or decision-making selection mechanism for organizational forms in Williamson's framework are also discussed.

There are two main aims in chapter 12, 'On transactions (costs) and markets and (as) hierarchies', by Christos Pitelis'. The first is to establish two interrelated propositions: that only the employment relation has a potentially legitimate claim in providing an explanation of the Coasean (multiple person, hierarchical) firm; and that all employment relationships are hierarchical, Coasean firms. The second aim is to assess critically Coase's own explanation of why Coasean firms. It is suggested that in order to explain why there are Coasean firms, one also has to address the fundamental question: why transactions, transaction costs, exchange, (thus) markets and firms, including the unitary (single producer) firm and the Coasean firm? It is claimed that an answer to these questions can be provided by focusing on production *and* exchange, which are inseparable as the latter presupposes the former and the former is realized through the latter. The reasons for the very existence of production, exchange and production for exchange, are then argued to be the benefits from the division of labour. The emergence of the Coasean firm is said to be explainable in terms of furthering the benefits from the exploitation of the division of labour. Coase's own early discussion of the importance of the division of labour is criticized as inadequate. Some further issues are then raised and concluding remarks follow.

1

Transaction Costs, Markets and Hierarchies: the Issues

CHRISTOS PITELIS

'The nature of the firm', Ronald Coase's classic 1937 article, is arguably transforming the nature of mainstream economic theory – from a mono-institutional theory to a duo-institutional, at first, and gradually to a poly-institutional one. In the pre-Coase era, economics was exclusively concerned with the analysis of the allocation of scarce resources through the price mechanism, 'the market'. The aim of economic theory in this mono-institutional world was the analysis of the existence, stability and optimality of *market* equilibrium. One of the greatest achievements of neoclassical general equilibrium theory was the provision of a proof that, under certain assumptions, the market could generate an equilibrium, which moreover was optimal, in the Pareto sense, i.e. no change in it could improve an agent's position without rendering that of somebody else worse (see McKenzie, 1989). As McKenzie observes, 'The institution whose phenomena are the primary subject of economic analysis is *the market*, made up of a group of economic agents who buy and sell goods and services to one another' (p. 1, emphasis added). Notable by their absence in this construct are *firms*. In the theory of price, Demsetz (1988) observes that firms are 'simply a rhetorical device adopted to facilitate a discussion of the price system' (p. 146).

Following Coase's article this was no longer true – not fully anyway. It might have taken some time before Coase's 'fundamental insight' was taken seriously (leading to more than one complaint from him; e.g. Coase, 1991), but when it was, economic theory had entered a new era – a duo-institutional one. In this new era resources are allocated by two *different* institutions, markets and firms. An important reason for the ultimate recognition of his contribution to the theory of the firm, Coase (1991) submits, was his other classic, the 1960 article on 'The problem of social cost'. In this Coase raised the issue of the third major institutional device in market economies, the law and the state. In this way, Coase has also been responsible for the third phase of economic analysis, (eventually) multi-institutionalism. In this phase it is acknowledged that the law and the state are also institutional devices for the allocation of resources, different to both markets and firms. This necessitates an analysis of the emergence, functions, evolution and possible failures of these three important institutions of market economies – the market, the firm and the state. Today, one could legitimately conceive of extending the list to include, among others, the family, norms and customs, 'clans', associations and even religion. Economics is becoming exciting now, and this is in large part due to Coase's two classics! His receipt of the 1991 Nobel Prize in economics confirms the profession's recognition of that.

What Coase said in print in 1937 (already there in embryo by 1932; Coase, 1991) was obvious enough for everyone to see – *ex post* as always! – namely that resource allocation in market economies was taking place not just through changes in relative prices (the market) but also not through such changes, but rather through 'entrepreneurial' decisions, unrelated to relative price changes. Such decisions would normally take the form of 'commands', or 'directions', making 'authority' the distinguishing feature of the firm from the market, in which no such authority was present. In this sense the price mechanism (market) and the firm were two *different* ways of resource allocation, and indeed not just different but *substitute*: 'the distinguishing mark of the firm is the supersession of the price mechanism' (Coase, 1937, p. 389). The firm, that is, replaces or supersedes the market, which raises the important question: *why?*

In his observation of the authority of the firm versus the 'democracy' of the market, Coase was certainly not the first (is one ever?). Karl Marx for one comments that 'Division of labour within the workshop implies the undisputed authority of the capitalist over men . . . . The division of labour within the society brings into contact independent commodity-producers, who acknowledge no other authority but that of competition, of the coercion exerted by the pressure of their mutual interests' (in Putterman, 1986, p. 56). Marx goes on to observe that, while 'division of labour in society at large . . . is common to economic societies most diverse, division of labour in the workshop, as practised by manufacture, is a special creation of the capitalist mode of production alone' (ibid., p. 57).

Where Coase's undisputed originality lay, however, was in the answer he provided to the 'why' above. In brief, he claimed that the very presence of the firm implied that the price mechanism had somehow failed. Had it not, firms should not have emerged at all. This failure of the market, moreover, should be attributed to the fact that allocating resources through the market costs something and that the supersession of the market through the authority of the firm helps to reduce such 'marketing costs'. In this sense, the firm *exists* because in certain cases it is a more efficient means of resource allocation than the price mechanism, in terms of 'marketing costs' (the cost of using the price mechanism; Coase, 1937, p. 403). The marketing costs mentioned by Coase were the costs of discovering the relative prices and of concluding separate contracts for each individual exchange-transaction. Costs of contracting, for example, could be reduced if a factor of production (entrepreneur) did not have to draw a series of contracts with other factors of production, but rather replaced a series of such contracts with one long-term contract, according to which the other factors agreed to obey the direction of the employer, within certain limits. This replacement of a series of spot contracts with just one long-term contract reduces the costs of contracting and (thus) increases efficiency in resource allocation. The emergent relationship is defined by Coase as a 'firm'. He goes on to observe that the emergence of a firm owing to reduced contracting costs is of more importance in the case of services – labour – than it is in the case of commodities.

Coase's paper was nearly totally overlooked for over thirty years. The first to provide an analysis reminiscent of Coase's was Stephen Hymer in his 1960 thesis on the 'multinational firm', which was not published until 1976. Hymer did not seem to be aware of Coase's views at the time, although he referred to Coase in a 1969 paper (see Pitelis and Sugden, 1991). Indeed, contributions along Coasean lines during the early 1970s were primarily by theorists of the multinational firm, (e.g. Hymer, 1970; McManus, 1972). In this same area, Buckley and Casson (1976) have explained the multinational firm in terms of failures in intermediate product markets in an apparent extension of the Coasean argument. At around the same time, Williamson (1975) published his *Markets and Hierarchies*, where Coase's analysis was explicitly developed.

As already mentioned, 1960 saw Coase's other classic 'The problem of social cost', where the emergence of law and the state is explained along much the same lines as the firm before it. Arrow (1970) has pursued further this type of analysis, generalizing for the first time the market failure theory of the state, in terms of 'transaction costs', defined as costs of running the economic system. Until that time, 'market failure' was widely recognized by economists to be a reason for the breaking down of the 'first fundamental theorem of welfare economics' (that a market economy can generate Pareto-efficient allocation of resources) but such failures were attributed to *instances* of market failures, such as externalities (interdependencies not conveyed through prices), public goods (characterized by jointness in supply and non-excludability) and/or oligopoly or monopoly (departures of prices from the competitive ideal). Arrow claimed that such instances could be attributed to a generic factor, *transaction costs*.

Following Williamson's 1975 contribution, the term transaction costs has now fully replaced Coase's early 'marketing costs'. Coase (1991) himself adopts this term and describes his analysis in the 1937 and 1960 papers respectively as follows: 'Transaction costs were used in the one case to show that if they are not included in the analysis the firm has no purpose, while in the other I saw, I thought, that if transaction costs were not introduced into the analysis . . . the law had no purpose' (p. 62). Besides his 1960 article, Coase considers Williamson's contributions as an important reason for the resurgence of interest in his work on the firm. Noteworthy is that the unearthing of the article on the firm has followed often independent transaction costs type contributions on the *state* and the *multinational* firm. Indeed, one could claim that contributions in the literature of the multinational are the third major factor for the current interest in transaction costs analysis.

Williamson's concern in his 1975 book and subsequent contributions (Williamson, 1981, 1986, among others) was to use transaction costs analysis to explain organizational (in particular market) failures, and (thus) the emergence of *hierarchies* (firms) from (failed) markets, for reasons related to their ability to economize in market transaction costs. Besides Coase's own focus on searching and contracting costs, transaction costs can also be taken to include costs of measurement, and policing and enforcing agreements (see Eggertson, 1991, for a survey). However, Williamson went beyond simply describing transaction costs, to explaining them in terms of human and environmental factors. These are bounded rationality (limits in the acquisition and processing of information), opportunism (self-interest seeking with guile) and asset specificity (the investment on specific assets by agents, which tends to lock them into transactions by generating sunk costs and thus high costs of exit, and (thus) leads them to protracted bargaining). For Williamson it is the pervasiveness of these factors that generates often excessive market transaction costs. The hierarchy (firm) can often attenuate the problems associated with the above factors for reasons related to both a reduction in the number of exchanges (e.g. Coase's long-term employment contract example) *and* the ability of authority to end prolonged disputes. Another reason is the alleged creation of a common viewpoint by the members of a hierarchy–firm: convergent expectations. To the extent that these factors can alleviate the problems generated from the three factors mentioned above, the hierarchy (firm) can replace the market and (thus) reduce market transaction costs and increase efficiency.

Following Coase (1937), Williamson observes that hierarchies do not fully eliminate transaction costs. Hierarchies have transaction costs of their own, in part resulting from their tendency to blunt the 'high-powered' incentives that market signals provide. In this sense, there will be a point where the advantages of internalization will be exhausted and no more of it will be observed. When the cost of organizing *the same* transactions within the firm or across the market (or another firm) is the same, no further internalization will occur, so the transaction will be 'left' to be 'organized' by the market. In this way the *transaction costs, markets and hierarchies* (TCMH) scenario can explain both hierarchies (the firm) *and* markets (the non-full supersession of the market by the firm) in terms of transaction costs economizing. In this sense the observed institutional mix (market, hierarchy) can be said to be one that is efficiency increasing.

Williamson has applied the TCMH perspective to explain a number of important issues relating to resource coordination, including the 'employment relation', vertical integration, the M-form organization, conglomerate diversification and the multinational corporation (e.g. Williamson, 1981, 1986). In all cases transaction costs related problems are seen to be alleviated through the internalization of markets: the labour market in the case of the employment relation; the external capital market in the case of the M-form; and the intermediate products market in the case of the conglomerate firm and the transnational corporation (TNC). With regard to the employment relation in particular, this can be explained in terms of idiosyncratic transactions and asymmetric knowledge. The acquisition of idiosyncratic experiences (job-related skills) increases employees' bargaining power over that of the employers. This and employee opportunism generate high transaction costs of external labour markets. Their internalization does not fully solve the problem of information asymmetrics, but alleviates problems of opportunism by the provision of incentives by employers to employees to cooperate, including the attachment of the wage rate to the job, not the workers, which is said to reduce individual bargaining and thus opportunism. Employer's opportunism is reduced because of the 'reputation' constraints, a point also stressed by Coase (1991), namely the fear that firms cheating will become known quickly and, for example, fail to attract good workers in the future. The existence of unions can be seen in this framework as an additional institutional device for monitoring the firm's commitments, thus facilitating the reduction of employer opportunism (see Malcolmson, 1982).

All in all, the TCMH perspective has provided an impressive research agenda. The multi-institutional nature of resource allocation and more generally of the coordination of economic and social activity is recognized, and the nature of markets, firms (including their internal organizational forms) and the state is being examined in terms of their transactional efficiency properties. Transaction costs economics are gradually finding applications in fields as (apparently) diverse as labour economics, public economics, economic history, industrial relations, industrial organization, organizational theory, 'human resources', micro- and macroeconomics, politics, sociology and law, thus allowing for once some hope for a unifying social sciences framework. This and some estimates that for the USA, for example, transaction costs may be as high as 50 per cent of the gross domestic product (North and Wallis, quoted in Coase, 1991) suggest that one can disregard the TCMH perspective only at a cost. To the above one should add the revolutionary policy implica- tions of the TCMH perspective, notably its challenge to the long held suspicion of monopoly and oligopoly in traditional welfare economics and the theory of industrial organization. To the extent that monopolies can result for transactional efficiency reasons, they may not be that bad after all. In this sense, the TCMH perspective could be seen as a complement to the neoliberal attack of traditional policy approaches, in line with Demsetz's 'differential efficiency' hypothesis, Schumpeter's 'differential innovation' hypothesis, Williamson's own early analysis of the efficiency gains from monopoly power and more recently the theory of 'contestable markets' (see Pitelis, 1991, for critical assessment).

Despite the widely acknowledged as revolutionary contribution of the TCMH perspective (or because of that), it has also become the subject matter of substantial criticism, from a number of perspectives. Such criticisms concern either the general framework, or particular applications of it, in particular those of Oliver Williamson. To start from the very beginning, concerns have been raised regarding: the very definitions of a transaction, transaction costs, market and hierarchy; the extent to which transaction costs are operationalizable and markets and firms separable; the assumption of pre-existing markets and, relatedly, that existing hier- archies imply failed markets; the substitutability between markets and hierarchies assumption; the process through which (efficient) firms replace (inefficient) markets; the agents (if any) involved in the process and relatedly whether the emergent institutions are (Pareto) efficient and whether the objectives of the agents involved in this process are separable from the *existence* issue; the possible role of power in this process; the possible links between transaction costs and power considerations; the focus of the TCMH perspective on *exchange* (and transaction costs) at the expense of production and production costs; the treatment of other institutions and conventions, such as associations, 'clans' and networks, but also trust and attributes other than pure self-interest; the focus on transaction *costs* at the expense of *benefits* possibly arising from different institutional forms; the role of the state in the TCMH scenario; the importance attributed by Williamson to asset specificity; and the treatment by the TCMH perspective of alternative explanations of institutions.

Many such critical assessments of and alternatives to the TCMH perspective can be found in a number of readers, edited volumes and books. For example, Putterman (1986) has an excellent collection of already published work on 'the economic nature of the firm'. Clarke and McGuinness (1987) have a number of contributions that compare and contrast transaction costs and more conventional approaches to the issues of vertical integration, the M-form, conglomerates, transnationals, etc. Williamson and Winter (1991) have Coase's own views of his contribution and a collection of articles from a 1987 conference, including very powerful critiques such as Harold Demsetz's. Thompson et al. (1991) have readings mostly from already published papers on 'markets', 'hierarchies' and 'networks', and comparisons between these three models. Thompson and Wright (1988) have a number of commissioned, mainly new, articles, many of which extend (some critically) transaction costs analysis to the issue of internal organization of firms. A good, sympathetic book on transaction costs developments is Ricketts (1987). Hodgson (1988) has a powerful critique of a number of aspects of the TCMH scenario. More recently, Eggertson (1991) provides what is, in my view, the most comprehensive survey of transaction costs developments, including analysis of the role of the state. These last three books ignore issues of transnational firms, which are covered in detail in the edited volume by Pitelis and Sugden (1991). Sympathetic but critical extensions of transaction costs economics to the analysis of the state, economic history and institutional change are in North (1981, 1990). Pitelis (1991) has an extension of transaction costs reasoning to the issues of the state and macroeconomics (including theories of failure–crisis), and a critique of the whole framework. Comprehensive as it may seem, the above list is not exhaustive. This in itself is strongly indicative of the interest in the TCMH perspective.

Besides readers, edited volumes and books, a large number of articles have appeared on TCMH, many extending or applying the framework, some attempting critically to assess it. Although both types of work are useful and necessary, the starting point of this volume was the view of the editor that a necessary condition for a successful extension of a framework presupposes a clear understanding of its strengths and weaknesses. In this sense it was felt that there was a pressing need for a volume with contributed articles that assess critically the TCMH scenario either with an eye to improving it or with an eye to replacing it. Such a volume should be comprehensive in its coverage of the existing or possible conceptual problems relating to the TCMH perspective. There is a clear gap in the literature, as evidenced by my brief survey of the nature of existing contributions.

As well as the aforementioned 'gap' in the literature, a second, and related, reason for this volume is that there have now been a number of interesting and important conceptual critical assessments of the TCMH scenario, which broadly correspond to the criticisms outlined above. Some of these have been published in established journals, some others have appeared in less well known journals, in books or as work in progress. It was felt by the editor that bringing these together could both fill a gap and make more widely accessible these contributions. However, given that the original existing works were not written with an eye to providing a comprehensive critical assessment of TCMH, complementary to other works, the authors of these works were commissioned to adapt and/or synthesize and extend their existing contributions for the purposes of the book. The result was the present volume.

The brief summaries in the Introduction provide the reader with a view of the contributors' own views on their contributions. They are intended to provide an overall perspective to the volume, and also to facilitate the reader's decision to focus on the chapters or issues of his or her particular interests. For my purposes here, it suffices to note the nature of their contributions and the logic of their inclusion, including their sequence. In brief, chapter 2, by Malcolm Sawyer, commences with a discussion of the nature and role of markets in economic theory in general and TCMH in particular. Given the nearly exclusive focus of neoclassical economics on markets and their crucial role in the TCMH framework, such an analysis is felt to be a necessary starting point. As already noted, the starting point of the TCMH scenario is that of markets and market failure. In chapter 3, Frederick Fourie assesses critically the assumption that 'in the beginning there were markets' and finds it deficient. Part of Fourie's contribution concerns the very definition of a firm in the TCMH perspective. This problematic is maintained in the next contribution (chapter 4), by Keith Cowling and Roger Sugden, on 'Control, markets and firms'. It is noted, among other things, that *control* rather than ownership is the *sine qua non* of firm's nature, which raises important questions about the TCMH definition of 'the firm' and its delineation from 'the market'.

Following some further comments on definitional issues, the next contribution (chapter 5), by Geoff Hodgson, deals primarily with the arguments of the TCMH perspective relating to the process of replacement of inefficient institutions by more efficient ones. Here again the TCMH scenario is found to be deficient and alternative views nearer to the 'old institutionalism' are being offered. In chapter 6, Gregory Dow maintains the focus on the replacement process. However, the emphasis here is on the assumption of the TCMH scenario that efficient institutions result in increased aggregate surplus. In the absence of costlessly transferable utility through side-payments among individual input suppliers –

members of a coalition – it is claimed, the *ex post* distribution of quasi-rents matters. In such cases appropriability constraints to institutional change render questionable the assumption of efficiency-enhancing institutional changes. The focus of TCMH on efficiency is also retained in chapter 7, where Paul Marginson compares and contrasts the efficiency versus power approach to the emergence of the firm. An important claim here is that hierarchy may be used in the interests of one party rather than both parties, broadly in line with Stephen Marglin's (1974) perspective.

In chapter 8 Michael Dietrich takes issue with what he considers an important implicit assumption in the TCMH scenario: that different organizational configurations can be explained purely in terms of trans-action costs minimization, while potential governance structure benefits remain constant (or are simply ignored). Accounting for governance benefits (revenues), it is claimed, facilitates the adoption of a dynamic perspective in which idiosyncratic advantages are arguably more im-portant than costs of governance structures in explaining the firm.

Despite Coase's own seminal 1960 contribution on law and the state, Williamson has put exclusive focus on the market–firm juxtaposition. This limitation was rectified in part by Douglass North's (1981, 1990) neoclassical theories of the state, where transaction costs theorizing and elements of the 'public choice' perspective were skilfully combined in an attempt to explain the persistence of inefficient property rights in history. North's attempt is very much a *sui generis* case, and potentially a source of a new and more expanded research agenda than that of Williamson in its width; history, ideology and the recognition of potentially differential power on the part of actors (principals, agents) sets North apart from the conventional TCMH perspective. For our purposes here, i.e. the critical assessment of this perspective, William Dugger, in chapter 9, points to some important implications for the role of the state flowing from trans-action costs economics, which are left rather unattended by the TCMH scenario. Dugger attempts to fill this gap by pointing to the importance of the state in institutionalizing exchange transactions, by defining, pro-tecting and enforcing property rights. Dugger takes the view that the state should be seen as a transaction costs minimizer, not an inefficient inter-vener, which questions, among other things, the validity of some argu-ments in favour of privatization. Moreover, given different types of states, Dugger suggests, a choice emerges for which state to rely upon, on the basis of their transaction costs minimization properties.

Despite the acknowledgement of the transaction costs associated with hierarchies, the TCMH perspective paid exclusive attention to the trans-actional efficiency of hierarchy. Indeed, on the basis of this, one could be legitimately excused for believing that the transition from market to hierarchy is both unidirectional and the natural way ahead. Such views have been challenged both conceptually and empirically. This is particularly true today, given that the existence and success of less hierarchical, more market-based, small, innovative, flexible, customer-oriented firms has been notable enough to be elevated by Michael Best (1990) to the status of a 'new competition' which challenges the reign of the large hierarchy (see also Pyke et al., 1990). There are a number of issues raised by this perspective, including the extent to which such developments are, in part at least, orchestrated by big hierarchies, e.g. transnationals, as indeed predicted by Hymer (1970); see also Cowling and Sugden (1987) and Pitelis (1991). Still, this does not dispute the observation that the move to hierarchy need not be either unidirectional or 'natural', due to its inherent advantages. The theme of chapter 10 relates to this issue. Steve Thompson and Mike Wright provide a sympathetic critique of the TCMH perspective, by observing that the latter downplays the advantages of *externalization*, going back to the market. The authors focus on the disadvantages of internalization and consider under which conditions externalization might occur, as well as the factors influencing this occurrence. The internalization–externalization choice is seen as being in part at least dependent on the achievement of appropriate incentive levels within firms and on organizational and other factors, which facilitate externalization.

Chapter 11 represents an internal critique of the TCMH perspective. Neil Kay argues that Williamson departs from Coase's own early focus, in representing the foundations of the TCMH perspective as being internal versus external markets. For Kay this represents a false construct of hierarchy. It is then suggested that Williamson's explanations of the M-form and the conglomerate, and his natural selection arguments, are logically flawed. Concerning the transnational firm, this is argued to be the result of non-specificity too, rather than just specificity of assets. This is in line with Demsetz (1988) and Coase (1991) himself, who have both critiqued Williamson's emphasis on asset specificity. Kay concludes by suggesting going back to Coase's focus on markets and firms as alternatives and retaining the term transaction costs for markets (as in Demsetz, 1988) but coordination costs for both exchange and organization costs. In this sense, Kay both returns to some of the original critiques of the TCMH perspective, and provides an overall comprehensive critique of the Williamsonian version of it.

In the final chapter, Pitelis focuses on two issues: first, the extent to which Coasean firms can be explained in terms other than the employment relation; second, if not, what explains Coasean firms, and also transactions, transaction costs, markets and firms, including the non-Coasean single-producer (or unitary firm)? It is suggested that to answer these questions one has to go back to the concept of the division of labour and that Coase's own early dismissal of this concept was on the basis of poor and even flawed reasoning. Going back to the division of labour allows the incorporation of production and production costs in the analysis, an acknowledged major limitation of the TCMH perspective (see, for example, Demsetz, 1988; Pitelis, 1991). The chapter concludes by pointing to other limitations of the TCMH perspective, some of which are addressed by other contributors in this volume.

This description of the chapter contents does not exhaust the issues covered by the contributors here. Other points raised in various chapters include the importance and role of opportunism versus trust, a critical assessment of the substitutability of markets and hierarchies assumption, and the existence of alternative organizing devices, e.g. networks etc. However, the volume is neither exhaustive in its treatment nor intended to be. I have already mentioned other readers – books where further discussion of some of the points raised here can be found. Where this volume is unique, however, is in its rather comprehensive, step-by-step, focus on the implicit and explicit assumptions of the TCMH perspective and their critical assessment. Admittedly, particular contributors are not always exhausting existing or potential problems of their subject matter, reflecting in part bounded rationality, opportunism and asset specificity, e.g. more simply the authors' attempts to be more original than exhaustive. There is, however, sufficient old knowledge surveyed and new knowledge provided here to make the volume, I believe, a very useful source of information to readers interested in this exciting area. The question of 'surveys' brings me to the existence of some overlapping between contributed chapters, particularly when surveying the TCMH perspective. This was not edited away for two reasons (besides convenience): first, in order to facilitate independent reading of the individual contributors; second, because the very nature and focus of each survey is in itself indicative of the authors' problematic and (thus) subsequent critiques.

The final issue I wish to discuss here is that of bias. The volume is consciously biased, as evidenced by its focus on *critical* assessments of the TCMH perspective. There are many reasons for this, including the fact that most existing published contributions tend to favour the perspective (which does not contribute to polyphony and pluralism) and also simply that such a product did not exist. More fundamentally, however, it is the belief of this author that application presupposes satisfactory understanding, including the limitations of any research programme. In this sense, this volume contributes towards this direction. Harold Demsetz (1988), in a powerful critique of TCMH, observed that the successes of this programme might have served a negative purpose: the lack of interest in alternative views. I believe that this volume serves Demsetz and the search for more and fresh views. There is a sense in which this volume is more biased that its editor had desired. It was originally hoped that Oliver Williamson would be able to reply to the critiques raised here in a 'reply' chapter. However, time constraints disallowed him from doing so. This makes the volume weaker to the bias criticism, which I am sure reviewers will not allow to pass unnoticed. I wish, however, to stress here, as many of the contributors in this volume individually do, that whatever the disadvantages of the TCMH perspective (and they are many), it has been important, influential and a catalyst of positive trans-formations in economic theory – if nothing else, economics is becoming exciting now!

REFERENCES

Arrow, K. (1970) The organization of economic activity: issues pertinent to the choice of market versus non-market allocation. In R. H. Haverman and J. Margolis (eds), *Public Expenditure and Policy Analysis*. Chicago: Markham.

Best, M. (1990) *The New Competition*. Cambridge: Polity Press.

Buckley, P. J. and Casson, M. (1976) *The Future of the Multinational Enterprise*. London: Macmillan.

Clarke, R. and McGuinness, T. (eds) (1987) *The Economics of the Firm*. Oxford: Basil Blackwell.

Coase, R. (1937) The nature of the firm. *Economica*, 4, 386–405.

Coase, R. (1960) The problem of social cost. *Journal of Law and Economics*, 3(1), 1–44.

Coase, R. (1991) The nature of the firm: meaning, and The nature of the firm: influence. In O. E. Williamson and S. G. Winter (eds), *The Nature of the Firm: Origins, Evolution and Development*. Oxford: Oxford University Press.

Cowling, K. and Sugden, R. (1987) *Transnational Monopoly Capitalism*. Brighton: Wheatsheaf.

Demsetz, H. (1988) The theory of the firm revisited. In *Ownership, Control and the Firm: the Organization of Economic Activity, Vol. I*. Oxford: Basil Blackwell.

Eggertson, T. (1991) *Economic Behaviour and Institutions*. Cambridge: Cambridge University Press.

Hodgson, G. (1988) *Economics and Institutions: a Manifesto for a Modern Institutional Economics*. Cambridge: Polity Press.

Hymer, S. H. (1970) The efficiency (contradictions) of multinational corporations. *American Economic Review Papers and Proceedings*, 60, 441–8.

Hymer, S. H. (1976) *The International Operations of National Firms: a Study of Foreign Direct Investment*. Cambridge, MA: MIT Press.

McKenzie, L. W. (1989) General equilibrium. In J. Eatwell et al. (eds), *The New Palgrave, General Equilibrium*. London: Macmillan.

McManus, J. C. (1972) The theory of the multinational firm. In G. Paquet (ed.), *The Multinational Firm and National State*. London: Collier-Macmillan.

Malcolmson, J. M. (1982) Trade unions and economic efficiency. *Economic Journal Conference Papers Supplement*.

Marglin, S. (1974) What do bosses do? The origins and functions of hierarchy in capitalist production. *Review of Radical Political Economics*, 6, 60–112.

North, D. C. (1981) *Structure and Change in Economic History*. New York: Norton.

North, D. C. (1990) *Institutions, Institutional Change of Economic Performance*. Cambridge: Cambridge University Press.

Pitelis, C. N. (1991) *Market and Non-market Hierarchies*. Oxford: Basil Blackwell.

Pitelis, C. N. and Sugden, R. (eds) (1991) *The Nature of the Transnational Firm*. London: Routledge.

Putterman, L. (1986) *The Economic Nature of the Firm: a Reader*. Cambridge: Cambridge University Press.

Pyke, F., Becatrini, G. and Sengenberger, W. (eds) (1990) *Industrial Districts and Inter-firm Co-operation in Italy*. Geneva: International Institute of Labour Studies.

Ricketts, M. (1987) *The Economics of Business Enterprise: New Approaches to the Firm*. Brighton: Wheatsheaf.

Thompson, G., Francis, J., Levacic, R. and Mitchell, J. (eds) (1991) *Markets, Hierarchies and Networks*. London: Sage.

Thompson, S. and Wright, M. (eds) (1988) *Internal Organization, Efficiency and Profit*. Oxford: Philip Allan.

Williamson, O. E. (1975) *Markets and Hierarchies*. New York: Free Press.

Williamson, O. E. (1981) The modern corporation: origins, evolution, attributes. *Journal of Economic Literature*, 19(4), 1537–68.

Williamson, O. E. (1986) *Economic Organisation: Firms, Markets and Policy Control*. Brighton: Wheatsheaf.

Williamson, O. E. and Winter, S. G. (eds) (1991) *The Nature of the Firm: Origins, Evolution and Development*. Oxford: Oxford University Press.

2

The Nature and Role of the Market

MALCOLM C. SAWYER

1 INTRODUCTION

The role of the market is a central feature of debates over the appropriate organization and coordination of economic activity. The purpose of this chapter is to raise questions on the way markets are conceptualized in economic analysis, and how far the theoretical conceptualization corresponds to what might be termed actual markets. It is argued that the theoretical conceptualization of markets in their 'pure' form is embedded in general equilibrium analysis (GEA). The rest of the chapter is concerned in a variety of ways with the issue of the appropriateness of that conceptualization of markets for understanding the operation of a market economy (i.e. an economy which includes extensive exchange between agents and decentralized decision-making on production).

Much discussion on economic organization has been plagued by the use of idealized forms, and the use of perfect competition as a representation of the market mechanism is a particular example of that. There is then a temptation to ascribe any deviation between the real world and the model to imperfections of the real world (e.g. to the existence of monopolies). My argument is rather different, namely that the 'pure' market system envisaged in GEA would not be sustainable and that some arrangements deemed to be imperfections in GEA (such as long-term contracts and deals based on trust) are required for the viability of a market economy. This, however, is not a blanket justification for any activity undertaken by independent firms in the pursuit of profits, but rather a plea for the development of a new analysis of a market economy.

This is a slightly revised version of a paper of the same title that oppeared in *Social Concept*, volume 6, no. 2, and appears here with the kind permission of that journal's editor.

Within a firm, relationships are generally not market ones and resources are allocated and activities coordinated by non-market means. Hence, firms themselves can be considered as imperfections (relative to the 'pure' market) from the standpoint of GEA. Thus it becomes necessary to discuss the relationship between firms and markets.

This chapter has eight sections, of which this is the first. In section 2, the question is raised as to how markets and the market mechanism have been conceptualized in economic analysis. It is argued that there is a conceptualization within GEA, though many doubts can be raised on the correspondence between that conceptualization and the exchange relationships in the real world. This leads into section 3, in which the general equilibrium analysis of the operation of markets is examined in some detail. In particular, it is argued that GEA reduces all transactions between people to exchange relations, with the only role of the price mechanism being seen as an allocative one. Section 4 reviews some arguments that a 'pure' market mechanism, operating along the lines envisaged in GEA, would not be sustainable, and that a range of non-price relationships between economic agents is necessary. The Coasean approach in which firms and markets are seen as alternative modes of coordination is considered in section 5. It is argued that this approach treats firms and markets as undertaking essentially the same functions, whereas firms and markets should be viewed as performing quite different functions. The final two main sections are concerned with the role of prices. It is argued in section 6 that prices considered as signals do not provide sufficient information for coordination purposes, while a range of non-allocative roles of price are considered in section 7. Section 8 is a brief concluding section.

2 THE CONCEPTUALIZATION OF MARKET AND THE MARKET MECHANISM

As Moss (1984) has observed, 'For all that is written about the market and market forces, it is remarkably difficult to find a definition of "the market" in the textbooks or other economic literature.'[1] Attention has been paid to the delineation of specific markets, and it is well known that in practice it is difficult to draw the boundaries with any precision. However, the concern here is rather different and is with the conceptualization of the market mechanism and of a market economy.

In economic analysis, words are used with meanings that diverge from the common usage of such words. Further, economic concepts and variables are given specific properties in a theory which do not fully reflect the properties of the entities in the real world to which they are intended to correspond.[2] It is inevitable that there is not an exact match between the properties of an economic concept in theory and of the corresponding concept in reality (or that part of reality to which the concept is intended to apply). But the domain of a theory is determined by the concepts on which it is based: a theory of firm behaviour is restricted to the behaviour of economic institutions labelled firms and is not intended to apply to households. The conception of a firm is contained, if only implicitly, within the theory of firm behaviour. Some institutions which would be labelled firms in the real world may fail to conform to the theory because on the basis of the concept of the firm in the theory they would not be considered as firms.

Davis (1989) in his discussion of GEA makes a similar point when he states: 'that a given concept can be reasoned *a priori* to have certain properties associated with it, does not imply that real examples of the object designated will also have those properties'.[3] The question here concerns the relationship between the theoretical concepts of firms and markets and actual firms and markets.

There is a prior question as to the extent to which markets actually exist rather than being a convenient (or otherwise) concept in economic analysis. The GEA concept of the market focuses on exchange relations. Raising the question of the existence of markets is not to deny that exchange transactions take place, but rather raises the question of whether they occur within institutional arrangements that approximate markets as conceptualized in GEA (and by extension in much of economic analysis). In order to discuss this, it is necessary to discuss the conceptualization of firm and market.

Some authors have argued that economists should not look for any correspondence between their theoretical constructs and apparently corresponding real world entities. Machlup (1967) appears to take this position concerning the concept of firm when he argues that 'The model of the firm in that theory [perfect competition] is not . . . designed to serve to explain and predict the behavior of real firms; instead, it is designed to explain and predict changes in prices . . . as effects of particular changes in conditions. . . . In this causal connection the firm is only a *theoretical link*, a mental construct helping to explain how one gets from the cause to the effect' Machlup (1967; italics added). Further, he argued that 'to confuse the firm as a theoretical construct with the firm as an empirical concept, that is, to confuse a heuristic fiction with a real organization like General Motors or Atlantic and Pacific, is to commit the "fallacy of misplaced concreteness"', which consists of using theoretic symbols as though they had an observable and concrete meaning. An underlying theme of this chapter is that this 'fallacy of misplaced concreteness' has been widely committed in discussion on the operation of markets.

The concept of the firm espoused by Machlup is akin to the transmitter of changes in specific variables (e.g. a shift in demand) to changes in other variables (e.g. price). The concept of the firm here is very similar to the 'black box' notion of the firm, which is frequently used in economic analysis, with the firm closely identified with a production function linking inputs to outputs. There are, though, many other concepts of firm employed; for example, the firm may be a coalition of interests (e.g. Cyert and March 1963), a social organization or a block of capital (for further discussion see Sawyer, 1989a, chapter 4).

Similar, though more difficult, problems arise over the conceptualization of a market. It is rare to find explicit discussion of the conceptualization of a market in economic analysis, but the implicit conceptualization has two important aspects. The first concerns the definition of a particular market in terms of the voluntary exchange of a well-defined commodity at a uniform price. The uniformity of price is, however, used as a characteristic both of a market for a particular commodity and of the equilibrium outcome. Marshall (1920) stated that 'the more nearly perfect a market is, the stronger is the tendency for the same price to be paid for the same thing at the same time in all parts of the market'. A perfect market would then have an infinite speed of price adjustment and hence always be in equilibrium. But out of equilibrium there will not be a uniformity of price and hence questions arise as to whether apparently similar commodities traded at different prices should be regarded as being in a single market.

A significant feature of the Walrasian auctioneer approach is that no trading is permitted while a market is out of equilibrium. The adjustment of price does not take place in historical time, but rather time is frozen while prices are adjusted to find their equilibrium values and then trading takes place instantaneously at the equilibrium prices. The use of historical, rather than logical, time generates a significant problem for the definition of a market. The definition of market derived from Marshall and others requires a uniformity of price, and this definition can be applied across time and space. In the Arrow–Debreu approach to GEA, physically identical commodities traded at different times and/or different places can be treated as different goods, and hence seen as traded in separate markets. Within each market there is uniformity of price, but differences in price for physically identical commodities across time and space are clearly possible when markets and goods are distinguished by time and place. When prices adjust in real time, then prices differ over time and it follows that the commodity at time t is to be considered as different from the commodity at time $t + 1$ (since there is non-uniformity of price). This indicates that the analysis of disequilibrium processes in real time in market situations is not just difficult, but rather is impossible. A disequilibrium process requires changes in price over time, whereas a market is defined in terms of a uniformity of price.

When a market is delimited in terms of uniformity of price, then the boundaries of a market can only be drawn when equilibrium has been reached. Different prices for a physically identical product may be a sign of disequilibrium or that there is more than one market (based, for example, on location) for that commodity: the problems would of course be greater when physically different (if similar) products are considered. This perspective also means that the definition of a particular market can only be made, in a sense, *ex post* by reference to the uniformity of price.

The second aspect relates both to a specific market and to the market mechanism in general, with the sole contact between individuals being seen to be through exchange at parametric prices. The concept of market embodied in GEA (and also in neoclassical partial equilibrium analysis) has those characteristics, and much of the discussion below relates to GEA. This concept of market will be referred to below as a 'pure' market, though it is not intended to imply anything about either the desirability or existence of such markets.

There need not be a close correspondence between that concept of a market and the actual process of exchange. For example, it can be observed that people are hired as, say, secretaries at (probably varying) wages, and it may be tempting to talk of a market for secretaries. But from the observation that firms seek to hire secretaries, that workers offer themselves as secretaries and that people are hired at some level of wages, it cannot be inferred that there is a market for secretaries comparable to the portrayal of a market in neoclassical economic theory. The way in which wages are settled and people are appointed as secretaries may deviate in important respects from the theoretical model. Further, it is not possible without investigation to say whether there is a unified market for secretaries (e.g. there may be localized rather than regional or national markets, or secretary may be too broad or narrow a classification). Indeed, the observation of one (or even many) exchange (in this example of secretarial services) can tell us nothing about the existence or otherwise of a single market, since the scope of a market is generally defined in terms of uniformity of price. Thus the definition of a specific market can only be made *ex post* by observing whether the actual set of exchanges conforms to the condition of uniformity of price.

It can be further argued that 'whatever difficulties we have in defining firms and households, they exist – they are *entities*. "Markets", on the other hand, are largely figures of speech in economics' (Auerbach, 1988).

This suggests that a comparison between the theoretical construct of a firm and real-world firms (or at least the legal entity called a firm) could be undertaken. There are different theoretical constructs of the firm, as suggested above, and drawing a precise boundary around a real-world firm presents its difficulties. Nevertheless, there is a sense in which we know that entities called firms exist. However, in the case of the term market, the difficulty arises as to what is meant by market in the real world (as well as what is meant by market in theory and the correspondence between the two). As indicated below, the term market is used in a number of different senses. There are some cases, such as the foreign exchange market or the stock market, where there is an entity called market which could be compared with the theoretical construct. But I would suggest that these examples are limited in number.

Neoclassical economics has been virtually synonymous with the analysis of exchange through markets and has neglected the production process. We may take the view that 'Of the enormous number of transactions in an economy, only a tiny fraction of them take place in what may literally be described as a "market"' (Auerbach, 1988) because of, for example, the scale of transactions within firms and within households. This would suggest that the range of application of neoclassical economic analysis was rather limited. But one response has been to describe a range of apparently non-market activities as market transactions. The term market has been applied to, for example, the internal labour market and the market for marriage ('a market in marriages can be presumed to exist'; Becker, 1976). But as Hodgson (1988) argues, in neither the internal labour market nor the market for marriage is there a price established on the basis of an anonymous market. In both hiring and marriage decisions, the 'quality' of one party to the transaction is usually of some relevance to the other party! Indeed, the central idea of an internal labour market is that in such cases wages are administratively determined and not set through an anonymous market. Thus the basic idea of the internal labour market is completely at odds with the usual concepts of a market. This is not to argue that what happens inside a firm is not influenced by what is happening outside, though it may suggest that there is no reason to prioritize the external influences over the internal influences. Firms' decisions will be influenced by a spectrum of relative prices, but in turn those prices will be influenced by the firms' decisions.

It is possible then to find a concept of market, albeit a very restrictive one, from GEA. However, the term market is used much more broadly in economic analysis, as just suggested. In common parlance, the term market can mean a geographical area (as in, for example, 'the Californian market'), a group of traders (for example, when talking of a 'nervous or confident market') or a range of products (for example, the 'car market').

Further, there is a considerable difference between the theoretical construct of a market (as in GEA) and the exchange processes which are observed in the real world.

3 GENERAL EQUILIBRIUM ANALYSIS AND MARKETS

GEA, based on perfect competition, dominates much economic thinking on the operation of markets. It is an analysis of a 'pure' market system in that all transactions between people are exchange relations, and production relations are omitted, with the price mechanism given a solely allocative role. GEA has strong overtones of 'perfection' in abstracting from any non-market restraints (such as custom, price norms etc.) and in the sense of being regarded as Pareto-optimal.

In GEA, the only contact between economic agents is an exchange relationship based on parametric prices. There are clearly many reasons for arguing that the exchange processes in the real world depart significantly from that. These reasons would include the ability of one party to impose a price in a position of market power and the benefits to the parties involved of contracts that extend over a series of transactions (as suggested in the implicit contract literature). The neglect of economic power in GEA is well-known and the existence of market power is seen as a major impediment to the achievement of the benefits of a competitive equilibrium. Within the neoclassical approach, economic power benefits one party at the expense of the other, with an overall net loss. However, the position with long-term contracts is rather different. Since such contracts are voluntarily entered into, they are presumed to benefit both parties. The relationship between the two parties is a continuing one and the terms of the contract (including price) are arrived at through negotiation rather than being externally imposed by an auctioneer.

GEA does not make any distinction between different types of goods and services and the only property required of goods and services is that they provide benefits to demanders and impose costs on suppliers. The general post-Keynesian approach, which is reflected in Keynes (1936), is that there are important differences between financial, labour and product sectors in the ways in which they operate. In the product sector, it is typically the case that a relatively small number of producers dominate the sector, and it is producers who decide on price, quality etc. In the labour sector, there may be a variety of forms of negotiation and bargaining. Further, the relationship between and the relative power of the different sectors are also relevant. The typical post-Keynesian approach portrays real wages as determined in (or at least strongly influenced by) the product sector and not in the labour sector, for although money wage is set in the labour sector the real product wage arises from the setting of product prices (relative to money wage). In that sense, the product sector could be said to dominate the labour sector in the matter of real wage determination. The financial sector is in many respects closer than the other sectors to operating like a collection of competitive markets, in which the prices respond quickly and the commodities are well-defined. However, prices of commodities in the financial sector appear to display considerable volatility and in many parts there are acute problems arising from asymmetry of information.

Economic agents are conceptualized in GEA as 'atom-like', with single, all-powerful brains. In the absence of 'atom-like' firms, the internal relationships between individuals within a firm become relevant for the allocation of resources (as suggested by the Coasean notion of the firm). The recognition that people are not 'unbounded rational' but rather may have 'bounded rationality' (and may also be 'irrational') clearly leads to a consideration of how people seek to cope with an inability to process all the available information in a world of considerable uncertainty. The use of long-term contracts, the adoption of routines of behaviour, and the use of price norms may be ways (among many others) that people use to help cope with uncertainty. Within the confines of GEA these modes of behaviour are viewed as 'imperfections', but such a view is clearly theory-dependent, for when viewed in some other theoretical contexts these responses are seen as beneficial and/or necessary (for example, adoption of routines is a way of coping with pervasive uncertainty).

GEA assumes that production takes place subject to non-increasing returns to scale, and many of its conclusions rest on this assumption – notably the proofs of the existence of an equilibrium, the viability of atomistic competition and the inverse relationship between real wages and employment of labour. The absence of economies of scale is a crucial assumption of GEA in the sense that the analysis would be inoperable without it, and is an assumption that cannot be modified as the analysis is refined.

The objectives of the economic agents are assumed to be utility and profit maximization. This imposes an 'economic man' view of the world and strongly biases the analysis towards a stress on the response of individuals to (monetary) incentives. This 'economic man' approach rules out by assumption any other approach to human behaviour. This is not to argue that monetary and other incentives have no role to play, but rather that feelings such as obligation to fellow workers and organization, pride in work and professional ethos can also be relevant.

The assumption of 'atom-like' economic agents removes any consideration of the internal organization of a firm. But when large corporations are discussed, then 'profit maximization involves a substantial contradiction. Those in charge forgo personal reward to enhance it for others. . . . [Hence] the technostructure, as a matter of necessity, bans personal profit-making' (Galbraith, 1967). Further, a successful organization requires some elements of cooperation between workers. Thus within the organization success is likely to depend on cooperation and an element of the suspension of pursuit of (short-run) self-interest. Indeed, it can be argued that satisficing behaviour would enable the reconciliation of competing interests to be arrived at more readily than if individuals each pursue optimizing behaviour. Alternatively, the firm can be viewed as being able to restrain opportunism rather better than market arrangements can (Williamson, 1975).

The role of price in GEA is a solely allocative one. Resources are allocated in response to prices, and price movements serve to coordinate economic activity. The auctioneer adjusts prices until equilibrium between demand and supply in each market is reached, and resource allocation follows. But since the auctioneer is a disinterested participant, variation of price is only to eliminate excess demand or supply, and not for any other motives, such as promoting self-interest. This will be used below in a consideration of the range of roles of price (which could be alternatively viewed as a range of motives governing the way prices are set). It is, of course, the case that GEA does not provide a convincing story of how prices move to perform this allocative role.

Finally, Say's law, the idea that 'supply creates its own demand', and the apparent impossibility of generalized excess supply, holds in GEA. Thus, there is a strong in-built tendency to conclude that full employment will be achieved, with any failure to achieve full employment ascribed to 'imperfections'. Any need for demand management policies is thereby ruled out by assumption. It is well known that GEA has found it impossible to find any convincing explanation for the existence of money. The significance of these remarks is that some possible sources of economic malfunctioning (e.g. money) are omitted and that the role for non-market forms of coordination (e.g. demand management policies) is excluded by assumption.

It is relatively easy to criticize GEA, and this discussion has only mentioned some of the criticisms that can be advanced. The purpose of this section has been to point to some important features of market economies (e.g. economies of scale, money, price-making behaviour) which cannot be comprehended by GEA.

4 THE GENERAL EQUILIBRIUM SYSTEM AS SUSTAINABLE PERFECTION

The thrust of arguments associated with the concept of workable competition (Clark, 1940; Sosnick, 1958) can be seen as a denial of perfect competition as a worthwhile attainable ideal. For some, while perfect competition may be an ideal, it is costly to attain fully. For others the obstacles of pervasive uncertainty and unknowability of the future, lack of knowledge and dynamic consideration (absent by assumption in GEA) would always prevent the full attainment of the benefits of perfect competition. Another group would not see perfect competition as an ideal, through for example the existence of economies of scale, externalities and product differentiation.

A few authors have argued that a 'pure' market mechanism (as defined above) would not be viable. Richardson (1960) argues that

> The theory of perfect competition ... [provides] under the guise of an equilibrium position, a particular configuration to which the organization of production and exchange could conform. ... But the theory provides us, neither with a satisfactory account of how this state of affairs might come about, nor with a blue-print of the institutional or market arrangements which would best promote it. The so-called equilibrium could be brought into being, in principle, by the allocative decisions of a central planning authority. ... The closest approximation to the configuration obtainable in practice, however, is likely to be reached by arrangements in which both competition and deliberate co-ordination – whether public or private – play some part.

Further, he argues that it seems 'to be the case that entrepreneurs would have access to the market information they require only if there existed a variety of restraints, of differing degrees of strength and durability, to which their freedom of action would frequently be subject. These restraints feature, in our accepted analysis, as imperfections or frictions which clog the competitive system; in fact, ... they play an important, and indeed an essential role in its successful operation.' Connections between firms take many forms, which 'may range from mere conservatism at one extreme to formal contracts or rigidly exclusive arrangements at the other; all of them may be regarded as the antithesis of competition ... but in fact they need not prevent the attainment of the objectives which competition is valued as serving, such as productive efficiency and the rational allocation of resources.'

One example of the requirement for non-market institutions is given in the context of labour markets by Marsden (1986) when he argues that 'the importance of apprenticeships in establishing occupational labour markets for general skills suggests that such skills also may be largely dependent on an institutional base, rather than being a natural state of affairs.' Further, the 'parallel between general skills and public goods means that the occupational labour markets built on them may be difficult to maintain in practice unless protected by institutional rules, or by social consensus.'

Hodgson (1988, pp. 187–94) deals with 'the impossibility of perfect competition', and one part of his argument is highlighted here. In the presence of uncertainty and bounded rationality, future markets may not exist and when they do exist they cannot work efficiently. Thus economic agents have to cope with a lack of information and/or an inability to process all relevant information, and will devise means of helping to cope with pervasive uncertainty. These may include explicit and implicit collusion and a variety of ' "frictions", "imperfections" and "restraints", which, although they appear to stand in the way of "free competition", are actually in some measure necessary to make the market system function at all'.

The evidence of the past 150 years or so is that there is a strong tendency in capitalist economies for the absolute and relative size of large firms to increase. This would appear to be strong evidence that a market system based on atomistic competition (in the structural sense of a large number of small firms) is unsustainable (or has never existed). Such observations serve to confirm Marx's analysis of the processes of concentration and centralization serving to break down the structural elements of atomistic competition. This does not mean that competition in the sense of rivalrous behaviour between firms or of the mobility of capital has declined.

Over a wide area of the twentieth-century capitalist economy, therefore, the adjustment of supply to demand is accomplished with the assistance of deliberate coordination, with or without government participation. Further, there are many forms of relationships between firms other than the arm's length parametric price relationship envisaged in GEA.

GEA strongly suggests that perfect competition has some desirable properties. In this section I have argued that there are theoretical and empirical reasons to believe that perfect competition would not be sustainable, and as such provides a poor benchmark against which existing economic arrangements should be judged.

5   FIRMS AND MARKETS

Coase (1937) drew the distinction between coordination through a decentralized market mechanism and coordination by a central decision-maker in discussing the function of a firm, which reflected a similar dichotomy between the market system and central planning. In this section I discuss the concepts of market and firm, and the nature of the relationship between market and firm, that are used. Coase, Williamson and others have treated market and firm as alternative ways by which resources are allocated, whereas it is argued here that market and firm perform quite different functions. In the Coasean approach, market and firm are regarded as substitutes, whereas the approach below portrays them more as complements.

Coase's view can be summarized by the following quote:

> For instance, in economic theory we find that the allocation of factors of production between different uses is determined by the price mechanism. The price of factor A becomes higher in X than in Y. As a result, A moves from Y to X, until the difference between the prices in X and Y, except in so far as it compensates for other differential advantages, disappears. Yet in the real world we find that there are many areas where this does not apply. If a workman moves from department Y to department X, he does not go, because of a change in relative prices, but because he is ordered to do so. (Coase, 1937)

The market and the firm, like the related dichotomy between price mechanism and central planning, are portrayed as two alternative polar extremes (for example, the market involves voluntary decisions while the firm involves compulsion). However, the market and firm are seen as serving the same purposes, namely the coordination of economic activity and the allocation of resources. It is argued below that the role of the firm is quite different from the role of the market.

The nature of the market implicitly involved here can be seen from a closer examination of the quote:

1 'The price of factor A *becomes* higher in X than in Y.' This assumes an anonymous market with an auctioneer who adjusts prices. For most exchanges in practice, there is not a disinterested auctioneer adjusting price; rather, the identity (e.g. producer or consumer) of the economic agent who declares prices is an important ingredient in the analysis of exchange. Further, there are many cases (particularly for labour services) where the lack of anonymity is highly relevant.

2 'As a result, A moves from Y to X, until the difference between the prices in X and Y . . . disappears.' The movement of A is ultimately not worthwhile in the sense that the prices (returns) in X and Y are the same. Thus a movement is only worthwhile if the returns before equilibrium is achieved are significant and compensate for any costs of movement. This is a reflection of the general difficulty of providing a convincing story of how markets reach equilibrium.

3 'If a workman moves from department Y to department X, he does
   not go, because of a change in relative prices, but because he is
   ordered to do so.' The dichotomy is drawn between voluntary decisions in response to price differences and obeying instructions within
   the firm. While some conceptions of a firm do emphasize the role of
   command within a hierarchical structure, there are many other ways,
   such as cooperation between workers, in which coordination of
   economic activity within the firm can take place.
4 It is assumed that the only contact between firms is that which takes
   place through the exchange process. In practice, there are many
   other forms of contact between firms, such as collusion, cooperative
   arrangements etc., some of which may be socially beneficial and
   some not. In contrast, it is argued in this chapter that a market
   system without some forms of non-price contact would not be able to
   function.

The 'transactions cost' approach to the firm (e.g. Williamson, 1975,
1981) is a development of the Coasean approach. The explanation of the
existence of firms is based on economizing on transactions costs, for it is
costly for firms to purchase from others. The growth of large firms is then
the replacement of the market by internal planning, and is explained in
this approach because 'managerial guidance or internal planning they
provide is more efficient than the price adjustment process the market
provides' (Dugger, 1983). One particular example, based on other work
by Williamson, is that of the large multi-divisional corporation, which
can be seen to allocate financial capital between the divisions, in effect
replacing the allocation of finance by the market that would have occurred
if the divisions were separate firms.

The general growth of the absolute size of firms over the past century
or so suggests a diminution in the role of the market as a coordinating
mechanism, and a growth of the role of administrative decisions in
coordination of economic activity and the allocation of resources: the
replacement of the invisible hand by the visible hand (Chandler, 1977).
This argument rests on the identification of the market with exchange
coordination. The decisions of those operating in the market lead to the
replacement of the market (in the sense just given). As Auerbach (1988)
argues, firms are devices both for avoiding market transactions and for
the extension of the market mechanism (in the sense that firms are, for
example, the vehicle through which market capitalism expands into
previously non-capitalist areas of activities).

The arguments of Coase appear to be based on the implicit assumption
that markets always exist, and against that background firms expand their
range of activities in order to economize on the costs of market trans-

actions. As Fourie (1989) argues, 'market relations are nothing but relations between already existing firms (or between such firms and customers). Without firms that produce, there are no products to be transferred and allocated by market transactions.' Thus in a temporal sense the existence of firms (even one-person firms) has to precede the development of markets in order that goods are produced which can be exchanged through markets. Further, since markets cannot produce, but only aid the exchange of goods and services produced by firms, firms have quite different functions from markets: specifically firms produce whereas markets cannot produce but may aid exchange. In this case, any analysis of an economy that deals only with markets (and not with firms) will be seriously misleading, since such an analysis may be able to explain the process of exchange, but cannot discuss the production of what is exchanged. Much neoclassical theorizing has, of course, focused on exchange, with the commodities available for exchange taken as given.

Thus, market transactions could not exist without firms, for markets exchange the commodities which the firms produce. In the absence of firms there would be nothing to exchange. There is clearly a sense in which resources are allocated within a firm as well as being allocated between firms. But that is to overlook an essential property of a firm, namely that it is a production unit. A (or the only) key activity of markets may be seen to be exchange and allocation; in contrast a key activity of a firm is production.

There are reasons (including those analysed within the 'transactions cost' approach) for a firm to produce something itself rather than buy it from elsewhere. But in order to make a comparison between own production and purchase from elsewhere, the two activities have to be placed on a par. In the 'transactions cost' approach this is achieved by comparing the relative costs: purchase from self is compared with purchase from elsewhere. This form of comparison overlooks the essential differences between exchange and production. But it also overlooks the wide range of activities, such as strategic planning, innovation and management of technical change, which can only be undertaken within firms.

The time horizons of the market and of the firm are also quite different. The market (at least in its 'pure' form) deals with instantaneous exchange. It is only firms that can adopt a long time horizon and make strategic decisions (which is not to say that they always do so). The eventual effect of those strategic decisions by firms is the nature of the market environment at some future date.

This discussion would indicate that firms undertake a much broader range of functions than markets do. The latter can influence the co-ordination of economic activity and the allocation of resources, while the former are additionally involved in production, innovation etc. In the next section, I consider the role of market and the price mechanism in the coordination of economic activity.

6   PRICE SIGNALS AND COORDINATION

In the work of Walras, an auctioneer was introduced to conduct the *tâtonnement* process by which prices and quantities could adjust to achieve an equilibrium. It is well known from the reappraisal of Keynesian economics literature that the absence of an auctioneer creates difficulties of coordination.[4] There is a failure of markets to clear instantaneously (in real time) and firms and households are confronted with quantity constraints. In such circumstances, they have to respond to quantity signals as well as price signals. However, much of the discussion on the operation of markets proceeds as though these difficulties do not arise and there is an auctioneer or the equivalent. This is particularly evident in the new classical macroeconomics, in which instantaneous market clearing is achieved through the assumption of 'rational' expectations, where the expectation that the market will clear leads to the market clearing instantaneously.

The auctioneer is portrayed as providing information to economic agents on both price and the excess demand/supply position (indirectly through price adjustments), and information when equilibrium is reached (when trading is permitted). This information is all that is available but is sufficient for the efficient coordination of economic activity. In the absence of a Walrasian auctioneer, there is no signal for market participants that equilibrium has been reached, and therefore it may not be realized when equilibrium is reached and the participants may continue to make changes, thereby moving away from equilibrium. A firm can judge whether it is itself in equilibrium, but is not able to judge whether there is an overall equilibrium. It also has to be the case that in all exchange situations someone has to change price, and may do so to equate demand and supply (as is generally portrayed in models of imperfect competition; see Sawyer, 1990).

Hayek (1945) argued that price is the only information that economic agents require. If the price of a commodity rises (falls), it is not necessary for a trader to know why the price has risen (fallen). 'It does not matter for our purposes . . . which of these two causes [increased demand, reduced supply] has made tin more scarce. All that the user of tin needs to know is that some of the tin they used to consume is now more profitably employed elsewhere, and in consequence they must economize tin' (Hayek, 1945).

It is clear that price does not convey sufficient information for the firms involved. The first point relates to the question of what the price refers to. In the case of products with no possibility of, for example, quality variation, the product is well defined. But in the general case when the product is not well defined, information on the nature of the product is required, and knowledge of the seller and conditions of sale may also be useful. This is particularly the case for labour services, where there are variations in skill, quality of labour service as well as the effort and intensity of work. The second point is that a rise in the price of tin may be temporary or permanent, arise from demand or from supply changes, involve quality changes etc., and hence the single signal of a price cannot convey the reasons why price has changed, though information on the reasons is generally useful for market participants. If prices did convey all necessary information, then specialists commenting on, for example, commodity market trends and prospects would not be required. Yet they are observed to exist in market economies.

When the price is not set by some anonymous market (or market-maker) but rather by one side of the transaction (or by both parties through negotiations), then the message contained in a price will to some degree reflect the objectives of the economic agent setting the price. For example, the setting of a limit price by incumbent firms is intended to deter entry into an industry, with the price set to convey the message that such entry would not be profitable. Further, much of the literature on the inflexibility of prices can be seen as suggesting a variety of ways by which the economic agents who set price believe that a change in price would provide a signal to be interpreted in a way unfavourable to the price setter. An obvious example here would be where the offer of a lower price may be interpreted by the consumer as indicating lower quality or by rivals as starting a price war.

In any economy where there are prices that influence decisions and the distribution of income, a relevant question is who sets and changes prices. Each such economy has a number of 'auctioneers' who do change prices, but the function of being an 'auctioneer' is generally combined with some other function, such as being a producer or distributor. Having the role of price-setter conveys some power, and which economic agents are the effective auctioneers will influence how the economy operates. Thus, it is usually the case that in product markets it is the producers who decide upon prices, and then prices are set in the interests of those producers (where they have sought to take into account the various impacts of the prices they set, including any effect on potential entrants).

Hirschman (1970) argues that consumers can signal their dissatisfaction to a firm either through the exit option (stop buying the firm's product) or through the voice option (express dissatisfaction to the firm). Similarly, workers can signal dissatisfaction by leaving the firm or by voicing their complaints. He further links exit with market forces and economic mechanisms and voice with non-market forces and political mechanisms.

The exit effect would work in rather different ways under a situation of perfect competition as compared with one of imperfect competition. In the former case, the fate of one firm is shared with other firms. A loss of demand by one firm signals a general decline in the demand for the product concerned, and does not signal anything about the firm's own operations. In the latter case, a loss of demand by one firm may signal a general decline in demand, or a shift in demand to other firms.

The signal sent by exercise of the exit option is a generalized one while that sent by exercise of the voice option is a much more specific one. Hirschman argues along similar lines when discussing Friedman's advocacy of a market mechanism in education. He argues that 'Friedman considers withdrawal or exit as the "direct" way of expressing one's unfavorable views of an organization. A person less well trained in economics might naively suggest that the direct way of expressing views is to express them!' (Hirschman, 1970). The relevance of this line of argument is that the exit option corresponds to the market mechanism in the sense of being exercised through an exchange relationship. The 'voice' option may be exercised through numerous routes, e.g. direct complaint, media pressure or organization of pressure groups.[5] It requires extra-market mechanisms through which it can operate, and suggests that freedom of expression is generally an important ingredient for the operation of an economy using the market mechanisms.

The final part of the title of Hirschman's (1970) work is 'loyalty'. It can first be noted that 'exit has often been branded as criminal, for it has been labeled desertion, defection, and treason' (Hirschman, 1970). In the absence of loyalty, a firm in apparent decline would find all its employees leaving, and hence the decline would occur. Some loyalty is required for 'voice' effects to be effective. This could be seen as an illustration of the point made above, namely that some departure from individual utility maximization may be required for the effective operation of a company. In this case, feelings of loyalty by individuals to an organization can help a firm overcome its short-term difficulties. The exercise of short-term opportunism would lead to individuals leaving the organization, whereas the long-term revival of the organization requires that some individuals stay.

The arguments of this section would suggest that coordination of economic activity by price signals alone will not work very well. The emergence of other means of coordination can then be understood as having a role to play.

7 ROLES OF PRICES

It was indicated above that the only role of price within GEA is the allocative one. In this section, I outline the argument that price plays a number of other roles. Gerrard (1989) argues that there are (at least) five roles of prices, namely the conductive, positional, strategic, financial and allocative. The conductive role relates to the passing on of costs as prices (with the addition of a mark-up) and, in the case of workers, the passing on of prices as wages. Full-cost pricing provides an example of the conductive role of pricing. The positional role obviously concerns the relativity of one economic agent with another: in the labour sector this has been seen as particularly important for groups of workers relative to other groups. The strategic role of price 'results from the need of firms to develop competitive strategies with which to achieve their marketing objectives in the face of competitive strategies adopted by their rivals' (Gerrard, 1989). The setting of a limit-price to deter new entrants is an example of the strategic role of price. The financial role is to enable firms to generate sufficient funds for their investment and other objectives. The post-Keynesian theories (e.g. Eichner, 1973) that portray firms as adjusting profit margins so as to generate internal finance for investment offer a clear case of the financing role of price.

These four non-allocative roles of price arise from the absence of a disinterested auctioneer, when economic agents themselves have influence over prices. The allocative role remains, in that when prices have been set there may be consequent demand adjustments leading to output adjustments (which may have been foreseen when the prices were set). Thus, this allocative role arises as a by-product of the other four roles. Further, the first four roles could be seen as deliberately adopted by firms, while the allocative role reflects the response of customers and arises from the interaction of the other roles.[6]

The allocative role of price depends heavily on a negative relationship between the demand for a commodity and its price (and similarly on a positive relationship between supply and price). One particular difficulty that arises here is that outside of perfect competition with parametric prices, demand and supply functions take on a different meaning in that prices and quantity are simultaneously set. However, it is possible to trace out a demand side (or supply side) relationship between price and quantity. The Sraffian approach has shown that the relationship between a measure of the capital stock and the rate of profit is not necessarily negative, and more recently Steedman (1985) has shown that a similar result can be obtained for employment of labour and the real wage. It is also the case that under conditions of imperfect competition (particularly with increasing returns of some form) the real wage/employment

Malcolm C. Sawyer

relationship can be positive and the output/price one can be negative.[7]

From this we can conclude that the allocative role of price will not be fully operational. Price is seen to play many other roles, which will interfere with the allocative role. Further, there are reasons to think that the negative relationship between price and demand required for the allocative role of price will not always hold.

8   CONCLUSIONS

The general purpose of this chapter has been to argue that the analysis of 'market economies' cannot be adequately undertaken solely in terms of arm's length exchange transactions. GEA, which underlies much discussion on the role of markets, is then seen as seriously misleading through its focus on the allocative role of markets, and on anonymous markets as the only mode of economic coordination. Instead it is argued that there are a range of other modes of economic coordination that require a full evaluation.

NOTES

1   Moss provides his own definition as follows: 'the market is here defined as the set of producers actually comprising an industry together with the set of users of the closely substitutable commodities produced by the industry and all economic agents who, directly or indirectly, buy these commodities from the producers only in order to sell them to users, or who arrange the direct sale of commodities to the users by the producers' (Moss, 1984). For further discussion see Hodgson (1988), especially chapter 8. The *New Palgrave* (Eatwell et al., 1987) does not have in its exhaustive treatment of economics any entries on markets or market mechanisms. Eckert and Leftwich (1988), in their best selling textbook, say that 'the concepts of demand, supply, markets and degree of competitiveness in markets are basic to a working knowledge of how a price system guides and directs, the economic activity of a private enterprise economy', but do not define markets in their glossary.

2   A convenient example of this is money, which in the conventional Keynesian analysis has properties of yielding zero interest, of being in fixed supply under the control of the Central Bank and of constituting net worth. Although these properties are crucial in the derivation of many of the conclusions of Keynesian macroeconomic analysis, nevertheless they are clearly far removed from those of currently existing money.

3   Davis (1989) also indicates that one of the characteristics of general equilibrium theory is that the concepts (e.g. of consumer) are set by the

requirements of the theory itself: for example, convexity of preferences is required to ensure the proof of the existence of equilibrium. Thus it may not be possible to modify the concepts in response to observations in the real world without undermining the basis of the theory.

4 The starting points for the re-appraisal of Keynesian economics literature are Clower (1965) and Leijonhufvud (1968).

5 A good example here is the reduction in the use of CFCs in aerosols. This required the exercise of the voice option, both in terms of spreading the relevant information and in securing a redution in the use of CFCs. The exit option would have signalled to a firm only that its demand was declining, not the reason for the decline.

6 The model developed in Dutt (1988) and used in Sawyer (1990) can be viewed as incorporating all four non-allocative roles of price.

7 A point made by Robinson (1933); see Sawyer (1989b) for elaboration.

REFERENCES

Auerbach, P. (1988) *Competition: Economic Analysis of Industrial Change*. Oxford: Blackwell.

Becker, G. (1976) *The Economic Approach to Human Behavior*. Chicago: University of Chicago Press.

Chandler, A. D. (1977) *The Visible Hand: the Managerial Revolution in American Business*. Cambridge, MA: Harvard University Press.

Clark, J. B. (1940) Towards a concept of workable competition. *American Economic Review*, 30, 241–56.

Clower, R. W. (1965) The Keynesian counter-revolution: a theoretical appraisal. In F. Hahn and F. Brechling (eds), *The Theory of Interest Rates*. London: Macmillan.

Coase, R. (1937) The nature of the firm. *Economica*, 4, 386–405.

Cyert, R. M. and March, J. G. (1963) *A Behavioural Theory of the Firm*. Englewood Cliffs, NJ: Prentice Hall.

Davis, J. B. (1989) Axiomatic general equilibrium theory and referentiality. *Journal of Post Keynesian Economics*, 11, 424–38.

Dugger, W. M. (1983) The transactions cost analysis of Oliver E. Williamson: a new synthesis? *Journal of Economic Issues*, 17, 95–114.

Dutt, A. (1988) Competition, monopoly power and the prices of production. *Thames Papers in Political Economy*, Autumn.

Eatwell, J., Milgate, M. and Newman, J. (eds) (1987) *The New Palgrave*. London: Macmillan.

Eckert, R. D. and Leftwich, R. H. (1988) *The Price System and Resource Allocation*. New York: The Dryden Press.

Eichner, A. (1973) A theory of the determination of the mark-up under oligopoly. *Economic Journal*, 83, 1184–200.

Fourie, F. C. v. N. (1989) The nature of firms and markets: do transactions approaches help? *South African Journal of Economics,* 57(2), 142–60.

Galbraith, J. K. (1967) *The New Industrial State.* Boston: Houghton-Mifflin.

Gerrard, W. (1989) *Theory of the Capitalist Economy: towards a Post-Classical Synthesis.* Oxford: Blackwell.

Hayek, F. (1945) The use of knowledge in society. *American Economic Review,* 35, 519–30.

Hirschman, A. O. (1970) *Exit, Voice and Loyalty.* Cambridge, MA: Harvard University Press.

Hodgson, G. (1988) *Economics and Institutions.* Cambridge: Polity Press.

Keynes, J. M. (1936) *The General Theory of Employment, Interest and Money.* London: Macmillan.

Leijonhufvud, A. (1968) *On Keynesian Economics and the Economics of Keynes.* Oxford: Oxford University Press.

Machlup, F. (1967) Theories of the firm: marginalist, behavioural, managerial. *American Economic Review,* 57, 1–33.

Marsden, D. (1986) *The End of Economic Man? Custom and Competition in Labour Markets.* Brighton: Wheatsheaf Books.

Marshall, A. (1920) *Principles of Economics*, eighth edn. London: Macmillan.

Moss, S. (1984) *Markets and Macroeconomics: Macroeconomic Implications for Rational Individual Behaviour.* Oxford: Blackwell.

Richardson, G. B. (1960) *Information and Investment.* Oxford: Oxford University Press.

Robinson, J. (1933) *The Economics of Imperfect Competition.* London: Macmillan.

Sawyer, M. (1989a) *The Challenge of Radical Political Economy.* London: Harvester-Wheatsheaf.

Sawyer, M. (1989b) On the relationship between real wages and unemployment. *Cyprus Journal of Economics,* 1, 69–88.

Sawyer, M. (1990) On the post Keynesian tradition and industrial economics. *Review of Political Economy,* 2, 43–68.

Sosnick, S. H. (1958) A critique of the concepts of workable competition. *Quarterly Journal of Economics,* 82, 380–423.

Steedman, I. (1985) On input 'demand' curves. *Cambridge Journal of Economics,* 9, 165–72.

Williamson, O. E. (1975) *Markets and Hierarchies.* New York: Free Press.

Williamson, O. E. (1981) The modern corporation: origins, evolution, attributes. *Journal of Economic Literature,* 19(4), 1537–68.

3

In the Beginning There Were Markets?

FREDERICK C. V. N. FOURIE

The relationship between individuals, markets and firms must be rated as one of the most basic questions in the transactions cost and (old, new and neo-) institutionalist literature.

In the transaction cost approach of Coase (1937) and Williamson (1973, 1975, 1981, 1985) the starting point is that the transaction is the ultimate unit of analysis, that 'in the beginning there were markets', and that firms emerge and therefore exist in order to internalize, and thereby economize on the cost of, market transactions between individuals. The nature of the firm is therefore understood through the prism of the market, which serves as ultimate and overarching point of reference, indeed as the most elemental building block of theoretical understanding of social institutions. Prominent topics in the transaction cost approach have been the reasons for the existence and growth of firms as well as the nature of the firm as opposed to the market, including the distinctions – if any – between employment, subcontracting and integration. Some of the most pertinent contributions are the work of Williamson on markets and hierarchies, and of Alchian, Demsetz, Jensen and Meckling on the role of inter-individual contracts (see Cohen, 1979; Fama, 1980; Cheung, 1983; Putterman, 1986).

The assumption that 'in the beginning there were markets' (Williamson, 1975, p. 20; 1985, p. 87) raises an issue that has become critical in the debate (Putterman, 1986, p. 18), and that will be pursued throughout this chapter. The question is whether it is methodologically legitimate and constructive (*and* successful) to attempt to explain the typical and distinguishing inner nature of the firm exclusively in terms of another, typically different relation, i.e. the market (transactions, contracts). Second, and related, is whether the singular focus on inter-*individual* transactions, found especially in the contracts approach, is appropriate. A broader question is whether the transaction costs approach as such is fruitful in the determination of the nature of firms and markets. These issues will be illuminated by critically analysing the contributions mentioned above.

1 THE NATURE AND EMERGENCE OF THE FIRM

A first question is whether the transaction approach provides a clear indication of the distinctive nature of the firm – not so much of particular, existing examples of firms, but of the firm as a distinctive societal institution, the firm as such. That is, the quest here is for the intrinsic, *generic* nature of the firm. The starting point for this issue is Coase (1937), critical analysis of which also provides the first indications of the limitations of the transaction approach.

1.1   The Firm as Market Superseder

Coase uses an internalization-of-external-transactions argument to explain the nature, existence and growth of firms. He makes two basic observations.

1   First, one can distinguish (but also observe the parallels) between the allocation of resources in the economic system as a whole (i.e. by the price mechanism) and within the firm (by a manager). Thus he observes that 'outside the firm, price movements direct production, which is co-ordinated through a series of exchange transactions on the market, while within a firm these transactions are eliminated and in place of the complicated market structure with exchange transactions is substituted the entrepreneur-co-ordinator, who directs production' (Coase, 1937, p. 388).

2   Second, asks Coase, if the market can coordinate production, why then do firms exist or emerge in the first place? Arguing that exchanges will be brought under the coordination of the firm whenever the cost of using markets exceeds that of using authority and direction, Coase concludes that firms exist because there are costs of using the market mechanism.[1] Therefore 'the distinguishing mark of the firm is the supersession of the price mechanism' (Coase, 1937, p. 389). Correspondingly the expansion of the firm is defined as the internalization of additional external transactions, with the equilibrium boundary of the firm being determined by marginal transaction cost calculations. (The larger part of Coase's paper is in fact devoted to the growth and boundary issue.)

While the observation that both markets and firms appear to have some coordination function is important, useful and perfectly legitimate, the attempt to go further and use this insight to derive and specify the typical, intrinsic nature of the firm runs into serious difficulties. This can be illustrated by considering the case of one-person firms.

1.2   The One-person Firm and Related Problems

If the firm emerges because it is a less costly way of handling the exchanges and transactions necessary to direct and coordinate production, then the existence of such production must logically precede the emergence and existence of the firm.

Although there is no consensus on exactly what a firm is, the management of some *production* (and/or distribution) process appears – both intuitively and in most textbook definitions of the firm – to be central to the nature of the firm. From this two lines of argument follow. If one argues that even the smallest production unit, a producing individual or artisan, is in principle (if only seminally) a firm, then such production can only take place if firms already exist.[2] Then the firm cannot emerge as a market-replacing institution to begin with. In this case Coase's definition and explanation of the firm in terms of market transactions is logically untenable. On the other hand one may argue that any producing individual cannot be regarded, without further ado, as a firm (also see section 3.5). For instance, while it is true that Coase's idea is presented and has been interpreted *as a general definition* and existential explanation of the firm, Hodgson (this volume) argues that one must assume that Coase has in mind what Marx calls 'the capitalist firm', i.e. a firm in which the capitalist owners own the product of the property, and hire and control labour power under a contract of employment. According to Hodgson, this definition of a (capitalist) firm would exclude the one-person firm. That would seem to protect Coase against the criticism voiced above.

While all producing individuals may not be regarded as firms, that does not eliminate the possibility of the one-person firm. One simply cannot decree that upon reduction of its personnel to one (e.g. through automation or retrenchment) a firm ceases to be a firm (even a capitalist firm). One must accept the one-person firm as a conceptual possibility and indeed as an often encountered empirical reality (also historically). For example, in South Africa a recent innovation in corporate law has been the creation of the so-called *closed corporation*, which is something between a partnership and a corporation, with fewer mandatory accounting and auditing procedures, intended to encourage the small business sector. A significant number of these closed corporations – which are formally constituted as separate corporate business entities legally distinct from the private financial assets of the persons involved – are one-person establishments. This lead is being followed in a number of industrialized countries.

Such one-person firms cannot in all circumstances be conceptualized as coming into being to supersede transactions between persons or firms, or as existing because of the costs of using the market mechanism. The one-person firm cannot *in general* have the supersession of the price mechanism as distinguishing characteristic.

The important point is not to guess what Coase meant, but to ask to what extent his concept can be used to construct a general definition of the intrinsic, *generic* nature of the firm – the common element distinguishing all firms, in all shapes, sizes and forms, capitalist or non-capitalist. Furthermore, and critically, if the Coasean framework cannot capture the generic nature of the firm as such, as a matter of course it cannot capture the generic nature of specific variations, versions or forms (e.g. the capitalist firm) either.

1.3 What Do Markets Do? Do Markets Produce?

A more general insight regarding the relation (or distinction) between firms and markets is that firms can exist without markets, i.e. without barter or trade. However, a market, unlike a firm, cannot produce. Therefore market relations can only *link* firms (producing units). Barring the theoretically moot case of producing individuals that are not firms, or the hypothetical possibility of a multitude of non-firm (self-employed) producer-individuals, market relations are nothing but relations *between already existing firms* (or between such firms and customers). Typically, without firms that produce there are no products to be transferred and allocated by market transactions. Thus markets and firms are not alternative modes of production, but are inherently and essentially dissimilar.[3] Therefore the firm as such cannot derive its inner nature from the market, or from superseding the market.

Therefore, although some firms may in practice be formed or adapted in order to eliminate or avoid market (exchange) transactions, *the emergence and existence of the firm as such – of all firms – cannot be explained by transaction cost considerations.* Accordingly the supersession of the price mechanism cannot be the distinguishing mark of *the* firm – that has to be sought elsewhere (see Fourie, 1981). Therefore Coase's analysis simply cannot provide the distinctive characteristics and intrinsic nature of the firm as opposed to the market – *or*, for that matter, as opposed to other social organizations. (Actually the latter is an important point, for the attribute of the supersession of the price mechanism, i.e.

the allocation of resources via non-contractual internal interrelations, can also be found in non-firm, non-economic organizations such as universities, schools or churches.)

The important distinction here is that between the generic nature of a social institution and the variable positive forms that it can assume under various circumstances while retaining that intrinsic generic nature that makes them all identifiable as, say, firms. Therefore, what Coase's analysis *can* explain, and most effectively, is the existence of, and especially the *particular characteristics* (but not intrinsic nature) of, more complex or more developed *forms* of the firm, which include those that have already internalized formerly external relations or production units, or those that explicitly came about in order to economize on transaction costs. (This would of course also include Hodgson's 'capitalist firm'.[4]) Such firms and markets may perhaps be viewed as different modes of internally and externally *coordinating*[5] relations between producing units (which may, in the market case, be either producer-individuals, one-person firms or multi-person firms). For these forms of the firm Coase's characterization is an apt (albeit partial) *description* of certain pertinent aspects. However, as a *general definition* and depiction of the distinctive, intrinsic, generic nature of the firm as such – of *all* firms – it does not hold.

1.4 The Market: Transactions and Rivalry Relations

Another problem with Coase's analysis is his exclusive focus on the exchange relations within markets. However, exchange relations and markets are not equivalent. Markets not only comprise exchange (transaction-type) relations, but are more complex, structured phenomena also encompassing *rivalry* relations, e.g. those between sellers (see Fourie (1991) for a comprehensive analysis of the structure and nature of the market).

Therefore, the incentive to form or expand firms in order to eliminate the irritations and friction of markets not only relates to market transaction (or exchange) relations. Just as often the incentive to form or adapt firms may lie in the elimination of rivalry relations between competitors. In eliminating such relations (e.g. by a merger) the objective of economizing on exchange or transaction costs is not directly at issue, and expansion of the firm does not amount to the internalization of external transactions. Yet such mergers are (and always have been) an important method for the creation of new firms.

Again, Coase's analysis is not universally applicable, in this case not even to reasons for the emergence and form of specific firms (including capitalist firms). This confirms the circumscribed (although still significant) import of his analysis, in this case largely owing to an unthinking equating of the market as a whole with exchange relations.[6]

1.5 Markets and Hierarchies/Firms – Which First?

The complexity of the market as economic phenomenon also has relevance for the question of the chronological order in which markets and firms (hierarchies) appeared historically. Obviously the scene is set by Williamson's assertion that 'in the beginning there were markets'.

This phrase suggests an individualistic, atomistic type of argument, akin to that often used in a Hobbesian (natural law-type) social contract depiction of the presumed emergence of the state. Such an approach may want to see a market-coordinated community of self-employed producers/individuals as the 'natural' state, with transaction costs leading to the spontaneous, social contract-style emergence of the firm out of this sea of inter-individual market transactions. This indeed seems to be in the mind of many a theoretical economist working on transaction costs. However, as is the case with the individualistic social contract theory of the emergence of the state, this sea-of-individuals scenario is contrary to the historical development of society. Historically, the development of more individualistic inter-individual relationships was preceded by periods in which communal relationships (sibs, ancient villages and medieval cities, guilds or religious communities) dominated society. The individualistic 'natural state' picture and emergence story is a myth. For example, as a business historian such as Chandler (1979) illustrates, historically the development of the firm as separate business unit was closely associated with an emancipation process from within the family community (i.e. small, family businesses becoming independent firms), and *not* from isolated individuals.

That would seem to settle the point, especially if one adds that the development of more individualistic inter-individual relations required the prior development of the civil (i.e. inter-individual) law sphere, which in turn was preceded by the emergence and existence of the state. Then there is also the more general remark of North (1981, p. 41) that the view of the firm as a substitute for the market 'ignores a crucial fact of history: hierarchical organization forms and contractual arrangements in exchange predate the price-making market'.

Despite this I would want to caution against the dangers of getting into an either/or type of argument regarding the chronology. 'Which first?' is perhaps the wrong question to ask, simply because the relation between various types of societal phenomena is much more complex than a simple linear progression – especially because in history these phenomena (institutions, organizations, etc.) themselves went through different phases of differentiation and development, varying from seminal forms to more complex forms. In the process the links between and interweaving of phenomena – and notably between exchanges, markets and firms – also differentiated and developed (see Fourie, 1991). Typically, firms and markets are unbreakably interwoven, especially the less trivial, non-seminal forms found in a modern, differentiated economy. The internal, production relation of a firm has as necessary external correlate the external market relations. Similarly, the existence of external inter-relations that constitute the market are inextricably linked to the internal relations of the firm.

For analytical purposes the critical insight is that *the existence and development of firms and markets are unbreakably correlated* (see Fourie, 1991). An analysis of the historical details of the unfolding of this cor-related coexistence can be most enlightening. Given the structural richness involved in such an analysis, a 'which first' question may be quite misleading, if not simply banal. In any case, what is clear is that one should not attempt to use such a (hypothetical) individualistic rational reconstructionist model to derive the inner nature of the firm. That is where Coase went so wrong.

1.6 The Market as Seminal Unit of Analysis?

Superficially the source of the limitations of Coase's analysis is his failure to consider the entire spectrum of positive forms of the firm, and the one-person firm in particular. Although his concern may have been the typical 'capitalist firm', as Hodgson argues, and although in some societies the one-person firm today may be a relatively unimportant empirical phenomenon, there can be no arguing that a definitive logical and empirical test for a *general* conceptualization or definition of the firm as such is its ability to accommodate all positive forms of the firm that occur and have occurred historically and in different economic systems. Limiting one's analysis to one particular form, e.g. the 'capitalist firm', as Hodgson argues, is much too restrictive and indeed may prevent important insights, notably if one's objective is to ascertain the intrinsic, the generic, with regard to the firm.

The one-person firm is not the real issue. More fundamentally, Coase's weakness does appear to lie in his attempt to derive and explain the typical and distinguishing inner nature of the firm exclusively in terms of another, typically different relation, the market. While the insight that both firms and markets appear to have some coordinating function is important – so that Coase may rightly depict markets and (some) firms as alternative ways in which production activities are coordinated – *the nature of the firm cannot uniquely be described as market-replacing or market-simulating.* Considering that markets cannot produce, one cannot really say that the firm, where production plays such an essential and typifying role, only exists to supersede the market (i.e. because of market failure). Remarkable as Coase's insight may be, pursuing it as a general way of understanding the inner nature of the firm as such may stretch the analytical content and applicability of that insight to such an extent that eventually the exercise may obfuscate rather than clarify, may hide that which is unique behind the less distinctive (also see Kay, this volume).

A key question is the following. If the nature of the firm is not to be derived from, or explained exclusively in terms of, the market, what exactly is its relation to the market? The challenge is to discover the intrinsic dissimilarity between firm and market amidst the apparent similarity in terms of coordinating functions. To achieve this, the difference between within-firm and between-firm (i.e. market) relations must be analysed.[7]

2 WITHIN THE FIRM AND BETWEEN FIRMS

If markets can *at most link* firms, market relations are necessarily external to any firm (whose production is internal to that firm). A clear conceptualization of internal and external relations is important, as is apparent when one considers the differences between the following: the employment relation (the employer–employee relationship), subcontracting, and vertical or horizontal integration (internalization).

2.1 Employment versus Integration

One fundamental step towards delineating the bounds of the firm, as well as the difference between firm and market, is a clear definition of employment and employeeship. An indication of problems that can arise in this context is provided by the critical analysis of contributions by Oliver E. Williamson.

In his pioneering focus on hierarchies Williamson (1973, 1975) expands on the internalization argument of Coase. He begins by noting that 'the transaction is the ultimate unit of microeconomic analysis' (1975, pp. xi, 20). Assuming that 'in the beginning there were markets' with ubiquitous contracting, he explores how the choice between handling a transaction in a market *vis-à-vis* within a firm (a hierarchy) hinges on transactional factors. He discusses three contexts.

1 *The labour market* Given 'autonomous contracting between individuals', these are impeded by transactional factors (bounded

rationality paired with uncertainty, opportunism paired with small numbers, and information compactedness). This is the reason 'for *workers* to be joined in simple hierarchies' (1975, p. 56; emphasis added). Hierarchy, which embodies authority and subordination, can overcome transactional impediments. Therefore 'simple hierarchy . . . can be regarded as substitutions of internal organization for failures in the *labour* . . . markets' (1975, p. xvi; emphasis added).

2 *The employment relation* Four alternative modes of 'labour contracting' between employer and employee are considered: contingent claims contracting, recurrent spot contracts, the Simon authority relation (Simon, 1957, pp. 184–5) and the internal labour market (Williamson, 1975, pp. 72–81). Of these only the last, being within a hierarchy, is free from transactional difficulties.

3 *Intermediate product markets* Given technologically separable production units and the exchange of components between them (under contingent claims or recurrent spot contracts), the same transactional factors impede these alternative types of sales contracts. This induces the merger of the production units into a hierarchy. Thus vertical integration 'can be regarded as [the] substitution of internal organization for failures in the . . . intermediate product markets' (1975, p. xvi; also pp. 56, 82 et seq.) and moreover as the extension of the employment relation to include department managers (for example, a former inside contractor) (1975, p. 4).

The question is whether Williamson actually succeeds in providing a consistent and clear distinction between (a) employing an individual within a firm, (b) subcontracting and (c) integrating a production unit on the opposite side of a market relation. First of all, Williamson appears to use the term employee to encompass both internal workers (members) of a firm and external subcontractor-individuals.[8] This is untenable, especially because he sees relations with the latter as labour contracting. Furthermore, it does not provide a distinction between what is inside and what is outside the firm.

Second, situation 1 describes *workers* joining in a hierarchy to overcome transactional failures in the *labour* market. If Williamson is describing the emergence of a firm along Coasean lines, his analysis suffers from the same flaws. Furthermore, here the firm (hierarchy) replaces labour markets (defined as transactions between workers). If he is describing the merger or integration of one-person firms, it is difficult to see why he treats it separately from situation 3, and why he calls it a labour market situation. If he is describing an employment process, why treat it separately from situation 2?

One must conclude that here Williamson fails to provide the necessary distinction between employment, subcontracting and integration. This evidently is because he, ironically, does not clearly distinguish markets and firms (i.e. hierarchies; also see Kay, this volume). In his analysis these simply become different degrees or classes of coherence between workers in the labour market, and this clouds his distinctions. (He also fails to distinguish workers/individuals and one-person firms.)

2.2 Employment versus Subcontracting: the Contract Approaches

A different approach to these matters is to ask whether one should try to distinguish firms and markets at all, whether they are not so similar that firms really should be regarded as quasi-markets. Indeed, it has been argued that the entire exercise of drawing firm–market contrasts is misplaced (see Klein, 1983, p. 373; Putterman, 1986, p. 18). To consider this question it is useful to contrast employment proper (i.e. of a worker within a firm) with subcontracting (in the market).

Alchian and Demsetz – and the grocer

The seminal contribution in this regard is that of Alchian and Demsetz (1972), who compare the relation between a grocer and his employee with that between a client and his grocer:

> The firm does not own all its inputs. It has no power of fiat, no authority, no disciplinary action any different in the slightest degree from ordinary market contracting between any two people. I can 'punish' you only by withholding future business or by seeking redress in the courts for any failure to honour our exchange agreement. That is exactly all any employer can do. He can fire or sue, just as I can fire my grocer by stopping purchases from him or sue him for delivering faulty products. What then is the content of the presumed power to manage and assign workers to various tasks? Exactly the same as one little consumer's power to manage and assign his grocer to various tasks. . . .
>
> To speak of managing, directing, or assigning workers to various tasks is a deceptive way of noting that the employer continually is involved in renegotiation of contracts on terms that must be acceptable to both parties. Telling an employee to type this letter rather than to file that document is like telling a grocer to sell me this brand of tuna rather than that brand of bread. . . .
>
> I have no contract to continue to purchase from the grocer and neither the employer nor the employee is bound by any contractual obligations to continue their relationship. Long-term contracts between employer and employee are not the essence of the organization we call a firm. (1972, p. 777)

The employee can terminate the contract as readily as the employer, and long-term contracts, therefore, are not an essential attribute of the firm. (1972, p. 783)

My grocer can count on my returning day after day and purchasing his services and goods . . . and he adapts his activity to conform to my directions to him as to what I want each day . . . he is not my employee. (1972, p. 777)

In essence Alchian and Demsetz argue that there is no fundamental difference between these two relations on the following points: the role and presence (rather absence) of authority and punishment, the voluntary and contractual nature of the relations, the equivalence of assigning tasks and continuously renegotiating contracts, and the relevance of the term of the contract (long versus short). The only substantial difference is that, with respect to employment relations, one party, the employer, is in a centralized position in the contractual arrangements with other 'inputs' (employees), and that there is team use of inputs in the (by assumption) joint-input production process. (Indeed, they argue that firms exist in order to exploit the advantages of such team work: the 'team process' induces 'the contractual form called the firm'.)

Internal criticism shows the following. First, their definition of the firm as a contractual team of inputs can only be valid, if at all, for multi-person firms and not for one-person firms. Conversely it has been pointed out in the literature that their definition cannot explain large complex hierarchical firms either (Williamson, 1981, p. 1565). Therefore it cannot serve a general conception of the firm.[9] Second, the centralized position of one party in internal contracts is just as true for the contractual relationships between their illustrative grocer and all his customers and suppliers.[10] *This leaves the (intra-firm) relationship between grocer and employee indistinguishable from the (extra-firm) relationship between grocer and customer or supplier.* Everything is reduced to market relations.

This causes a dilemma for these authors. Given their viewpoint, on what grounds can they themselves call one person employee and another supplier or (inside or outside) contractor (or customer), i.e. how can they distinguish between employment and subcontracting? In the absence of a clear distinction between internal and external relations such terms cease to have legitimacy.

Jensen and Meckling

These kinds of problems are most apparent in an equally seminal paper by Jensen and Meckling (1976), who treat the firm under the theory of principal–agent relationships. Like Alchian and Demsetz they emphasize the contractual nature of firm relationships: 'contractual relations are the essence of the firm, not only with employees but with suppliers, customers, creditors, etc.' (p. 370). They do so, however, in a stricter way that concentrates exclusively on the contractual aspect. The firm is viewed, as are organizations in general, simply as a legal fiction that serves 'as a nexus for a set of contracting relationships among individuals';[11] it is an 'artificial construct under the law' that allows the organization to be treated as an individual (pp. 310–11). For them there is only a multitude of inter-individual contractual relationships. All structures or organizations are artificial. Accordingly, 'the behaviour of the firm is like the behaviour of the market, i.e. the outcome of a complex equilibrium process' (p. 311).

This view implies truly no distinction between internal and external relations of the firm, as the authors readily admit (claim?): 'Viewed this way, it makes little or no sense to try to distinguish those things which are "inside" the firm (or any other organization) from those things that are "outside" of it (Jensen and Meckling, 1976, p. 311).[12] However, a denial of any difference cannot be made as easily as that. The inevitable consequence of dissolving everything into a series of interpersonal transactions is to eradicate any distinction between institution and non-institution, between firm and market. As a general theory of the distinctive nature of firms and markets this approach must fail. If everything is reduced to an ocean of inter-individual market relations, one cannot legitimately talk about the firm or about the market, cannot distinguish managers, employees or outsiders, cannot talk of owning a firm, residual claims on a firm, the inside or outside equity of a firm, factors exogenous to an organization, etc. – terms Jensen and Meckling use all the time. Therefore their view is inconsistent with concepts they themselves use and cannot avoid using.

The untenability of this approach is borne out by the fact that it is inconsistent with the historical order of events. Legal contracts became possible only after the dissolution of primitive undifferentiated society into a differentiated society with different institutions, notably the state, whose public legal order makes such contracts possible and enforceable. However one wishes to interpret history, the existence of meaningful contracts requires the existence of a public legal order, which in turn presupposes the emergence and existence of at least the state (and by implication other institutions). But this is contrary to Jensen and Meckling's own view that all structures, including the state, are actually non-existent and but a legal fiction masking a multitude of purely inter-individual contractual relationships. Their denial of the real existence of structures like the state thus precludes the very contracts that are at the core of their argument.

3   INTERNAL AND EXTERNAL RELATIONS: AN ALTERNATIVE VIEW

3.1   Sources of Failure: the Market and Individualism

As suggested before, the four contributions share a key feature that is simultaneously a common source of problems. What it amounts to, albeit in varying degrees, is the theoretical hegemony of the market concept – a tendency to define everything in terms of, or reduce everything to, market transactions. Starting with Coase they progressively posit an increasing extent of similarity between market relations and within-firm relations. Coase finds a common element in a process of resource allocation, but flounders when attempting to explain the nature of the firm entirely in terms of the market – the firm is reduced to a proxy for, or a simulation of, the market.[13] Williamson places even less emphasis than Coase on the difference between markets and hierarchies. In his 'employment relation' both categories are seen as forms of employment in the labour market – any difference is only a matter of degree, blurring any distinctiveness between firms and markets. Alchian and Demsetz as well as Jensen and Meckling find the common element in the contractual nature of inter-individual market relations, a correspondence between firm and market so absolute that any real difference is denied: interindividual markets (contracts) become the only relevant economic entities.

More specifically, these approaches cannot explain or consistently accommodate a number of elements that appear to be essential in the determination of the distinctive nature of firms and markets. These elements are:

* All the kinds and forms of firms and markets. All these authors have a problem with this: some, for example Coase, cannot accommodate the one-person firm, while others acknowledge 'producing individuals' (one-person firms?) and nothing more.
* What is inside versus what is outside the firm. This is the critical question that Coase, Williamson and the other authors are attempting to face up to. The former two do acknowledge some distinction, although their analysis is not entirely successful. The other authors deny the importance of and need for this distinction. This causes their predicament, as shown above.
* The relation between individuals and structures (institutions, organizations). Both Coase and Williamson seem to accept the real existence of organizations or hierarchies. While Coase does not focus on individuals as such, Williamson has trouble distinguishing a one-person firm and an individual. The other authors cannot, given

their premises, do anything but deny the real existence of organizations to a lesser or greater extent; hence they cannot clarify the relation between individuals and such organizations.

- The unity and durability of firms *vis-à-vis* the absence of any durable unity in inter-individual or market relationships. In particular, Alchian and Demsetz and Jensen and Meckling fail to explain and take this into account when they reduce all organizations to a series of market transactions.

On the whole the result of conceptualizing the firm exclusively in terms of the market (i.e. as a market analogue) is that in the end no uniquely different attributes of the firm can be identified. *If the firm is nothing but another variant of the market, a quasi-market, the firm as societal institution has not been, and cannot be, uniquely typified.* The distinctiveness of the firm is obscured behind certain apparent similarities with the market. In addition severe logical and historical inconsistencies are encountered.[14]

The tendency to reduce everything to market relations is closely linked to a highly individualistic approach to the theoretical analysis of society – the dominance in economics of 'methodological individualism' (Boland, 1982). Alchian and Demsetz and Jensen and Meckling adopt a strictly individualistic explanation of all 'structures' when they attempt to analyse exclusively in terms of the simplest elements, the elementary interactions between autonomous individuals (atoms). Without any regard for any structure or 'societal form' within which individuals may operate, they effectively deny the existence of societal structures like firms. In a sense they only acknowledge one-person firms or, actually, producing individuals, despite the existence of multi-individual firms. This leads them straight into dilemmas and inconsistencies.

3.2   The Alternative: the Firm as a Durable, Cohesive Structure

The results above lead one to shy away from efforts to consider firm and market as mere alternatives, as equivalent ways of organizing economic activity, and to argue for the acceptance of the reality of firms as separately recognizable, cohesive societal structures and as something quite different from market relations. Without in any way denying the pivotal role of individuals and inter-individual interaction within these structures, such a view recognizes *firms as cohesive, durable institutions with members (individuals) who are bound together in a solidary whole that has a durability of existence amidst changes in membership*. It implies that in their capacity as members of such a whole, individuals do not have a detached, linked-only-by-market-transactions existence.

This is accepted for at least three reasons. The first is its intuitive appeal: if such institutions did not really exist, if they were fictitious, if there were only a multitude of individuals, why is it that one can observe and immediately recognize them as firms? Obviously there are people (individuals) everywhere, but why are one and all intuitively aware of these and other institutions *as institutions*? And let it not be argued that the real existence of organizations/institutions is not at issue here.[15] The ultra-individualistic views of Alchian, Demsetz, Jensen and Meckling deny exactly that. As shown below, had they in fact accepted such existence and its consequences, their analyses would be rid of much weakness.

A second reason for adopting this stand is the dilemmas and inconsistencies revealed by internal criticism of views that do deny the real existence of any structure. This strongly suggests that there is a reality that cannot be disregarded at will or forced into a favoured intellectual framework – in this case extreme individualism. Third, and conclusively, the simple step of accepting the existence of the firm as a cohesive institution at once suggests a way out of most of the difficulties highlighted before. The basic points, to be elaborated below, are these:[16]

- The firm's internal relations can be defined as those between members (including managers) and/or sub-units within the firm. This allows one to distinguish, as a correlate of these internal relations, market relations as an external exchange relation between firms (or firm and customer/supplier).
- The main distinction of the market relation is that it does not unite the participants into a cohesive whole, but leaves them to interact independently in cooperation, neutrality or antagonism.[17] This interaction – or 'coordination by the market' – remains external to any institutional whole such as the firm. Such a two-participant non-cohesive relationship also guarantees no continuity amidst changes in participants. Any change in participant implies a new relationship, implying recurring formation and disintegration of such relationships.
- When such an external, market relationship is internalized by a firm (as in Coase's analysis) its character changes to a within-firm, i.e. an intra-whole relation, with the initially separate firms or units becoming bound together and coordinated within one institutional whole. Such coordination as exists is distinctively characterized by the cohesiveness and durability of the firm as institution (see below).

Without any pretence of providing insight into all aspects of the distinctive nature of the firm, these results enable important first steps: they preserve a clear difference and distinction between internal and external units/individuals/relations, and pave the way for legitimate and meaningful distinctions between firm and market, inside and outside, employee and supplier, and so forth. This can now be demonstrated.

Employment: authority, voluntarism and the durability of contracts

At this point it is useful to introduce the concept of a *voluntary association*. Such an organization contrasts with, for example, the family – into which one is born and thus becomes and remains a member independently of one's will – and the state, where citizenship automatically derives from birth and normally cannot be changed arbitrarily, and, if at all, only subject to restrictions imposed unilaterally by that state. Membership of a voluntary association always originates from an (implicit or explicit) voluntary contract of membership.

Once the firm is conceived of as a durable, cohesive structure encompassing individuals, one can recognize that the firm in fact is a voluntary association. One can then apply the concept of membership: in this case the contract of membership is a contract of *employeeship*. This provides a clear definition of an employment or labour contract proper: an employee is internal to the firm, and is a person who has voluntarily entered into a contract of membership with the employer. (He or she is, of course, simultaneously a member of other structures and institutions, such as the church, state and family, fulfilling particular functions in each.)

This is why, as observed by Alchian and Demsetz, the employment relation typically displays a voluntary and contractual nature, similar to the market relation. However, a crucial insight is that each actualization of tasks in the continuing employer–employee relationship itself is not, *ab initio*, per contract. Only the initial *establishment* of this relationship is.

This concerns the durability or non-durability of employment and market contracts (Putterman, 1986, p. 7), and specifically the presence or absence of authority. Since the firm as cohesive structure has a more or less durable existence, membership implies durability in the employment relation – as against a more or less instantaneous non-durable relation in a market exchange. Durable membership implies a *durable contract*, which covers and allow a range of tasks within certain limits – if the firm has to negotiate a separate exchange contract for each task as it arises, no 'worker' becomes a member. Whereas such a system of establishing separate exchange contracts implies the absence of any authority and subordination, durable contracts that allow a range of possible tasks imply the presence of authority.[18] A true employment contract therefore enters the individual into a durable societal whole under a single (membership) contract that allows the employer to assign the employee to particular tasks.[19] That is, the employer has authority over the employee.

Alchian and Demsetz, therefore, are correct when they say that an employer has no authority over a person with whom he or she contracts, spot-contract style, for a single and specific task. However, such a person is not an employee proper, not a member of the firm. What they say amounts to the truism that an employer has no authority over a non-employee, for example a subcontractor. The latter remains external to the firm: there is no durability, no membership and especially no authority in this and other market relationships.[20]

Thus: (a) with employment only the establishment is by contract, not each task in the day-to-day variable actualization of the relation that the durable contract allows for and sets bounds for; (b) with market exchanges both the establishment and momentary realization are essentially contractual. The problem in the analysis of Alchian and Demsetz stems from their failure to recognize and incorporate this distinction. Their 'employee' is no real employee, no member of the firm. To paraphrase them, to speak of the employer being continually involved in renegotiation of (spot) contracts with 'employees' is a deceptive and incorrect way of noting that the employer is managing, directing and assigning employees to various tasks under a single durable membership contract with an implied authority relation.

The fact, noted by Alchian and Demsetz (1972, p. 783), that an employee can readily terminate his membership does not affect this conclusion. The voluntary nature of membership does not imply that it may not be durable nor that the employer may not assign employees to tasks during their voluntarily entered into membership of the firm. In voluntarily accepting membership the employee just as voluntarily accepts the authority of the employer for the duration of his membership. As Williamson (1975, pp. xv and 54) notes, the employment relation is associated with voluntary subordination (also Putterman, 1986, p. 7).[21]

Employment, subcontracting and integration

The basic source of confusion regarding employment and vertical integration is that they occur together so often that they are confused with each other. However, the definition of employment that flows from the distinction between firm and market above enables one to distinguish them and at the same time clarify the nature of subcontracting.

Integration in the first instance involves the inclusion, by an integrating firm, of new functions – previously performed by a subcontractor, say – in its range of functions. If a subcontracting firm as such becomes part of this firm, it is a merger as opposed to internal expansion. Both are acts of integration or internalization. New functions require employees to perform them. But only if new hiring takes place (or if there is a merger) do new employment relations concur with integration. Integration as such does not necessarily imply (new) employment. It is but one instance when employment *may* occur. Similarly, employment as such does not imply integration, only membership of an additional individual. In principle these two processes are distinct, even though and even when they occur simultaneously. One internalizes an individual, the other internalizes a firm. This is true, notably, in the case of integrating a one-person firm: such integration can be seen to involve, in principle, both of these different processes.

Moreover, in terms of the internalization of transactions the two processes differ markedly. When a producing unit (firm) is vertically integrated a formerly external exchange relation is simultaneously internalized, with transaction cost considerations most relevant. Employment *per se*, however, does not comprise internalization of a transaction relation. While employment can be regarded as the internalization of an individual (but not of a one-person firm) the transition is from the absence of any exchange or transaction relation to the existence of an employment relation. Consequently *the decision to employ* per se *cannot be explained by transaction costs considerations*.

This analysis shows that a likening of employment 'under authority' (i.e. within the firm) and employment 'in the market' is not meaningful. Employment proper is by nature and in principle within-firm (notwithstanding everyday, non-scientific use of the term as in 'employing a subcontractor'). Subcontracting, by contrast, is an external, market relation. This is the main misconception in Williamson's treatment of employment and vertical integration, and explains the inconsistencies outlined before.[22] Once the proper distinctions are used to amend his analysis, it gains considerably in clarity and explanatory power.

Jensen and Meckling do not and cannot provide any distinctions between employment, integration and (sub-) contracting. This is inevitable and intentional, since all but the latter class are defined out of existence. If only inter-individual market exchanges and a multitude of individual producers are acknowledged, the choice between integration and subcontracting does not exist.[23] As a matter of course their analysis excludes the existence of employment proper – all that exists is subcontracting.

3.3   Digression: the One-person Firm Again

It may be felt that the notion of a one-person firm is not consistent with my own definition of the firm, in particular that a one-person firm is not durable since it dies with the person, that there are not 'members bound together' and that it is not an organization.

The durability of firms should not be misunderstood as permanency of existence. What it means is that if the single owner-manager sells the firm to another person, the change in occupancy does not affect the uninterrupted existence of that firm. (This is particularly obvious in the case of an incorporated one-person firm, e.g. in the closed corporation.) Similarly, if the single owner-manager dies, ownership/management of the business can be transferred to another person while that particular firm continues to exist. This contrasts with, say, a marriage, where a change in partner necessarily destroys the first marriage and necessarily requires the creation of a new marriage. In this sense a marriage does not have durability amidst changes in membership, whereas a firm has.

The absence of multiple membership does not present a problem *if* one has a developmental perspective on more and less complex forms of the firm, *and if* one realizes that in a differentiated society membership never implies a total subsumption of the whole person, rather his or her fulfilling a specific function within the context of that particular organization. In the more developed forms of the firm separate persons fulfil the functions of manager, worker and shareholder. By contrast, in simpler forms of the firm, e.g. a partnership, the capacities of manager and worker are situated in one person or persons (they act as both manager and worker). That is, whereas in more developed firms these capacities (or functions) are separated out (differentiated) and situated in different persons, in simpler forms they still overlap. Yet these *capacities* (if not persons) can still be distinguished in these 'collapsed' or seminal versions of the firm.[24]

The one-person firm is the ultimate seminal firm, where all capacities/functions overlap and situate in one person – the person (in one capacity) employs himself (in another capacity). Therefore the cohesiveness and bounding together of 'members' – or, more accurately, of members *in their particular capacities/functions* – is automatic. That the latter attribute is somewhat trivial in this simple, polar case does not prevent one from identifying this as a crucial feature in more complex forms of the firm. In this regard the term 'self-employed producer', used by Hodgson for example, in itself reveals more than one may suspect. The ironic point is that use of the term 'self-employed' is a Freudian slip suggesting that this 'person' is indeed implicitly viewed as a seminal firm, with at least two capacities involved, as noted above.

Of course this argument does not imply that all producer-individuals have to be viewed as firms. One must leave room for a non-firm producing individual. Exactly when such a producing activity becomes a firm is still unsettled. However, the number of persons involved will probably not be decisive, but the extent to which the particular production activity becomes differentiated from the private (or family) life of the person, i.e. begins to function as a primarily *economic* entity separate from the (primarily non-economic) family institution.

As for the term organization, the reader is probably used to the use of this term, for example in organization theory, in the context of the problems of managing and coordinating a large number of people. However, in a wider sense the term just denotes the activity of using power to structure, arrange, order and coordinate recources, i.e. using formative (economic) power actively to shape and direct a production process. This may or may not involve people/employees, and in any case is also applicable to the management of (real and financial) capital. In this sense a one-person firm is also an organization, for its foundation indeed is the organization of capital and other resources in a production process.

4   CONCLUSION

One purpose of this chapter has been to highlight the usefulness and limitations of the transaction and contract approaches in analysing the nature of, and relation between, firms and markets. Essentially these approaches focus on two aspects: the role of *transactions* (markets, contracts), and the *inter-individual* nature of these. Both angles have much insight to offer. However, they do have definite limitations. These appear when one attempts to explain firms and markets almost exclusively in terms of inter-individual market relations.

In general it has been shown that:

- The generic firm, the firm *as such*, cannot be defined or distinctively characterized exclusively in terms of market transactions.
- Therefore the distinguishing mark of the firm as such (as against markets and as against other organizations) cannot be the supersession of the price mechanism.
- More particularly the existence of the firm as such cannot be explained by transaction cost arguments.
- The employment decision of a firm cannot be explained by transaction cost considerations either.
- On the other hand both the decision to integrate and the extent of integration can be explained in this way (as has been done most fruitfully in recent contributions of, for example, Williamson (1985)).
- Not only transactions (exchanges), but also rivalry relations within markets are relevant in the determination of the boundary of the firm.

The development of an alternative approach has as starting points: (a) the intrinsic, generic dissimilarity between the firm and the market, and (b) the real existence of the firm as a cohesive, durable institutional whole within which individuals play their pivotal role. One important reason for accepting this viewpoint is that such a perspective clarifies most of the problems and pitfalls exposed earlier, pinpoints the usefulness of transaction insights, and provides consistent characterizations of differences between firms and markets, between internal and external relations, and between employment, integration and subcontracting. Without acceptance of the firm as a cohesive structure these distinctions cannot be drawn consistently.

While much has been said above about what the firm is *not*, relatively little has been contributed positively about what the distinctive nature of the firm actually *is* (see Fourie, 1981). However, establishing the futility of searching for the distinctive nature of the firm in that of another, very different thing, the market, is most useful. It forewarns against nonproductive avenues of inquiry, in particular those instinctively most tempting for economists, given the dominance of the market concept in conventional economic thinking. It shows that if the market is to be used at all in the search for the distinctive nature of the firm, its most useful role is probably in determining what the firm is *not*. That, rather than conceptually trying to model the firm on the market, may be the methodologically most sensible meaning of the expression 'using the market as a benchmark'. Everything simply cannot be explained in terms of market relations (see note 15).

Another, more fundamental methodological inference is that an exclusively individualistic explanation that attempts to disregard the existence of real societal structures encounters debilitating problems. The difficulties encountered severely limit the potential of these approaches to give insight into the nature of the various kinds of relations and structures one finds in society, including – ironically – the place of individuals and markets in these. A less extreme approach is called for.

NOTES

1 Williamson (1975, 1985) provides an exposition of the transactional factors underlying the costs of markets. Klein et al. (1978) provide additional insights.
2 That leaves still unsettled the question of whether an individual producer or artisan is to be regarded merely as a 'producing person' or as a firm, albeit a seminal one; alternatively, when such a 'producing unit' becomes a (one-person) firm. This is discussed in section 3.5.
3 Although Coase himself does not put it this way, Marris and Mueller (1980) have characterized Coasean approaches as viewing markets and firms as alternative modes of production.

4   In fact, that Hodgson's viewpoint is problematic is also suggested by the fact
    that even a multi-person partnership where all the partners are both
    managers and workers, and where there is no real employment relation,
    would not qualify as a (capitalist) firm. Meanwhile, a business history such as
    Chandler (1979) shows that the partnership is and was an important form of
    the (capitalist) firm in, for example, the United States. Also see section 3.5.

5   In this context the term *coordinate* should be used, not *organize*, as Hodgson
    does (this volume) or *direct*, as Coase does. Markets cannot organize (*or*
    direct), for the latter term denotes, and requires, active decision-making
    capability, power and authority. The market is not a person, and has no such
    capabilities. The market can at most lead to a rather loose, non-managed,
    spontaneous linking or coordination of voluntary participants (in which the
    market power of participants can of course play an important determining
    role) (see Fourie, 1991).

6   See also North (1981, pp. 42–3), who distinguishes between markets and
    price-making markets. In this context it is important to have a developmental
    perspective on the positive form of markets, i.e. a spectrum of forms from
    simple, even seminal markets to complex markets. Correspondingly price has
    various, differentiated functions, depending on the complexity of the market
    (Fourie, 1991).

7   While Coase does not incorporate all consequences of the difference between
    within-firm and between-firm relations (see below), he does suggest that they
    differ in that internalized transactions are carried out using the direction and
    authority of an entrepreneur-coordinator, while in external (market)
    transactions coordination is by the price mechanism. The role of authority is
    discussed below.

8   He also describes the employment agreement as the substitution of a single
    incomplete contract for many complete ones with suppliers (1975, p. 4).

9   For related points of criticism, see Jensen and Meckling (1976, p. 310) and
    Williamson (1975, pp. 49–50).

10 They moreover fail to consider inter-employee and inter-subunit relations
    and transactions, internal to the firm, where there need be no centralized
    party.

11 The firm in particular is also characterized by the existence of divisible
    residual claims on the assets and cash flows of the organization which can
    generally be sold without permission of the other contracting individuals
    (Jensen and Meckling, 1976, pp. 310–11).

12 In similar vein Klein (1983, p. 373) has stated that the question concerning
    the essential characteristic of the firm appears to be unimportant, that it is a
    fundamental advance to think of all organizations as groups of explicit and
    implicit contracts.

13 Coase does preserve some difference since authority is present in the case of
    within-firm allocation; see note 8.

14 These problems are less apparent in Coase's analysis, but their seriousness in
    the more extreme versions of Alchian and Demsetz and Jensen and Meckling
    alerts one to the presence of similar problems in Coase's analysis.

15   Putterman (1986, p. 24) refers to analysts who indeed are embarrassed by the existence of real institutions and therefore attempt to develop new institutional analyses of highly neoclassical flavour where 'markets are found to surface at every pass and markets *work*' (italics in original).

16   It is not necessarily implied here that all the approaches discussed fail to achieve all these ends. In particular, Coase's analysis, being less extreme, is less vulnerable.

17   For an analysis of the intrinsic nature of the market, including a detailed analysis of aspects mentioned here, see Fourie (1991).

18   This is indicated by Coase (1937, p. 39) and Simon (1957, pp. 184–5), and acknowledged by Williamson as well as Alchian and Demsetz – the latter when they argue that recurrent spot contracting, and not durable or long-term contracts, is typifying the employer–employee relation, and that accordingly authority is absent from the firm.

19   In the quotation from Alchian and Demsetz above, the employee's typing the letter or filing a document are both covered by one membership contract. By contrast, buying tuna or buying bread from the grocer implies two different, non-durable exchange relations/contracts.

20   A so-called long-term sales contract is not a durable exchange relation as such, but only as an agreement to repeat the non-durable exchange at certain intervals. The supplier remains external to the firm, is not a member and is not under the authority of management.

21   The intrinsic voluntarism of the firm does have implications for the nature of its authority relation, in particular that it is radically different from that of other institutions, notably the state. That the firm does not have physical force or power as foundation of its authority does not imply that the firm does not have any authority relation at all. Such a misunderstanding can explain the denial by Alchian and Demsetz of authority in the firm. See Fourie (1989, p. 156).

22   His discussion of the 'labour' market – individuals being joined in simple hierarchies to overcome transactional impediments – can now be seen actually to concern the joining of one-person firms. It is thus simply another view of integration, not of the labour market proper. His 'employment relation' harbours a confusing mix of employment proper and subcontracting: he regards recurrent spot or contingent claims contracting as alternative modes of employment, while they really are alternative modes of subcontracting (market relations). His definition of vertical integration as the extension of the employment relation to include department managers ('inside contractors') confuses employment proper and integration.

23   The latter is the only real choice facing the firm in this regard. Employment versus either integration or subcontracting are not as such relevant options. Employment merely accompanies integration in some instances and is not the real alternative to subcontracting, even of a one-person firm.

24   The coincidence of different capacities or functions in one person is the necessary counterpart of the fact that one person can simultaneously be a member of different societal institutions, i.e. have a variety of differentiated

functions in different institutional contexts. Again, this is so because, in a differentiated society, his membership of one institution never implies a total subsumption, rather his fulfilling a specific function within the context of that institution. It is imperative not to think of the individual in an undifferentiated way.

REFERENCES

Alchian, A. A. and Woodward, S. (1988) The firm is dead; long live the firm. A review of Oliver E. Williamson's The Economic Institutions of Capitalism. *Journal of Economic Literature*, 26(1), 65–79.

Alchian, A. A. and Demsetz, H. (1972) Production, information costs, and economic organization. *American Economic Review*, 62(5), 777–95.

Baumol, W. J. (1967) *Business Behaviour, Value and Growth*, revised edition. New York: Harcourt, Brace & World.

Boland, L. A. (1982) *The Foundations of Economic Method*. London: George Allen & Unwin.

Caves, R. E. (1980) Industrial organization, corporate strategy and structure. *Journal of Economic Literature*, 18(1), 64–92.

Chandler, A. D. Jr (1979) *The Visible Hand*. Cambridge, MA: Harvard University Press.

Cheung, S. N. (1983) The contractual nature of the firm. *Journal of Law and Economics*, 26(2), 1–21.

Coase, R. H. (1937) The nature of the firm. *Economica*, 4, 386–405.

Cohen, L. R. (1979) The firm: a revised definition. *Southern Economic Journal*, 46(2), 580–90.

Cyert, R. M. and Hedrick, C. L. (1972) Theory of the firm: past, present, and future; an interpretation. *Journal of Economic Literature*, 10(2), 398–412.

Cyert, R. M. and March, J. G. (1963) *A Behavioral Theory of the Firm*. Englewood Cliffs, NJ: Prentice-Hall.

Dugger, W. M. (1983) The transactions cost analysis of Oliver E. Williamson: a new synthesis? *Journal of Economic Issues*, 17(1), 95–114.

Fama, E. F. (1980) Agency problems and the theory of the firm. *Journal of Political Economy*, 88(2), 288–307.

Fourie, F. C. V. N. (1981) *A structural theory of the nature of the firm*. Unpublished PhD Dissertation, Harvard University.

Fourie, F. C. V. N. (1989) The nature of firms and markets: do transactions approaches help? *South African Journal of Economics*, 57(2), 142–60.

Fourie, F. C. V. N. (1991) The nature of the market: a structural analysis. In G. M. Hodgson and E. Screpanti (eds), *Rethinking Economics*. Aldershot: Edward Elgar.

Jensen, M. C. and Meckling, W. H. (1976) Theory of the firm: managerial behaviour, agency costs and ownership structure. *Journal of Financial Economics*, 3, 305–60.

Klein, B. (1983) Contracting costs and residual claims: the separation of ownership and control. *Journal of Law and Economics*, 26(2).

Klein, B., Crawford, R. G. and Alchian, A. A. (1978) Vertical integration, appropriable rents, and the competitive contracting process. *Journal of Law and Economics*, 21, 297–326.

Machlup, D. (1967) Theories of the firm: marginalist, behavioral, managerial. *American Economic Review*, 51(1), 1–33.

Marris, R. (1964) *The Economic Theory of 'Managerial' Capitalism*. Glencoe, IL: Free Press of Glencoe.

Marris, R. and Mueller, D. C. (1980) The corporation, competition, and the invisible hand. *Journal of Economic Literature*, 18(1), 32–63.

North, D. C. (1981) *Structure and Change in Economic History*. New York: W. W. Norton.

Putterman, L. (ed.) (1986) *The Economic Nature of the Firm: a Reader*. Cambridge: Cambridge University Press.

Simon, H. (1957) *Models of Man: Social and Rational*. New York: Wiley.

Williamson, O. E. (1963) Managerial discretion and business behaviour. *American Economic Review*, 53(5), 1032–57.

Williamson, O. E. (1964) *The Economics of Discretionary Behavior: Managerial Objectives in a Theory of the Firm*. Englewood Cliffs, NJ: Prentice-Hall.

Williamson, O. E. (1973) Markets and hierarchies: some elementary considerations. *American Economic Review*, 63(2), 316–25.

Williamson, O. E. (1975) *Markets and Hierarchies: Analysis and Antitrust Implications*. New York: The Free Press.

Williamson, O. E. (1981) The modern corporation: origins, evolution, attributes. *Journal of Economic Literature*, 19(4), 1537–68.

Williamson, O. E. (1985) *The Economic Institutions of Capitalism*. New York: The Free Press.

4

Control, Markets and Firms

KEITH COWLING AND ROGER SUGDEN

1 INTRODUCTION

The aim of this chapter is to present some foundations for an alternative theory of the firm. The basic justification for doing this is that although the theory of the firm is the subject of a vast literature dating back many years and including numerous seminal contributions, there remain fundamental issues which are being misunderstood and indeed ignored, while other concerns are receiving inappropriate attention.

The chapter has two main sections. Section 2 focuses on Coase (1937), the (at least implicit) starting-point for most economists' work in this area. Section 2 uses a critique of Coase (1937) as a springboard for an alternative theory. It discusses the definition of a firm. Section 3 then advances the argument by turning to the ideas in Williamson (1975), the work that has revitalized Coasean analysis for many researchers. We compare the questions posed in Williamson (1975) to those posed by our analysis. Although there is some overlap, both the questions and the suggested answers are significantly different in the two approaches. Section 3 also comments on Aoki's (1990) discussion of Japanese firms, important for the attention they are receiving and for the challenging view that they are fundamentally different. Clearly the chapter falls short of presenting a complete theory and we thus conclude with some suggestions for future activity.[1]

The authors would like to thank Christos Pitelis for comments on an earlier draft of this chapter.

2 THE BEGINNINGS OF A THEORY OF THE FIRM[2]

The obvious starting point for a theory is to define a firm. This is considered by Coase (1937), who sees firms as the means of coordinating production without using market transactions. This is suggested by the following observation: 'Outside the firm, . . . production . . . is coordinated through a series of exchange transactions on the market. Within a firm those market transactions are eliminated' (Coase, 1937, p. 388).

The idea of firms as means of coordinating production is acceptable (with a qualification[3]), as in some sense is the view that production entails a set of transactions. However, we reject the focus on market versus non-market transactions. In querying this dichotomy we are not alone. For instance, Imai and Itami (1984) talk of non-market exchange using 'market principles', while agreeing that market exchanges occur only between firms or between firms and consumers – See also Brown (1984) on firm-like behaviour in markets and Richardson (1972) on inter-firm cooperation. But our concerns go much deeper than these, challenging Coase (1937) at a more fundamental level.

Focusing on the type of transaction used in production – be this market, non-market or any other, perhaps composite, type – is to focus on an essentially superficial attribute. It ignores the important insight that the crucial factors distinguishing transactions are their essential qualities. The very nature of a transaction is what matters. Whether or not the market is involved is of no fundamental relevance; it should be some underlying qualities that are the foundation for analysis because it can only be the essential characteristics that really distinguish transactions. This approach corresponds to that used by Marglin (1974, 1984, 1991) in his discussion of the transition from putting-out system to factory in the English textile industry. Marglin focuses in detail on what is happening in production, in particular on control of the work process, and does not get diverted into the market/non-market distinction.

Hence the key problem in devising a better theory of the firm is to determine the essential characteristics distinguishing transactions. With this in mind, particularly interesting has been the concern of a very extensive literature with firms' decision-making. This is significant because analyses of decision-making tend to concentrate directly on what is actually happening when production takes place; they tend to go to the heart of production, cutting through superficialities. This is precisely what we need. In general, this is seen in such seminal works as Simon (1959), arguing that satisficing is the norm, and Cyert and March (1963), which develops an analysis closely associated with all behavioural theories of the firm (see also the literature in the organizational behaviour tradition, e.g. Drucker, 1961; Channon, 1979; Andrews, 1980). More specifically – and for us more importantly – it is also seen in analyses of the control of firms.

Following Zeitlin (1974), control implies the ability to determine broad corporate objectives despite resistance from others. In other words, to control is to have the power to make decisions over strategic issues and hence to take a firm in a particular direction even though others would prefer something different. This is not to say that what actually happens in production is determined solely by these strategic decisions. Rather, they are the pinnacle of a hierarchical system of decision-making. They constrain the operational, day-to-day decisions over such tactical issues as the choice of a particular project from a subset of alternatives. Moreover, they also constrain the choices made by everybody in a firm over work intensity, etc. Thus what actually happens in production is determined by all three sets of decisions. Nevertheless, it is the strategic decisions that play the prime role because, by definition, they determine a firm's broad direction (see Pitelis and Sugden, 1986).

What all of this suggests is that the concept of strategic decision-making goes to the core of the way in which production is carried out in a firm. It implies that the crucial distinguishing feature of transactions within a firm is that they are subject to strategic decision-making from one centre. It also leads us to the suggestion that while we have thus far been content to go along with Coase's focus on transactions, and without denying that recognizing their presence can provide important insights into an understanding of firms' activities, this is not something to be retained in a definition concentrating on the real essence of a firm. What really matters is strategic decision-making. Accordingly we propose the following definition:

> A firm is the means of coordinating production from one centre of strategic decision-making.

To compare and contrast our definition with Coase's alternative, consider a simple illustration. Suppose an economy is characterized by one consumption good being produced without any market exchange and under the coordination of an operation with centralized control. For Coase this operation would be a firm: it is the means of coordinating production, there is no market exchange, and therefore it is 'the means of coordinating production without using market exchange'. We, too, would see the operation as a firm, but because of the centralized control. However, the critical difference between the approaches is seen by relaxing one of the simplifying assumptions: suppose now that there are market exchanges in production. For instance, if the consumption good is clothing, one stage of production may require the putting together of a sales catalogue containing a sample of the cloth used. One possibility is to bring workers into a factory where they literally sit down and glue squares of cloth on to a piece of card. For Coase, this would be a non-market activity. Another possibility is to subcontract the work to homeworkers. For Coase, this would involve a market exchange. For example, a home-worker may be contracted to carry out the task in consideration of one pound for each batch of one hundred completed cards. Such a transaction would therefore fall outside the ambit of a Coasean firm but inside the ambit of a firm as we see it. We prefer this view because production is still being coordinated from one centre of strategic decision-making whether or not there is a market exchange. In ignoring this the Coasean approach denies the especially important role of strategic decision-making in coordinating production. We suggest that the Coasean concern with superficial attributes misrepresents the activities of firms and can lead to misunderstanding and error, for instance underestimating the span of a particular firm's production and consequently, perhaps, underestimating the extent of monopoly power in an economy (among other things).

3 DEVELOPING THE INSIGHT

Our analysis also implies that reliance on the ideas in Williamson (1975) can lead to misunderstanding and error. This should be expected, given the association between the work of Williamson and Coase (although see Kay in this volume for differences). Nevertheless, it is worth comparing our approach to that in *Markets and Hierarchies* because this does advance the argument quite considerably.

Williamson (1975) poses two basic questions:

1 Why markets versus hierarchies, i.e. why carry out a transaction in a hierarchy rather than on a market?
2 What organizational form within a hierarchy, i.e. why carry out a transaction in a hierarchy in one way rather than another?

Both questions are aspects of the same general issue – the choice between alternative ways of completing a transaction – and thus it is not very surprising that his answers to both employ the same factors used in the same way. He concentrates on transactions costs and their alleged causes – more specifically bounded rationality, uncertainty and complexity, opportunism and small numbers – and is concerned with efficiency.

Consider, for instance, his analysis of a transaction being 'shifted out of a market and into a firm' (i.e. a hierarchy) (p. 20). His general approach is that 'whether a set of transactions ought to be executed across markets or within a firm depends on the relative efficiency of each mode' (p. 8). The source of efficiency gains is savings in transactions costs, the idea being that transacting on a market has different costs to transacting in a firm. These savings are associated with bounded rationality, etc.

3.1 Our Questions

Like that of Williamson (1975), our analysis clearly sees firms as hierarchies; indeed our definition of a firm focuses on strategic decision-making, seen as the pinnacle of a hierarchical system of decision-making. However, we see firms as hierarchies that can include what Williamson distinguishes as market and non-market transactions. This was illustrated by the case of homeworkers fixing cloth samples to sales catalogues. Providing production is being coordinated from one centre of strategic decision-making, a person carrying out this task is an employee of the firm whether working according to a market or non-market exchange: in either case the transaction would still be taking place within a hierarchy, there would still be a hierarchical relationship between a worker and the controllers of the firm. The crucial point is that what Williamson views as market versus non-market does not alter the essence of the transaction.

Accordingly, in the light of our definition, counterposing markets and hierarchies in the theory of the firm is not merely deficient, it is wrong. The market *versus* hierarchy question is fundamentally flawed because we are simply not faced by markets *rather than* hierarchies. It is a false dichotomy.

Williamson's markets versus hierarchies dichotomy is a specific form of the more general question: why are some transactions performed inside a firm and others performed outside a firm? Williamson's specific form simply follows from his view of markets and firms. The more general question is clearly interesting – for example, its answer explains why there is vertical integration (an issue given considerable attention by Williamson). Accordingly we can usefully address the more general question. Given our view of markets and firms it becomes, more specifically: why are some transactions coordinated from one centre of strategic decision-making and others not? This is the question we would ask in place of the markets versus hierarchies issue.

Williamson's second basic question is relevant to our theory of the firm. However, unlike for Williamson, for us the question does not merely compare non-market transactions. Rather it can be broken down into various issues, some of which Williamson (1975) cannot accommodate. We can sensibly ask: Why carry out a transaction in a hierarchy in one non-market way rather than another non-market way? Why carry out a transaction in a hierarchy in one market way rather than another market way? Why carry out a transaction in a hierarchy in a non-market way rather than in a particular market way? Whereas the first of these questions is the one that Williamson (1975) is really asking, neither of the others can arise in his analysis.

3.2 Our Answers

To ask why some transactions are coordinated from one centre of strategic decision-making while others are not is to focus on the essential characteristic of a transaction, not its type and not merely its cost. Thus the question asks why some transactions are of one nature and others of a different nature. This follows from the argument used to establish our definition.

Put like this it is clear that our answer is not going to concentrate on transactions costs. The whole point is that we are addressing why transactions are of different natures, i.e. do essentially different things. This is not an issue of merely finding the cheapest way to do something, which is the concern of transactions costs analysis. When we answer the second basic question (about organizational form within a firm), the factors identified in Williamson (1975) and the way he uses them have some interest but on both counts the work is of extremely limited relevance and contains fundamental flaws.

To illustrate the argument, consider Marglin's (1974) explanation for replacing the putting-out system with factories in the English textile industry during the Industrial Revolution – an argument about alternative organizational forms within firms as we have defined them. He argues that the desire of capitalists – i.e. strategic decision-makers – to supervise and discipline workers was all-important.[4] One interpretation of this is as follows. Under the putting-out system workers in the woollen industry, for instance, concealed imperfections in spinning to deceive capitalists – they behaved opportunistically. Accordingly capitalists brought workers into factories where they could be supervised. Assume for now that supervision in the putting-out system was impossible. What we have here is a transaction that could be carried out in a factory but could not be carried out in the putting-out system. Thus the costs of this particular transaction are finite in a factory and infinite under the putting-out system. Consequently the move to the factory saves transactions costs – it is efficient. But this is a trivial and very deceptive conclusion. It merely says that the factory is more efficient than something which cannot exist! As an explanation of organizational form within a hierarchy this is virtually worthless.

In contrast, Marglin emphasizes the importance of concentrating on what is really going on in production, and of appreciating distributional considerations. His analysis is in tune with our view of the firm and implies that focusing on transactions costs and opportunism misses the point. For Marglin, what really matters is the concept of supervision. True, opportunism makes supervision necessary (from the viewpoint of capitalists) and is therefore relevant. But it is the idea of supervision – an understanding of what is really going on in production – that provides the critical insight. As with the comparison between Coase's definition of the firm and ours, there are significant differences between an analysis concerned with superficialities and one concerned with essential characteristics. By getting bogged down in superficialities it is all too easy to miss the point. If Marglin is correct, the factory succeeded the putting-out system because it facilitated the supervision and discipline of workers; in other words, because it was to the advantage of capitalists. Moreover it is vital to appreciate that in Marglin's analysis the advantage to capitalists is obtained at the expense of workers. The welfare implications of this as compared to the transactions costs approach are enormous. Rather than having an efficiency implication, his analysis focuses on distribution.

Suppose supervision in the putting-out system was possible; would this change our understanding? The transactions costs analysis and its efficiency implication make more sense, because the factory and putting-out system are genuinely alternative means to an end, but they are still deficient and deceptive. It would certainly be wrong to argue that the factory was simply an efficient outcome because again this misses the crucial point that supervision and discipline is about capitalists gaining at the expense of workers.

More generally, in the light of our definition of the firm our answer to the organizational form question is very different to Williamson's (1975). The logic of our focus on strategic decision-making as the pinnacle of a hierarchical system of decision-making is that, essentially and in general, the choice of organizational form suits the strategic decision-makers. In making this choice, opportunism and so on will be relevant. Furthermore, insofar as strategic decision-makers could obtain an identical outcome except for greater cost some other way, the choice is concerned with transactions costs and is efficient. However, if no other method yields an identical outcome this efficiency claim is trivial. Even more importantly, in this case and even where there is another finite-cost means to contemplate, the benefit to strategic decision-makers is always the critical factor. This puts distributional considerations on centre stage. The choice suits strategic decision-makers. By definition of control, they are in a position to take the firm in directions that others would prefer to avoid. Hence it is a foregone conclusion that at least on some occasions their choice will yield them advantages at the expense of others, for instance workers.[5] The only thing to prevent this would be for these others to have a veto over outcomes that they dislike. However, this would mean that they are strategic decision-makers, which would be a contradiction. Moreover, even in situations where the chosen form does not leave others worse off, this is essentially coincidence; the point is that benefit to strategic decision-makers is the fundamentally important factor.

We have treated the firm as a homogeneous, hierarchical entity, but recent attempts have been made to distinguish a different type of firm characterized by a non-hierarchical coordination of production (see, for example, Aoki, 1990). This alternative mode, the so-called J-mode, being allegedly descriptive of the central features of a Japanese firm, is one in which management is secure in delegating coordination to lower levels, because employees are rewarded according to their contribution to organizational goals. Thus all employees actively participate in decision-making. Is this then worker control? Aoki is clear that this is not so. He argues that corporate decisions in the Japanese firm are subject to the dual control of financial interests (ownership) and employees' interests. However, Aoki fails to make a distinction between employee participation in operational decision-making and strategic decision-making. There is nothing in Aoki that would suggest that the strategic oversight of the Japanese firm is determined by any more than a tiny minority of those involved with the firm. While fuller participation in decision-making represents a real gain for its employees, that participation is sought for its contribution to the achievement of organizational goals set by those in strategic control. The fact that both employees and owners may, under certain conditions, gain from the J-mode of organizational form as compared with the H-mode, the term used by Aoki to refer to the standard hierarchical form of the contractual literature, does not deny the more fundamental point that the choice of organizational form suits the strategic decision-makers. We would therefore reject Aoki's notion of dual control: employee participation in operational decision-making does not constitute a dualism of control. Thus adaptations towards J-mode structures currently being made in Western H-mode firms do not undermine our central thesis. Worker participation will only constitute control when that participation extends to the realms of strategic decision-making, and the J-mode would appear to fall well short of that.

4   CONCLUSION

This chapter has proposed an alternative definition of the firm, going beneath an obsession with markets and based on centres of strategic decision-making.[6] It has identified a different set of research questions to Williamson (1975) and also indicated significant differences in the way these questions should be analysed. Without presenting a complete theory of the firm we have laid some foundations for an alternative approach. For the future, there are many areas to explore, not least the identification of a full research agenda and the more detailed exploration of even the items on that agenda focused upon in this chapter. A more specific requirement is to pursue the implications of our proposals, for example as regards the design of government industrial economic strategies.[7] There is also a need to position the approach in the context of a thorough appraisal of the existing literature. This should include a thorough critique of Williamson's work and ideas, going beyond the *Markets and Hierarchies* volume. It should also include examination of ideas from the likes of Alchian and Demsetz, i.e. from the other oustanding contributors to the field. This would both explain and develop out suggestions.

NOTES

1 We are currently engaged in an ongoing research programme that analyses sequentially different contributions to the theory of the firm. This chapter is an early product of that programme. A wider appraisal and development of tthe theory is in our plans for the future.

2 This section relies on Cowling and Sugden (1987a,b), which contain further analysis.

3 In practice firms are also a means of consuming goods and services but, as a first approximation, concentrating on production is reasonable.

4 The old question of why capital hires labour and not the other way around decomposes into two: why hierarchy, and why capitalists at the pinnacle of that hierarchy? 'The second question, put another way, asks why the rich do not simply lend their money out instead of undertaking production under their own supervision and control' (Eswaran and Kotwal, 1989). Their answer lies in the moral hazard in capital markets in the presence of limited liability: supervision is profitable. Thus hierarchical organizations will exist even when efficiency does not demand team production or the division of labour.

5 There is a dispute over who controls a firm. For example, some argue that it is senior managers, others that it is a subset of shareholders. However, there is widespread agreement that control rests with a subset of those involved with a firm and certainly not the general workforce.

6 Simon has recently returned to the fray to denounce the new institutional economics as seriously incomplete, retaining as it does 'the centrality of markets and exchanges' (Simon, 1991, p. 26), whereas 'the economies of modern industrialized society can more appropriately be labeled organizational economies than market economies' (p. 26).

7 See, for instance, Cowling and Sugden (1987a, 1991) for discussion of government strategies that build upon our alternative analysis of the firm.

REFERENCES

Andrews, K. R. (1980) *The Concept of Corporate Strategy*. Homewood, IL: Richard D. Irwin.

Aoki, M. (1990) Toward an economic model of the Japanese firm. *Journal of Economic Literature*, 28, 1–27.

Brown, W. B. (1984) Firm-like behaviour in markets: the administered channel. *International Journal of Industrial Organization*, 2, 263–73.

Channon, D. F. (1979) *Multinational Strategic Planning*. London: Macmillan.

Coase, R. H. (1937) The nature of the firm. *Economica*, 4, 386–405.

Cowling, K. and Sugden, R. (1987a) *Transnational Monopoly Capitalism*. Brighton: Wheatsheaf.

Cowling, K. and Sugden, R. (1987b) Market exchange and the concept of a transnational corporation: analysing the nature of the firm. *British Review of Economic Issues*, 9(20), 57–68.

Cowling, K. and Sugden, R. (1991) A strategy for industrial development as a basis for regulation. Mimeo, Research Centre for Industrial Strategy.

Cyert, R. N. and March, J. G. (1963) *A Behavioral Theory of the Firm*. Englewood Cliffs, NJ: Prentice-Hall.

Drucker, P. (1961) *The Practice of Management*. London: Mercury.

Eswaran, N. and Kotwal, A. (1989) Why are capitalists the bosses? *Economic Journal*, 99, 162–76.

Imai, K.-I. and Itami, H. (1984) Interpenetration of organisation and market: Japan's firm and market in comparison with the US. *International Journal of Industrial Organization*, 2, 285–310.

Marglin, S. A. (1974) What do bosses do? *Review of Radical Political Economics*, 6, 60–112.

Marglin, S. A. (1984) Knowledge and power. In F. Stephen (ed.), *Firms, Organizations and Labour: Approaches to the Economics of Work Organization*. London: Macmillan.

Marglin, S. A. (1991) Understanding capitalism: control versus efficiency. In B. Gustafsson (ed.), *Power and Economic Institutions: Reinterpretation in Economic History*. Aldershot: Edward Elgar.

Pitelis, C. N. and Sugden, R. (1986) The separation of ownership and control in the theory of the firm: a reappraisal. *International Journal of Industrial Organization*, 4, 69–86.

Richardson, G. B. (1972) The organisation of industry. *Economic Journal*, 82, 883–96.

Simon, H. (1959) Theories of decision-making in economics and behavioral science. *American Economic Review*, 49, 253–83.

Simon, H. (1991) Organization and markets. *Journal of Economic Perspectives*, 15(2), 25–44.

Williamson, O. E. (1975) *Markets and Hierarchies*. New York: Free Press.

Zeitlin, M. (1974) Corporate ownership and control: the large corporations and the capitalist class. *American Journal of Sociology*, 79, 1073–119.

5

Transaction Costs and the Evolution of the Firm

GEOFFREY M. HODGSON

Economic theory has suffered in the past from a failure to state clearly its assumptions. (Ronald Coase, 1973, p. 386)

This chapter is not only a plea for precision of language in the theory of the firm, as cited above in the very first sentence of the famous article on 'the nature of the firm' by Ronald Coase (1937). It is also argued that there are conceptual problems with the 'new institutionalist' theory of the firm advanced by Oliver Williamson (1975, 1985), relating to its individualist mode of analysis and its implicit but underdeveloped evolutionism.

After some general remarks are made about the transaction cost theories of Coase and Williamson, the argument in this chapter proceeds in the following steps:

1 Following earlier work by Carl Dahlman (1979), Richard Langlois (1984) and myself (Hodgson, 1988, chapter 9), it is reiterated that the concept of transaction costs must refer in the main to problems of radical uncertainty and lack of knowledge.
2 It is argued that the informational substance of transaction costs implies that the concept cannot be simultaneously combined with both the notion of omniscient calculation and Herbert Simon's idea of bounded rationality.
3 Hence, given transaction costs, retaining the concept of bounded rationality means the rejection of the idea of omniscient calculation. But this then means that we are in want of an explanation as to why a governance structure associated with lower transaction costs should predominate over another.
4 Accordingly, a comparative statics analysis is ruled out, and the main

The author is grateful in particular to Michael Dietrich, Frederick Fourie, Chris Pitelis and Mo Yamin for discussions and comments on earlier drafts of this chapter.

viable alternative mode of transaction cost analysis would seem to be an evolutionary one.

5   However, an evolutionary analysis poses a problem as to whether the individual or the firm is the unit of selection, and this is related to the 'appropriability critique' of Gregory Dow (1987).

6   To protect against the appropriability critique, the firm itself must be regarded as a unit of selection, rather than the individuals within it.

7   The most viable arguments for regarding the firm as such a collective entity bring us closer to the propositions of the 'old' rather than the 'new' institutionalism.

8   Furthermore, the evolutionary framework of analysis does not give support to some key propositions concerning hierarchy and efficiency advanced by Williamson.

The conclusion is that it might be more fruitful to examine the firm with some of the presuppositions of the 'old' institutionalist tradition, emanating in particular from the work of Thorstein Veblen and John Commons, in which the assumption of the given, hedonistic individual is abandoned.

1   THE COASEAN ARGUMENT

The famous work of Coase (1937) does not only include an explanation of why firms exist, it also (and necessarily) makes a conceptual distinction between the firm and the market. For Coase the key feature of the firm is its internal 'supersession of the price mechanism' (p. 389) and the allocation of resources by command rather through price. The question as to why firms exist then becomes the question as to why it is that the price mechanism is not used to allocate resources within the area of production taken over by the firm. For instance, why is it not normally the case that each worker, or group of workers, trades the semi-finished product with colleagues, until it reaches completion? Instead, the firm supplants such a mechanism by organizing relations differently, without such exchanges. As Coase (1937, p. 338) puts it: 'Within a firm, these market transactions are eliminated and in place of the complicated market structure with exchange transactions is substituted the entrepreneur–co-ordinator, who directs production.'

Coase (1937, pp. 390–1) then argues that:

> The main reason why it is profitable to establish a firm would seem to be that there is a cost of using the price mechanism. . . . It is true that contracts are not eliminated when there is a firm but they are greatly reduced. A factor of production (or the owner thereof) does not have to make a series

of contracts with the factors with whom he is co-operating within the firm, as would be necessary, of course, if this co-operation were as a direct result of the working of the price mechanism.

Following on from this approach, Williamson (1985, p. 1) has developed his central thesis that economic institutions such as the firm 'have the main purpose and effect of economizing on transaction costs'. Thus Williamson's explanation of the existence of non-market institutions is that they arise because they are less costly than continuous recourse to the market or exchange. Thus he too endorses a conceptual difference between the market itself and the non-market institution of the firm.

2 THE CONCEPT OF THE FIRM

All the foregoing is familiar, but even at this preliminary level there are some possibilities of misinterpretation. Consider the argument raised by Frederick Fourie (1989, p. 145), who writes that:

> Although there is no consensus on exactly what a firm is, the management of some *production* or distribution process appears to be central to the firm. Consider, however, that a market, unlike a firm, cannot produce. . . . If this is true, markets and firms are not alternative modes of production, but are inherently and essentially dissimilar.

Unfortunately, this is a misreading of Coase's argument. Note, first, that by a 'firm', Coase and Fourie mean different things. Coase himself is partly responsible for this confusion, for the bulk of his 1937 essay describes the firm in the vague terms of an 'entrepreneur–co-ordinator, who directs production' and who employs 'factors of production'. Towards the end of his essay (pp. 403–4) Coase does talk specifically about the employment relationship. Fifty years later, Coase (1988) stressed that his main concern was to see the essence of the firm in terms of organizational coordination.

Contrary to Fourie, while the management of production is central to the firm, production does not always involve firms in Coase's sense. For Coase, the firm involves the organization and coordination of multiple agents; the firm is essentially a multiple-person agency. In contrast, it is possible to conceive of ways of organizing production other than under the rubric of the firm. The obvious case is the market-coordinated community of self-employed producers, in which individual producers also trade their products directly on the market. This is referred to by Marx in *Capital* (depending on the translation) as a system of 'simple' or 'petty' commodity production.

Nowhere does Coase (or Williamson) suggest or imply that the self-employed producer can constitute a firm; clearly, by the firm, he has multiple-person entities in mind. Fourie, contrary to Coase, sees the self-employed producer as an example of a 'firm', and as a result their argument is at cross purposes. For Fourie, production *always* involves firms. In contrast, Coase conceives of the firm in terms of an organization encompassing at least one person. Hence it is quite reasonable for Coase to advance the proposition that the market is an *alternative* way of organizing production to the firm. At least two alternatives are possible: there can be a community of self-employed producers organized by the market, or there can be a capitalist firm organizing the same segment of productive activity through an employment relationship. Essentially, Fourie's 'criticism' stems from a different definition of 'the firm'. To avoid confusion, we must adopt either Fourie's or Coase's terminology: we cannot have both.[1]

For clarity, when we refer to the firm it should always be in terms of an enduring productive organization of two or more persons. With this definition of the firm, it is evident that all active firms engage in production, but not all production need involve firms.

A special case is 'the capitalist firm'. This is best defined in the terms of Marx (1976, pp. 291–2) in *Capital*, as an institution where:

- 'the worker works under the control of the capitalist to whom his labour belongs'; and
- 'the product is the property of the capitalist and not that of the worker'.

Clearly, this definition of a capitalist firm involves an employment relationship and excludes one-person firms. As Marx himself made clear, a worker cooperative is another example of a firm, but one which is not capitalist.

Coase and Williamson write mainly about capitalist firms, but their analysis would apply to *any* firm involving *multiple* agents, organized together in some manner – hierarchical, cooperative, participatory (Aoki, 1988), or whatever – but not through the market. In its most general form, the Coase–Williamson transaction costs analysis addresses all such (multiple-agent) firms, but not the single, self-employed producer.

It is also clear that Coase (1937) is comparing the capitalist firm as a system for organizing production with a system of market-coordinated, self-employed producers. Consequently, the Coasean explanation of the nature of the firm points to the higher transaction costs involved in the market-coordinated mode.

This leads to a another issue in the post-Coasean literature. Coase makes a straightforward comparison between the organization of production through a series of market contracts and the organization of production under the rubric of the firm.[2] Inspired by Coase, Williamson goes further by comparing different kinds of firm 'governance structures' in terms of their supposed relative efficiency. For Williamson and others, the transaction costs idea is not used simply to compare a market-coordinated system of production with a firm-coordinated one, but to compare different types of firm, be they hierarchical, participatory, U-form, M-form, or whatever. This would not be so problematic if the concept of transaction costs was clearly defined. But unfortunately, as discussed in the next section, it is not.

3 THE CONCEPT OF TRANSACTION COSTS

The concept of transaction costs seems to elude clear definition. As such, the term does not actually appear in Ronald Coase's original (1937) article. Importantly, Robert Clower (1969) argues that the reduction of 'bargaining costs' is the main factor determining the relative efficiency of a monetary over a barter economy. Perhaps its first appearance of the term itself is in an article by Kenneth Arrow (1969, p. 48), where he refers to transactions costs as the 'costs of running the economic system'. Yet, beyond this, the term is not clearly explicated or defined.

Despite using the term extensively, Williamson has still failed to provide an adequate definition of transaction costs. It is not that he ignores the problem. In one article it is noted that 'the concept wants for definition' (Williamson, 1979, p. 233) but he then proceeds not to define the term, but to list a set of 'factors' which relate to this mode of analysis. These 'factors' include sundry observations, such as that 'opportunism is especially important for economic activity that involves transaction-specific investments', and that 'the assessment of transaction costs is a comparative institutional undertaking'. He then goes on to note: 'Beyond these general propositions, a consensus on transaction costs is lacking.' But Williamson does not help to generate such a consensus under the illumination of a clear definition.

In another work, instead of a definition, Williamson (1985, p. 19) provides us with an analogy: 'Transaction costs are the economic equiva-lent of friction in physical systems.' This mechanical analogy suggests that we are moving from a simpler model in which friction is absent to one in which it is present. In contrast, however, transaction costs are supposed to be greater in markets than in firms. Hence in attempting to explain the existence of the firm in terms of transaction costs, Coase and Williamson are examining a sphere where transaction costs, and by analogy 'friction', are diminished, not increased. Hence models of markets must include greater 'friction' than models of firms. Coase and Williamson are not, therefore, introducing the analogue of friction with their analysis of the firm. Instead they are casting our eye on the relatively 'frictionless' zone of the firm, and by contrast highlighting the 'friction' associated with market transactions. Further, whatever the value of this friction analogy, it is still not a definition of transaction costs.

Given this lack of clarity with regard to a core concept, it is not surprising that Stanley Fischer (1977, p. 322 n.) can write: 'Transaction costs have a well-deserved bad name as a theoretical device, because solutions to problems involving transaction costs are often sensitive to the assumed form of the costs, and because there is a suspicion that almost anything can be rationalized by invoking suitably specified transaction costs.' Similarly, Dahlman (1979, p. 144) notes that the idea of trans-action costs 'has become a catch-all phrase for unspecified interferences with the price mechanism'. Furthermore, as Dahlman points out, the typical formal representation of transaction costs among mathematical economists, as a proportion of the value of the goods that are exchanged, differs in no significant way from a regular transportation cost. This hardly seems to be a sound innovation upon which an economic theory of institutions can be based.

4   TRANSACTION COSTS AND LACK OF INFORMATION

Overall, Dahlman offers us a useful lead into the further analysis of transaction costs. He suggests that three types of cost are involved, corresponding to three different, sequential phases of the exchange process, namely: 'search and information costs, bargaining and decision costs, policing and enforcement costs'. However, 'this functional taxonomy of different transaction costs is unnecessarily elaborate: fundamentally, the three classes reduce to a single one – for they all have in common that they represent resource losses due to lack of information' (Dahlman, 1979, p. 148).

It can be accepted that for purposes of theoretical clarification, Dahlman's argument is an important step forward; but many problems still remain and it is not entirely clear what a complete reduction of costs to those of information could mean. Indeed it could be fitted neatly into a neoclassical framework. Following the lead of George Stigler's classic (1961) article, search and information costs could be accommodated alongside, and treated similarly to, other costs in a probabilistic frame-work. In this approach information is treated just like any other com-modity, and subject to the marginalist rule that its consumption is optimal when the marginal cost of information search and acquisition is equal to its expected marginal return.

On reflection, however, the very idea of a rational calculus of information costs is open to objection. If we lack a piece of relevant information then how can we have any firm expectation of its marginal return? The very fact that the information is lacking means at most that such expectations are hazy and ill-defined. Clearly there is a problem of circularity here. As Brian Loasby (1990, p. 227) remarks: 'Transactions cost analysis appears to make the choice of administratively rational procedures itself a substantively rational choice.'

Furthermore, with such a treatment of information it is not clear why, for informational reasons, market contracting is superseded by the organization of the firm. After all, if information is simply a commodity like any other, there is no apparent special rationale for the firm to act as the minimizer of these information-related, transaction costs. Seemingly it would be possible to deal with such information problems through the due process of contract and trade.

Consider a model of productive organization of individual contractors all trading semi-finished products with each other, and each making marginal adjustments to deal with information costs along the lines proposed by Stigler. What has to be shown in this case is that some kind of economy of information costs can be obtained by organizing the agents together under an institutional umbrella. But it is still not clear why such an institution should be a firm, and not merely an association of producer-traders who pool relevant information.

More specifically, 'search and information costs' could be reduced substantially by a market research agency under contract from the producer-trader association, 'bargaining and decision costs' could be reduced by a team of consultants, and 'policing and enforcement costs' could be brought down by pooling information regarding the credit, performance and other reliability ratings of the agents involved. If informational economies of scale are substantial, why is it that such syndicates of independent producers should not arise to minimize the information costs that they would each face on their own, and thus obviate the need for the firm?

It is not immediately clear that such a syndicate would be more or less efficient than the firm in reducing such costs, but it is clearly more efficient than a mere aggregation of producer-traders. Thus the 'information costs' version of the transaction costs argument still fails to supply a convincing reason for the existence of the firm and for the relative rarity of alternative arrangements, such as the syndicate, in real life.

Not only is the above type of argument ineffective in providing a rationale for the firm, the treatment of information is itself unsatisfactory.

There is no distinction made between sense-data, i.e. the jumble of neurological stimuli which reach the brain, and information or knowledge, which involve the imposition of a conceptual framework. There is no regard given to the processes of assessment or computation with given information, which can lead to different conclusions depending on the method of calculation and the cognitive framework. It is well known, for example, that the firm's balance sheet is capable of different interpretations and even different 'bottom line' statements of profit and loss, depending on the interpretations and methodology of the accountant. These examples raise the problem, as Jim Tomlinson (1986, p. 239) points out, of treating 'information in a "positivist" manner, i.e. as a set of facts, indifferent to any problems of the conceptual frameworks which are necessarily involved'.

The 'information costs' version of the transaction costs argument does not appear to supply a convincing reason for the existence of the firm and for the relative rarity of alternative arrangements in real life. As Loasby (1976) has argued, there is no need in theory for non-market forms of organization in the general equilibrium model. Even the probabilistic version of general equilibrium theory, which implies information problems of a stylized and limited kind, provides no reason why firms, as such, should exist.

Langlois's (1984) solution to this problem is to make a distinction between different kinds of information problem, which parallels Frank Knight's (1921) famous distinction between risk and uncertainty. The essence of the argument is that 'parametric uncertainty' (akin to Knight's 'risk') cannot be used to find the source of transaction costs which are relevant to the explanation of the relative efficiency of organizations such as a firm. A similar argument has been offered by Neil Kay (1984, chapters 2–4), who has shown that, in a neoclassical world of perfect knowledge, the firm is stripped of most of its familiar structures and functions. The outcome is the same if problems of probabilistic risk (or 'parametric uncertainty') are introduced, because there 'is a close affinity between perfect knowledge and risk in terms of homogeneity and replicability of associated events'. The argument leads inexorably to the consideration of true or radical uncertainty as an essential concept to understand economic institutions such as the firm.

By emphasizing true uncertainty (as opposed to risk), but with different features and qualifications, Loasby, Kay and Langlois are all returning to Knight's *Risk, Uncertainty and Profit* and a core idea in its discussion of the firm that its 'existence in the world is the direct result of the fact of uncertainty' (Knight, 1921, p. 271). An answer to Coase's question as to why firms exist has re-emerged in terms of a non-probabilistic concept of uncertainty. Transaction costs may or may not remain an intermediate category in the argument. But it is clear that transaction costs as a category are not meaningful without some concept of true or radical uncertainty. Following Knight, there is a *prima facie* case for seeing the concept of uncertainty as a necessary – but not sufficient – concept to explain the existence of any kind of firm.

5 EVOLUTION OR COMPARATIVE STATICS?

If the concept of transaction costs is tied up with the existence of real uncertainty then there are important implications for the type of analysis involved. We may reach the same conclusion by noting Williamson's apparent reliance on Herbert Simon's (1957, 1959) concept of 'bounded rationality'. Williamson (e.g. 1985, p. 32) writes repeatedly in the following terms: 'Economizing on transaction costs essentially reduces to economizing on bounded rationality.'

Simon's argument, of course, is that a complete or global rational calculation is ruled out, and thus rationality is 'bounded'; agents do not maximize but attempt to attain acceptable minima instead. But it is important to note that this 'satisficing' behaviour does not arise simply because of inadequate information, but also because it would be too difficult to perform the calculations even if the relevant information was available.

Given this point, a prevailing orthodox interpretation of Simon's work, following William Baumol and Richard Quandt (1964), can be faulted. Contrary to this 'cost minimizing' interpretation, the recognition of bounded rationality refers primarily to the matter of computational capacity and not to additional 'costs'. Simon's concept of 'satisficing' does not amount to cost-minimizing behaviour. Clearly, the latter is just the dual of the standard assumption of maximization; if 'satisficing' was essentially a matter of minimizing costs then it would amount to maximizing behaviour of the orthodox type.[3]

Essentially, the Coase–Williamson type of transaction costs analysis involves comparative static comparisons of different types of governance structure.[4] Coase compares the market, viewed as a kind of disorganized governance structure, with the firm. Williamson compares different types of firm structure as well. In each case the reference is to a comparison of transaction costs across two or more equilibrium situations.[5]

It is important to emphasize, however, that if governance structure A is associated with lower transaction costs than governance structure B this does not itself explain why more A-type governance structures should exist in the real world. Apart from the logical problems with such an argument (Ullmann-Margalit, 1978), there are no omniscient agents doing comprehensive cost calculations. Indeed, given the considerations of bounded rationality, it is impossible for any entrepreneurial agent to perform the cost calculations to identify the lower transaction costs involved with A. Both uncertainty and limited computational capacity prevent such an assessment.

Williamson has a choice. He can either accept or reject the assumption that transaction cost minimization is assumed to be performed by a deliberative agent. However, if he accepts this assumption he cannot simultaneously embrace the concept of bounded rationality. If 'economizing on transaction costs' is cost-minimizing behaviour by a calculating agent, then this is inconsistent with Simon's concept.

It has been argued, however, that the concept of transaction costs is tied up with information problems and uncertainty. Consequently, we cannot dispense with bounded rationality: it is the omniscient, calculating agent that has to go. This creates a further problem. Without anyone knowing the full comparative costs of two governance structures, we lack an explanation of why the governance structure associated with lower transaction costs should predominate over the other. We have comparative statics, but without the means of explaining any real-world process of comparison.

One ostensible means of overcoming this difficulty is to drop the assumption of a fully deliberative agent and situate the analysis in an evolutionary rather than a comparative statics framework. In fact, although Williamson's work is mainly in terms of comparative statics, he alludes to an evolutionary explanation in several passages.[6] However, the invocation of the analogy with natural selection is generally casual, and is not accompanied by a detailed explanation of the causal linkages involved.

6   ARE FIRMS THE UNITS OF EVOLUTIONARY SELECTION?

One of the first issues that must be addressed in an evolutionary framework is that of identifying the unit of selection. Clearly, in this context it must be assumed that governance structures are the entities being sifted and selected in the evolutionary process. But this assumption is problematic. Indeed, it raises the whole controversial question of the viability of group selection. In biology, 'genetic reductionists' such as Richard Dawkins (1976) argue, along with methodological individualists from the social sciences such as Viktor Vanberg (1986), that the notion of group selection is incoherent.

The prominent argument against group and cultural selection – endorsed by Dawkins, Vanberg and many others – is that there is no clear mechanism to ensure that an advantageous pattern of behaviour for the group will for some reason be replicated by the actions of the individuals concerned. In particular, such a mechanism must ensure that 'free-riders' do not become dominant in the more productive groups. Free-riders would have the benefits of being members of a group whose other members together worked in a more productive manner, but bear no personal costs or risks in terms of self-sacrificial behaviour themselves. Consequently, in the absence of any compensating mechanism, it is likely that free-riders within the group will expand in numbers, crowd out the others, and alter the typical behaviour of the group as a whole. Thus, despite the possible benefits to the group of self-sacrificial behaviour, it appears that there is no mechanism to ensure that groups with these characteristics will prosper above others. What seems crucial is the selection of the constituent individuals and not the groups as a whole.

This is essentially a problem that Gregory Dow raises in his 'appropriability critique' of transaction costs analysis. He writes:

> A central dogma of transaction cost economics is that only the aggregate cost of a governance structure, and *not* the incidence of those costs among agents, affects the likelihood that the structure will be adopted. . . . Before the efficiency postulate of transaction cost economics can be justified in selection terms, one must come to terms with the fact that selection forces do not act on the costs or benefits experienced by arbitrary social aggregates. These forces operate only through the private payoffs of the entities selected upon, just as natural selection acts only upon individual organisms, rather than for the good of the species or the ecosystem. (Dow, 1987, p. 32–3)

However, the statement that 'natural selection acts only upon individual organisms' is not universally accepted within biology. Indeed, some biologists, such as Dawkins, argue that the gene, not the individual, is the unit of selection. Conversely, many biologists and philosophers of biology argue that several different levels of selection, including group selection, are viable.[7]

Biologists who argue the case for the possibility of group selection do not suggest that group selection will always operate; it depends upon the processes and structures involved. Essentially, group selection is seen to act if all organisms in the same group are 'bound together by a common fate' (Sober, 1981, p. 107). A population of (diverse) units is so interlinked, with spillover effects and externalities, that it is selected upon as an entity.

What if the behaviour of this interlinked group could somehow be explained in terms of the individuals involved? Philosophers of biology such as Elliott Sober (1981) point out that a reductionist explanation in terms of genes – if one were possible – leaves open the question of what causes the gene frequencies themselves to alter. Although all information about ostensible group selection may be reduced to and represented by selection coefficients of organisms or genes, such a formal reduction to the genic or individual level leaves the question unanswered as to what causes the frequency of genes in the gene pool to change. Likewise, we may remark, methodological individualist explanations leave open the questions of the origin or moulding or composition of a population of individuals, with their preferences and purposes.

Given the possibility of group selection in biology, it can be conjectured that the same phenomenon might occur in the socio-economic sphere. Considerations of institutions, rules, norms and culture are apposite. Assume that a particular characteristic affects all members of a group to a similar degree, such as the enforcement of different modes of diet, dress or behaviour. Assume further that this characteristic affects the future growth and prosperity of the group. Then there may be grounds for considering that group selection is at work.

7   GROUP SELECTION AND THE FIRM

For the firm to be considered as a unit of selection, similarly appropriate considerations must be involved. There must be something going on within the firm which 'binds its members together by a common fate', as Sober puts it. Clearly, all employers and employees within a firm have a stake in its prosperity and survival. However, the appropriability critique is still relevant if the owners of capital or labour power can desert the ailing firm for a more profitable alternative. The viability of these 'exit' options depends upon the state of the labour and capital markets. Their attraction may depend, in part, on asset specificity (Pagano, 1991). Especially with the textbook assumptions of self-seeking individuals and competitive environments, there is little adhesive to bind the members of the firm together. One option, of course, is to abandon the textbook assumptions and examine the firm in a more realistic light.

There are additional reasons why the firm can be considered as a collective or systemic entity. Consider the question of the skills embodied in the firm's routines. Sidney Winter (1982) argues that the capabilities of an organization such as a firm are not generally reducible to the capabilities of individual members. He points out that:

> The coordination displayed in the performance of organizational routines is, like that displayed in the exercise of individual skills, the fruit of practice.

> What requires emphasis is that . . . the learning experience is a shared experience of organization members. . . . Thus, even if the contents of the organizational memory are stored only in the form of memory traces in the memories of individual members, it is still an organizational knowledge in the sense that the fragment stored by each individual member is not fully meaningful or effective except in the context provided by the fragments stored by other members. (Winter, 1982, p. 76)

Clearly, there is an important question here concerning the possibility of collective knowledge. This is a matter of controversy within social theory. For instance, Ward Goodenough (1981, p. 54) writes that: 'People learn as individuals. Therefore, if culture is learned, its ultimate locus must be in individuals rather than in groups.' In contrast, there is the 'collectivist' position of anthropologists such as Marvin Harris (1971, p. 136), more in accord with that of Winter: 'Cultures are patterns of behavior, thought and feeling that are acquired or influenced through learning and that are characteristic of groups of people rather than of individuals.' Winter's own argument suggests that although tacit or other knowledge must reside in the nerve or brain cells of a set of human beings, its enactment depends crucially on the existence of a structured context in which individuals interact with each other. Otherwise, no such knowledge can become manifest. Furthermore, because organizational knowledge is tacit knowledge, no individual can express it in a codified form. The knowledge becomes manifest only through the interactive practice of the members of the group.

There are many cases where the organizational knowledge is maintained within a structure, perhaps even for long periods of time, despite the turnover of its individual members. Just as our personal memory of past events is retained, despite the loss and renewal of our brain cells, organizational knowledge may survive the gradual but complete replacement of the individuals comprising the organization.

Clearly both individual and organizational outcomes depend upon the nature of any such organizational knowledge. Here is a clear case of the fates of a number of individuals being bound together in a single group. Such organizational learning is thus feasibly associated with group selection. Organizational knowledge can relate to a subset of the workers within a firm. If the knowledge relates to all the workers in a firm, or crucial aspects of its management, then the organization in which that particular organizational knowledge resides is the firm as a whole.

Consideration of organizational learning has raised the question of culture within the firm. Arguably, an important feature of the firm is the 'trust dynamic' (Fox, 1974) that it engenders between its members. In contrast, in the sphere of the competitive market, trust and long-term cooperation, while present to some degree, are undermined by competition between the many different and transient agents. In the market there is a changing and volatile population, where each individual is pursuing his or her objectives largely in accord with the overt calculus of profit and loss. In distinction, opportunistic and self-seeking behaviour is certainty present and significant within the firm, but, contrary to Williamson, it is diminished and kept under check within its boundaries. The firm, by engendering loyalty and trust to some degree, encourages people to act differently. By trust or compulsion, that is by the use of social power, the managers of the firm may succeed in imposing their will on the employees. Without this ability to generate more cohesive and less atomistic behaviour the firm would not be able to function.

Given that capitalism is not a system of slavery, workers, unlike machines, may be hired but not bought. This means that capitalists face the ongoing problem of losing workers with acquired skills. In part, this may explain a relatively greater inclination for firms to invest in machines rather than people (Pagano, 1991, pp. 324–5). In addition, capitalists have an incentive both to provide incentives for workers to remain with the firm, and to engender loyalty and greater social cohesion within the institution.

Hence a key to understanding the nature of the firm is its ability to mould human preferences and actions so that a higher degree of loyalty and trust are engendered. In contrast, following the tradition of individualistic social scientists, Williamson puts forward a model of individual human nature (i.e. 'opportunism') and recklessly assumes that this applies equally to quite different forms of institutional arrangement, and that in particular it applies equally and universally to the market and all types of firm. No recognition is made of the effect of the institutional environment in moulding actions and beliefs.

Samuel Bowles (1985) has appropriately described the view of the human agent in this individualistic tradition as one of 'malfeasance', with its obsessions with self-seeking behaviour and with derivative phenomena such as 'shirking' at work. In contrast, as Bowles points out, the work performance function should not be regarded as exogenously given, as partly a consequence of immutable 'human nature'; it is endogenous and partly a function of the institutions, cultures and power structures involved.

If the firm has the effect of moulding the preference functions of the actors within it, by engendering loyalty and the like, then we cannot explain the firm by an individualistic framework where all preference functions are taken as given whatever the institutional context. Furthermore, the effect of culture on perceptions and preferences may act to bind agents together to some extent in a common group. Even if there are subcultures, involving antagonisms within the firm, the common culture binds the members together as a selectable group. In sum, there are reasons to suggest that the firm may be a (group) unit of selection, but many involve abandoning individualistic theoretical premises.

With endogenous preferences, and in an evolutionary context, the role of the concept of transaction costs is marginalized somewhat.[8] Instead, much more emphasis is put on the role of the firm as a durable social institution, incorporating its own culture, and acting as a protective enclave from market forces (Nelson, 1981; Dore, 1983; Hodgson, 1988).

8 CONTEXT DEPENDENCE AND SUBOPTIMALITY

Given that an evolutionary framework of analysis is more promising than comparative statics, we may re-examine Williamson's own invocation of evolutionism in his work. Along with his theoretical argument that hierarchy should be more efficient, Williamson frequently appeals to the empirical evidence of the preponderance of hierarchical firms in the real world to support his claim that such forms are more efficient than other types of organization, such as participatory or cooperative firms. He argues that the competitive process has led to the selection of hierarchical firms and for this reason they must be assumed to be more efficient than their rivals.

A closer inspection of evolutionary theory undermines Williamson's claim.[9] Even if the 'selected' characteristics of firms were the 'fittest' then they would be so with regard to a particular economic, political and cultural environment only; they might not be the 'fittest' for all circumstances and times. Consider the following illustrative example of a type of context dependence where the chief effect is of the frequency of the population on fitness, called 'frequency dependence' in biology (Lewontin, 1974). Assume two types of firm, type A and type B. The population as a whole is a mix of type A and type B firms, with the associated culture and inter-firm relations. Given that a new entrant can be of either type, their profits can be given by one of the following formulae:

Profit of type A entrant firm = 50 + (percentage of type B firms)
Profit of type B entrant firm = (percentage of type B firms)

Such illustrative profit values can be justified in terms of the different types of organization form and inter-firm relations. For instance, type B firms can be associated with more open and participatory structures and more cooperative inter-firm behaviour, including, for instance, the informal exchange of technical know-how (von Hippel, 1987, 1988). Accordingly, there could be positive externalities associated with a firm of such a type.[10]

Assume, first, that the initial (large) population is composed entirely of type A firms. In this case the profit for each type A new entrant will be 50, and for each type B new entrant will be 0. Clearly, type B firms are unlikely to become established if type A firms are dominant. However, if the initial population is composed entirely of type B firms then the profit for each type A new entrant will be 150, and for each type B new entrant will be 100. Consequently, in this case, type A firms can successfully invade the type B population. In sum, type A firms are likely to become or remain dominant, whatever the starting position. This will happen even if average profits are greater in an industry composed entirely of type B firms than one composed entirely of type A. Assume that the above equations apply to all firms, and not simply new entrants. Then the average profits of a type A population will be 50 and of a type B population will be 100. Yet type B firms are always at a relative disadvantage.

Furthermore, if the industry was dominated by type B firms then the situation might not last because new entrants of type A would be at a great advantage in those circumstances. Unless corrective action was taken – such as some arrangement for formal or informal regulation of the industry by the state or by an industrial association – the greater overall benefits related to type B dominance would eventually be undermined and destroyed by incoming type A firms.

This hypothetical example illustrates a number of general points. First, given that pay-offs are dependent on the nature of the industry as a whole, then the selected characteristics likewise depend on the overall environment. Indeed, research on cooperatives suggests that their success is highly dependent on the type of financial and cultural regime that prevails in the economy as a whole (see, for example, Thomas and Logan, 1982). Second, 'natural selection' does not necessarily favour the more efficient units, nor always the optimal or near-optimal outcomes. The low density of cooperative or participatory firms in the real world should not be taken to mean that either individual firms of this type, or an industry dominated by them, are necessarily less efficient.

9   PATH DEPENDENCY AND SUBOPTIMALITY

The historical evolution of the factory system and the modern firm is not simply a question of the quasi-natural selection of the most efficient organizational forms. Issues of path dependency (Arthur, 1989), as well as context dependence, may be significant. For example, some historical research has suggested that the factory system was influenced at its origin by the military structures of the time: the hierarchical regimentation of the soldiery has its parallel in the similar organization of the workforce.[11]

Charles Sabel and Jonathan Zeitlin (1985) argue on the basis of historical evidence that in Europe there was an alternative path to industrialization based on small-scale firms and flexible specialization. Also looking at the evolution of the factory system, Maxine Berg (1991) compares explanations based on the supposed dictates of technology with the idea of such an alternative road. She concludes that industrialization could have taken many possible pathways and occurred in different sequences. Ugo Pagano (1991, p. 327) considers the two-way and cumulative interaction of technology with property rights, pointing out that: 'In this context, simple efficiency stories may well lose their meaning. Each outcome is likely to be path dependent and inefficient interactions between property rights and technology are likely to characterise the history of economic systems.'

In the context of modern industrial structures, Richard Langlois (1988) argues explicitly that path dependency may be relevant in the evolution of organizational form. Likewise, and contrary to his earlier view, Douglass North (1990) now accepts that path-dependent processes also apply to institutions, and therefore the surviving arrangements are not necessarily the most efficient. The issue of path dependency is raised explicitly by Michael Everett and Alanson Minkler (1991) in their study of the legal and financial impediments to the formation of labour-managed firms in the earlier phases of the industrial revolution.

The Williamsonian hypothesis that existence implies greater relative efficiency would deem the military–industrial parallel to be irrelevant: whatever the original circumstances the more efficient forms would prosper and survive. The alternative industrial roads of flexible specialization or labour-management would be deemed to have been avoided because of their inefficiencies. On the contrary, the possibility of path dependency suggests that alternative, less-hierarchical or less-regimented forms of organization could have been just as viable. Only painstaking historical research, rather than bold evolutionary generalizations based on dubious 'biological laws', can adjudicate on this and related questions.

Above all, in the present context, much further examination of the performance characteristics of various types of hierarchic and less-hierarchic firm is necessary before generalizations concerning the efficiency of one organizational form rather than another can be made.

10   IN CONCLUSION: THE 'OLD' AND THE 'NEW' INSTITUTIONALISM

It has been suggested here that there are several questions of clarity, and theoretical problems and dilemmas, involved in the Coase–Williamson type of explanation of the nature of the firm in terms of transaction costs.[12] It has been indicated that the inclusion of endogenous preference functions, in which individuals are moulded by the internal culture of the firm, may be necessary for a viable theoretical explanation of the nature of that institution. It is precisely on points such as these that the 'old' institutionalism differs from the 'new' (see Hodgson, 1989, 1993).

It is often insinuated, however, that Williamson's work is close to that of the 'old' institutionalist John Commons. Note Williamson's (1975, pp. 3, 254) repeated and often cited (e.g. Langlois, 1986, p. 4 n.) suggestion that he is following the work of Commons in taking the transaction as the 'ultimate unit of analysis'. For Commons (1934, p. 55), however, the transaction is a *'unit of economic activity'* (emphasis in original), forming others, such as the 'larger unit of economic activity, a Going Concern'. Although there is a very superficial resemblance of terminology, Williamson's mode of analysis differs profoundly from that of Commons. For Williamson the unit of *analysis* is the given, abstract, atomistic and 'opportunistic' individual, whereas Commons stresses the organic and collective quality of institutions.

Commons's reason for describing the transaction and the 'going concern' as units of economic *activity,* is to break from the classical idea that the units in economics should be the *'commodities owned* and the *individuals* who owned the commodities, while the "energy" was human labour' (ibid., p. 56). Commons makes an analogy to quantum theory in support of his view that it is not mechanistically related entities or 'particles' but processes and events that should be the stuff of economics. Furthermore, in stressing the notion of activity, Commons is attempting to break from an atomistic mode of thought: 'These going concerns and transactions are to economics what Whitehead's "organic mechanism" and "event" are to physics, or the physiologists' "organisms" and "metabolism" are to biology' (ibid., p. 96). It should be clear that Commons's organicism bears no significant resemblance to Williamson's atomistic and individualistic line of thought.

Furthermore, while both Williamson and the 'old' institutionalists appeal, to different degrees, to an evolutionary metaphor in their work, it does not support the kind of Panglossian interpretation to be found in the work of Williamson and many others. In contrast to much 'new' institutionalist writing, the work of Thorstein Veblen (1919), for instance, does not involve the notion that evolution always works towards progressive or optimal outcomes.

In sum, while the work of Coase and Williamson has had an enormous positive effect in stimulating our thinking about the firm, the transaction costs theory, as it stands, is nevertheless still in want of further clarification and subject to some points of theoretical criticism. The line of argument developed here tentatively points to an alternative theoretical framework in which the firm can be analysed. It is again to Williamson's credit that by acting as a founder of the 'new' institutionalism he has, perhaps unwittingly, directed renewed attention to the 'old'. Unfortunately, we do not discover an adequate theory of the firm in the work of Veblen and Commons. Nevertheless, there are enough methodological and theoretical indications to suggest that further work may be productive using 'old' institutionalist tools.

NOTES

1   Christos Pitelis (1991, p. 52) correctly identifies the contentious question here as being 'whether single producers qualify as firms', this depending crucially on the definition of the firm 'one is willing to adopt'. However, Fourie's criticism has found its supporters, including Michael Dietrich (1991, pp. 41–2), who writes that: 'to assert that firms *replace* markets, as Coase does . . . suggests that trading can take place without production and distribution (i.e. without firms), which is clearly impossible.' Dietrich, like Fourie, sees production as inextricably linked to 'the firm', ignoring the fact that by 'the firm' Coase means a multiple-person organization, and disregarding the possibility of (non-firm) productive units consisting of single persons.

2   Coase (1988, p. 47) makes it clear that his 1937 article was intended to compare the firm with the market, rather than firms with firms: 'I did not investigate the factors that would make the costs of organizing lower for some firms than for others.'

3   Thus Jensen and Meckling (1976, p. 307 n.) are in error when they write that 'Simon's work has often been misinterpreted as a denial of maximizing behavior. . . . His later use of the term "satisficing" . . . has undoubtedly contributed to this confusion because it suggests rejection of maximizing behavior rather than maximization subject to costs of information and decision making.' Indeed, the misinterpretation of Simon's work is Jensen and Meckling's. The term 'satisficing' is employed by Simon precisely to distance his conception from 'substantive' rationality and maximizing behaviour. It is symptomatic that Williamson, for example, uses the term 'bounded rationality' much more often than 'satisficing'.

4   Nutzinger (1982) points out that the transaction costs associated with each governance structure are not independent of coexisting institutions. Hence the relative efficiency of different institutions is compared only by making strong *ceteris paribus* assumptions, and in a partial equilibrium framework. Such efficiency comparisons do not have the greater generality of a general equilibrium analysis.

5   Dietrich (1991) argues that the 'transaction benefits' of each governance structure must be taken into account as well as the 'costs'. While this point is valid, it points to another ambiguity in the definition of transaction costs. The term could be defined net (by deducting transaction benefits from costs), or

gross (exclusive of transaction benefits). Clearly, the net definition of transaction costs is the one that is relevant to the Coase–Williamson theory of the firm. On the contrary, Dietrich implies that Williamson has a gross definition in mind, but this is not demonstrated by reference to Williamson's work.

6 For example, Williamson (1985, p. 22–23, 394). Nevertheless, there are adjoining appeals for the development of a 'fully developed theory of the selection process' (Williamson, 1985, p. 23) and statements of the need to assess such propositions 'more carefully' (p. 394 n.).

7 These arguments are reviewed more extensively in Hodgson (1991a).

8 In this regard also note Julio Rotemberg's (1991) argument that under certain conditions the internal organization of the firm may be suboptimal, even if the firm is profit maximizing. This also challenges the view that the reason for the existence of the firm is its capacity to reduce transaction costs.

9 For a more extensive discussion of the issue of suboptimality in evolution, with references to both biology and economics, see Hodgson (1991b). For the flavour of the argument from biology see, for example, Gould (1980, 1989) and Gould and Lewontin (1979).

10 In a study of Italian cooperatives, Gherardi and Masiero (1990) argue that the development of a close-knit system of intra-organizational trust relations and networking activities has been crucial to their success.

11 With variations, this idea is proposed in Mumford (1934), Nef (1950), J. M. Winter (1975), McNeill (1980) and Smith (1985), among others.

12 Pagano (1991, p. 318 n.) provides an argument why the hierarchy in the firm may be advantageous even in a situation of zero transaction costs, because of the advantages resulting from putting those with management skills in charge of the coordination of production.

REFERENCES

Aoki, M. (1988) *Information, Incentives and Bargaining in the Japanese Economy*. Cambridge: Cambridge University Press.

Arrow, K. J. (1969) The organization of economic activity: issues pertinent to the choice of market versus nonmarket allocation. In *The Analysis and Evaluation of Public Expenditure: The PPB System*, vol. 1, US Joint Economic Committee. Washington, DC: US Government Printing Office, 59–73.

Arthur, W. B. (1989) Competing technologies, increasing returns, and lock-in by historical events. *The Economic Journal*, 99(1), 116–31.

Baumol, W. J. and Quandt, R. E. (1964) Rules of thumb and optimally imperfect decisions. *American Economic Review*, 54(2), 23–46.

Berg, M. (1991) On the origins of capitalist hierarchy. In B. Gustafsson (ed.), *Power and Economic Institutions: Reinterpretations in Economic History*. Aldershot: Edward Elgar.

Bowles, S. (1985) The production process in a competitive economy:

Walrasian, neo-Hobbesian, and Marxian models. *American Economic Review*, 75(1), 16–36 (reprinted in Putterman, 1986).

Clower, R. W. (1969) Introduction. In R. W. Clower (ed.), *Monetary Theory*. Harmondsworth: Penguin, 7–21.

Coase, R. H. (1937) The nature of the firm. *Economica*, 4(4), 386–405.

Coase, R. H. (1988) Lectures on 'The nature of the firm'. III: Influence. *Journal of Law, Economics, and Organization*, 4(1), 33–47.

Commons, J. R. (1934) *Institutional Economics – Its Place in Political Economy*. New York: Macmillan (reprinted 1990 with a new introduction by M. Rutherford, New Brunswick: Transaction Publishers).

Dahlman, C. J. (1979) The problem of externality. *Journal of Law and Economics*, 22(1), 141–62.

Dawkins, R. (1976) *The Selfish Gene*. Oxford: Oxford University Press.

Dietrich, M. (1991) Firms, markets and transaction cost economics. *Scottish Journal of Political Economy*, 38(1), 41–57.

Dore, R. (1983) Goodwill and the spirit of market capitalism. *British Journal of Sociology*, 34(4), 459–82.

Dow, G. K. (1987) The function of authority in transaction cost economics. *Journal of Economic Behavior and Organization*, 8(1), 13–38.

Everett, M. J. and Minkler, A. P. (1991) Evolution and organizational choice in 19th century Britain. Mimeo, Department of Economics, University of Connecticut.

Fischer, S. (1977) Long-term contracting, sticky prices, and monetary policy: a comment. *Journal of Monetary Economics*, 3, 317–23.

Fourie, F. C. V. N. (1989) The nature of firms and markets: do transactions approaches help? *South African Journal of Economics*, 57(2), 142–60.

Fox, A. (1974) *Beyond Contract: Work, Power and Trust Relations*. London: Faber and Faber.

Gherardi, S. and Masiero, A. (1990) Solidarity as a networking skill and a trust relation: its implications for cooperative development. *Economic and Industrial Democracy*, 11(4), 553–74.

Goodenough, W. H. (1981) *Culture, Language and Society*. Menlo Park, CA: Benjamin/Cummings.

Gould, S. J. (1980) *The Panda's Thumb*. New York: Norton.

Gould, S. J. (1989) *Wonderful Life: the Burgess Shale and the Nature of History*. London: Hutchinson Radius.

Gould, S. J. and Lewontin, R. C. (1979) The Spandrels of San Marco and the Panglossian paradigm: a critique of the adaptationist programme. *Proceedings of the Royal Society of London, Series B*, 205, 581–98 (reprinted in Sober, 1984).

Harris, M. (1971) *Culture, Man and Nature*. New York: Crowell.

Hodgson, G. M. (1988) *Economics and Institutions: a Manifesto for a Modern Institutional Economics*. Cambridge: Polity Press.

Hodgson, G. M. (1989) Institutional economic theory: the old versus the new. *Review of Political Economy*, 1(3), 249–69 (reprinted in G. M. Hodgson, *After Marx and Sraffa: Essays in Political Economy*, Macmillan: London).

Hodgson, G. M. (1991a) Hayek's theory of cultural evolution: an evaluation in the light of Vanberg's critique. *Economics and Philosophy*, 7(1), 67–82.

Hodgson, G. M. (1991b) Economic evolution: intervention contra Pangloss. *Journal of Economic Issues*, 25(2), 519–33.

Hodgson, G. M. (1983) Institutional economics: surveying the 'old' and the 'new'. *Metroeconomica*, 44(1).

Jensen, M. C. and Meckling, W. H. (1976) Theory of the firm: managerial behavior, agency costs and ownership structure. *Journal of Financial Economics*, 3(4), 305–60 (reprinted in Putterman, 1986).

Kay, N. M. (1984) *The Emergent Firm: Knowledge, Ignorance and Surprise in Economic Organization*. London: Macmillan.

Knight, F. (1921) *Risk, Uncertainty and Profit*. New York: Houghton Mifflin.

Langlois, R. N. (1984) Internal organization in a dynamic context: some theoretical considerations. In M. Jussawalla and H. Ebenfield (eds), *Communication and Information Economics: New Perspectives*. Amsterdam: North-Holland, 23–49.

Langlois, R. N. (ed.) (1986) *Economics as a Process: Essays in the New Institutional Economics*. Cambridge: Cambridge University Press.

Langlois, R. N. (1988) Economic change and the boundaries of the firm. *Journal of Institutional and Theoretical Economics*, 144(4), 635–57.

Lewontin, R. C. (1974) *The Genetic Basis of Evolutionary Change*. New York: Columbia University Press.

Loasby, B. J. (1976) *Choice, Complexity and Ignorance: an Enquiry into Economic Theory and the Practice of Decision Making*. Cambridge: Cambridge University Press.

Loasby, B. J. (1990) The firm. In J. Creedy (ed.), *Foundations of Economic Thought*. Oxford: Basil Blackwell, 212–33.

McNeill, W. H. (1980) *The Pursuit of Power: Technology, Armed Force, and Society Since A.D. 1000*. Chicago: University of Chicago Press.

Marx, K. (1976) *Capital*, vol. 1 (translated by B. Fowkes from the fourth German edition of 1890). Harmondsworth: Pelican.

Mumford, L. (1934) *Technics and Civilization*. New York: Harcourt, Brace and World.

Nef, J. U. (1950) *War and Human Progress: an Essay on the Rise of*

Industrial Civilization. Cambridge, MA: Harvard University Press.

Nelson, R. R. (1981) Research on productivity growth and productivity differences: dead ends and new departures. *Journal of Economic Literature*, 29, 1029–64.

North, D. C. (1990) *Institutions, Institutional Change and Economic Performance*. Cambridge: Cambridge University Press.

Nutzinger, H. (1982) The economics of property rights – a new paradigm in social science? In W. Stegmuller, W. Balzer and W. Spohn (eds), *Philosophy and Economics*. Berlin: Springer-Verlag, 169–90.

Pagano, U. (1991) Property rights, asset specificity, and the division of labour under alternative capitalist relations. *Cambridge Journal of Economics*, 15(3), 315–42.

Pitelis, C. (1991) *Market and Non-market Hierarchies: Theory of Institutional Failure*. Oxford: Basil Blackwell.

Putterman, L. (ed.) (1986) *The Economic Nature of the Firm: a Reader*. Cambridge: Cambridge University Press.

Rotemberg, J. J. (1991) A theory of inefficient intrafirm transactions. *American Economic Review,* 81(1), 191–209.

Sabel, C. and Zeitlin, J. (1985) Historical alternatives to mass production: politics, markets and technology in nineteenth century industrialization. *Past and Present*, 108, 132–76.

Simon, H. A. (1957) *Models of Man: Social and Rational*. New York: Wiley.

Simon, H. A. (1959) Theories of decision-making in economic and behavioral sciences. *American Economic Review*, 49(2), 253–83.

Smith, M. R. (ed.) (1985) *Military Enterprise and Technological Change*. Cambridge, MA: MIT Press.

Sober, E. (1981) Holism, individualism and the units of selection. In P. D. Asquith and R. N. Giere (eds), *Philosophy of Science Association 1980*, vol. 2. East Lansing, MI: Philosophy of Science Association, 93–121 (reprinted in Sober, 1984).

Sober, E. (ed.) (1984) *Conceptual Issues in Evolutionary Biology: an Anthology*. Cambridge, MA: MIT Press.

Stigler, G. J. (1961) The economics of information. *Journal of Political Economy,* 69(2), 213–25.

Thomas, H. T. and Logan, C. (1982) *Mondragon: an Economic Analysis*. London: George Allen and Unwin.

Tomlinson, J. (1986) Democracy inside the black box? Neo-classical theories of the firm and industrial democracy. *Economy and Society*, 15(2), 220–50.

Ullmann-Margalit, E. (1978) Invisible hand explanations. *Synthese*, 39, 282–6.

Vanberg, V. (1986) Spontaneous market order and social rules: a critique of F. A. Hayek's theory of cultural evolution. *Economics and Philosophy*, 2, 75–100.

Veblen, T. B. (1919) *The Place of Science in Modern Civilisation and Other Essays*. New York: Huebsch (reprinted, 1990, with a new introduction by W. J. Samuels, New Brunswick: Transaction Publishers).

von Hippel, E. (1987) Cooperation between rivals: informal know-how trading. *Research Policy*, 16, 291–302.

von Hippel, E. (1988) *The Sources of Innovation*. Oxford: Oxford University Press.

Williamson, O. E. (1975) *Markets and Hierarchies: Analysis and Anti-Trust Implications. A Study in the Economics of Internal Organization*. New York: Free Press.

Williamson, O. E. (1979) Transaction-cost economics: the governance of contractual relations. *Journal of Law and Economics*, 22(2), 233–61.

Williamson, O. E. (1985) *The Economic Institutions of Capitalism: Firms, Markets, Relational Contracting*. London: Macmillan.

Winter, J. M. (ed.) (1975) *War and Economic Development*. Cambridge, MA: Harvard University Press.

Winter, S. C. Jr (1982) An essay on the theory of production. In S. H. Hymans (ed.), *Economics and the World around It*. Ann Arbor, MI: University of Michigan Press, 55–91.

6

The Appropriability Critique of Transaction Cost Economics

GREGORY K. DOW

1 INTRODUCTION: EFFICIENCY AND APPROPRIABILITY

Transaction cost economics (TCE) has grown into a remarkably powerful intellectual force over the past two decades. It has reshaped the way economists think about the theory of the firm, to the point where TCE ideas are routinely taught in intermediate micro theory courses. Together with the related work of property rights theorists, TCE has extended its influence to scholars in the neighbouring disciplines of sociology, political science, law, business administration and even anthropology.

Most influential intellectual movements rest upon a simple but controversial core premise, and TCE is no exception. Two key proponents observe that TCE owes its 'distinctive powers' to 'its unremitting emphasis on efficiency' (Williamson and Ouchi, 1981, p. 367). More specifically, Oliver Williamson (1991, p. 95) asserts that organizational forms ('governance structures') mainly serve to economize on transaction costs. The claim that existing modes of organization enhance economic efficiency has become a rallying cry for TCE advocates, as well as a lightning rod for critics.

Here I want to sharpen this debate by advancing a specific counterclaim: governance structures frequently serve as vehicles for the appropriation of quasi-rent. This proposition requires a bit of conceptual background. The transactions considered by TCE usually demand prior investments in specialized physical or human capital. Since such assets

This research was funded by the Social Sciences and Humanities Research Council of Canada. Christos Pitelis and Louis Putterman provided helpful comments on an earlier draft. All opinions are those of the author.

cannot easily be transferred to other uses once they are in place, the revenues generated by production typically exceed the sum of the *ex post* opportunity costs facing input suppliers. In a competitive market this difference between revenue and cost represents a quasi-rent (the return to the sunk component of the initial investment expenditures). A governance structure, loosely speaking, is a decision-making procedure used by the production coalition after sunk costs have been incurred. Among other things, governance structures determine (directly or indirectly) how any available quasi-rent will be distributed *ex post* among the individual members of the production coalition.

My claim can now be formulated in a more precise way. Those governance structures that enable essential input suppliers to appropriate large *ex post* quasi-rent streams will thrive. Other structures will be selected against, because they will be unable to attract certain key inputs. 'Essential input suppliers' are those who incur large sunk costs before production commences, and are indispensable to the production process. This assertion will be amplified and qualified throughout the remainder of this chapter.

If the appropriability hypothesis is correct, the *ex post* distribution of quasi-rent generated by a particular governance structure has consequences for that structure's market viability. TCE denies this, holding instead that governance structures are chosen to maximize the aggregate gain from production and trade (or equivalently to minimize overall transaction costs, treating production costs as fixed).[1] TCE must therefore assume that the members of a production coalition can costlessly transfer utility among themselves, so that the distribution of this aggregate gain within the coalition can be ignored.

Side-payments which induce input suppliers to participate in a transaction when they would not otherwise do so are especially important for TCE's efficiency hypothesis. I will refer to such payments as *participation bribes*. In practice, the feasibility of participation bribes depends on the context. Some possible impediments include:

1 The non-contractibility of specialized investments.
2 Adverse selection and moral hazard problems among potential coalition members.
3 Collective action problems associated with large, diverse production teams.

When participation bribes are infeasible, anticipated flows of *ex post* quasi-rent operate as direct *ex ante* inducements to join in the transaction. The viability of each governance structure then turns on the magnitude of the inducements it offers.

In criticizing orthodox theories of the firm, Winter notes that economists usually adhere to the principle of methodological individualism, which warns against 'the practice of grounding theories on assumptions about the behavior of social groups, organizations, or institutions'. He goes on to observe:

> This dedication to methodological individualism – and, relatedly, to the study of non-cooperative equilibria – is abruptly suspended when the workings of the firm itself are discussed. There, fully cooperative relations among the diverse interests organized in the firm are routinely, though implicitly, assumed to be easily achieved through voluntary exchange.
> (Winter, 1991, p. 181)

The same criticism applies to TCE, which implicitly assumes away any obstacle to side-payments among the members of a production coalition. The appropriability hypothesis calls for a larger dose of methodological individualism. Only by descending from the social to the individual level of analysis can we hope to discover whether efficient structures will emerge, because only then can we determine whether individual strategic behaviour is compatible with efficient organizational outcomes.

Williamson (1991, p. 105) correctly states that 'all failures to allocate resources to highest value uses invite redress'. He adds in a footnote: 'The collision of strategic purposes and efficiency purposes sometimes prevents this from going through, although strategic purposes themselves then need to be unpacked. What prevents value-enhancing deals from being reached whereby strategic distortions are eliminated?' (p. 112). This is a fair question. Anyone who criticizes TCE's efficiency claim should show why private agents cannot implement efficient structures in practice.[2] In the present context, this means that we must explain why agents often cannot pay participation bribes, even when they would like to do so. I will defend this assertion both theoretically and empirically in later sections.

My argument will *not* be that participation bribes are *never* feasible. Instead, I maintain that they are most easily arranged in precisely those cases where TCE has had its greatest empirical success: vertical integration and the creation of multi-divisional corporations. TCE 'works' here because it is relatively easy to transfer title to physical assets in exchange for a side-payment (although some one-time haggling over price may be needed). By contrast, I will argue that participation bribes are frequently difficult or impossible to arrange in the labour market. It thus comes as no surprise that applications of TCE to the organization of work have met with considerable scepticism.

The use of the term 'efficiency' in the TCE literature has produced a good deal of confusion and controversy. The orthodox economic defini-tion is that of Pareto efficiency: no reallocation of resources can make any agent better off without simultaneously making some other agent worse off. A weaker test is Kaldor–Hicks efficiency, which merely requires that no reallocation would pass a social cost–benefit test (regardless of the actual effects on the welfare of individuals). When utility is transferable among individuals, the Kaldor–Hicks criterion reduces to maximization of the sum of the individual utilities. After the aggregate pie has been maximized, slices can be distributed in any desired way through side-payments.

Because TCE proponents almost always assume that preferences have this transferability feature, I interpret TCE's efficiency claim in a Kaldor–Hicks manner: equilibrium governance structures yield more total utility than any feasible alternative structure. If all of the participants in a given transaction have exogenous reservation utilities, this means that the equilibrium structure maximizes the overall surplus derived from the transaction (that is, total utility minus total *ex ante* opportunity costs).

With this background in hand, we can specify the empirical content of TCE's efficiency hypothesis. An *efficient* governance structure is one which would be chosen in a world where agents are well informed about the pay-offs generated under each feasible structure, and participation bribes are unconstrained. When such structures are actually found, TCE is vindicated. An observed structure is *inefficient* if some alternative structure would have provided a larger total surplus, but was not chosen because some input suppliers could not be bribed to participate. TCE is then falsified and the appropriability hypothesis is vindicated.

Several points need to be made about this criterion for the validity of TCE. First, we are not ruling out an 'as if' view of the TCE efficiency hypothesis. It may be that boundedly rational agents are incapable of identifying efficient structures *ex ante*, but efficient structures nevertheless emerge in some evolutionary fashion. Provided that the observed structure *would have been chosen* by sufficiently knowledgeable agents, TCE is vindicated.

Admittedly, it is difficult to test propositions involving comparisons with a hypothetical world (one where side-payments are unrestricted). However, the test is clear in principle: one looks for evidence that the infeasibility of participation bribes is a binding constraint on organizational choice. If *ex ante* side-payments are actually observed, this is naturally evidence for TCE. Failure to observe such payments raises the possibility that they are infeasible (though they might also be unnecessary, if the efficient structure happens to give sufficient quasi-rent to each coalition member). One then searches for corroborating evidence. The appropriability hypothesis becomes plausible, for example, if variations in the feasibility of side-payments are reliably correlated with variations in governance structure.

It is necessary at this point to dispose of a definitional objection: why should a structure be called inefficient if any improvement would require side-payments, and these side-payments are infeasible in the real world? Isn't it more accurate to say that the existing structure is efficient, relative to the set of alternatives that can actually be implemented? After all, the participants are doing the best they can under the circumstances.

This objection runs aground on the shoals of tautology. One can always rationalize an equilibrium structure as 'efficient' by adding enough constraints to the optimization problem. One could equally well say that outcomes in the one-shot prisoner's dilemma are 'efficient' because the prisoners cannot escape their fate by signing a binding contract. Semantic moves of this sort deprive TCE of its empirical content. If there are no imaginable reasons for calling an observed governance structure 'inefficient', then TCE becomes a form of theology rather than a scientific research programme. In keeping with Williamson's own emphasis on refutable implications, I henceforth treat efficiency claims as assertions about the world which might conceivably prove false.[3]

Section 2 describes the premises of TCE in greater detail. I draw primarily upon various chapters of Williamson and Winter (1991) for a contemporary statement of TCE. A short review of this useful volume appears elsewhere (Dow, 1992a).

Sections 3 and 4 develop and refine the main appropriability critique of TCE. Section 3 deals with specific investments that are non-contractable and generate shared *ex post* quasi-rents. I show that equilibrium governance structures must enable coalition members to recoup sunk investments, but need not maximize overall surplus. Section 4 addresses the externality problems associated with unrepresented agents: that is, stakeholders whose interests are affected by the choice among governance structures, but who are not in a position to influence this decision. Some examples include future quasi-rent recipients and members of an existing coalition whose quasi-rents are eliminated through defection by a sub-coalition. Section 5 distinguishes circumstances where TCE provides a useful first approximation from situations where appropriability factors typically dominate.

2 THE PREMISES OF TRANSACTION COST ECONOMICS

Before giving a detailed exposition of the appropriability hypothesis, we need to lay out the analytic framework of TCE more systematically. I review the choice between market and hierarchy in section 2.1. Section 2.2 examines the TCE explanatory scheme at a more abstract level.

Bounded rationality issues are taken up in section 2.3. Section 2.4 closes with some brief remarks on the subject of 'standard contracts' as public goods.

2.1   The Paradigmatic Case: Market versus Hierarchy

The paradigmatic issue for TCE is the choice between market exchange and hierarchy (Williamson, 1975). Although this simple dichotomy neglects intermediate organizational forms, it provides a useful format in which to review some key ideas.

First, we need to clarify the meaning of the terms 'market exchange' and 'hierarchy'. I will take market exchange to mean transactions between two independent owners of related physical assets (e.g. a supplier and customer in a vertical production relationship). These agents may sit atop hierarchical firms of their own, but I treat them here as individual transactors for simplicity. The alternative to market exchange is hierarchy, defined as an arrangement where one agent takes over ownership of all relevant physical assets and supervises the activities of the other party. This latter agent thus functions as the subordinate of the asset owner.

With independent ownership, transaction costs arise through bilateral bargaining between asset owners in an environment where frequent adaptation to new contingencies is needed. Because each party has an independent profit stream, coordinated responses to new states of the world are difficult to arrange. Instead, each side distorts information in pursuit of its own self-interest.[4]

Integrated ownership limits these distortions by merging the profit streams of the two parties, making it less attractive to behave opportunistically. But this remedy is a two-edged sword: incentives to supply effort also fall since each agent now shares in a collective profit stream. The resulting free-rider problem is usually resolved by having one party become the sole residual claimant, while the agent who is bought out now serves as a hired employee. This solution obliges the owner to use up resources in policing the efforts of his or her subordinate. Thus although it is true that hierarchy permits coordinated responses to changing circumstances, this gain in flexibility trades off against lower effort and costly monitoring. Distortions of the latter type are among the principal transaction costs of hierarchy.[5]

The central explanatory hypothesis of TCE is that governance structures having lower transaction costs will be adopted, other things equal. Market exchange emerges when bargaining costs are small (assets are short-lived and unspecialized) but hierarchial distortions would be large (effort is costly to monitor, or the firm would be hard to manage).

Conversely, hierarchy emerges when bargaining costs loom large (assets are durable and specialized), but the incentive problems arising under hierarchical control are mild and authoritative coordination is easily achieved.[6]

2.2 An Interpretive Framework

The market versus hierarchy problem illustrates the style of reasoning commonly used in TCE. Several general propositions can be distilled from this example. After listing these in summary form, I will expand upon each point in turn.

1 A *transaction* requires that certain actions be carried out by the members of a coalition. The resulting aggregate gains vary with the actions chosen by individual agents.
2 Some of these actions are *contractable*. Third parties are willing and able to enforce agreements concerning actions of this sort. Long-term contracts are generally incomplete, however. Non-contracted actions are chosen by individual agents according to their own self-interest.[7]
3 A *governance structure* is a binding agreement regulating the con-tractable actions of coalition members, and specifying an authority structure to decide actions not explicitly covered in advance. A governance structure also usually distributes claims on contractable payment streams and may determine the pattern of physical asset ownership.
4 The *transaction cost* associated with a governance structure is the difference between the aggregate surplus generated by that structure and the first-best surplus level arising in a hypothetical world where agents can costlessly contract on all relevant actions. Comprehensive contracting is thus the efficiency benchmark. A governance structure gives rise to transaction costs because (and to the extent that) it is an imperfect substitute for complete and costless contracts.
5 An *efficient* governance structure (that is, a structure with minimum transaction cost) will be adopted. Since real-world contracts are incomplete, first-best outcomes are generally unattainable. Observed governance structures are therefore efficient only in a second-best sense.

These five ideas represent the analytic core of TCE. Each point will now be scrutinized a bit more carefully.

Transactions

The forms of exchange which are of greatest interest to TCE involve sustained interactions over time. One-time trades, although possibly bedevilled by problems of adverse selection or moral hazard, do not typically warrant construction of a specialized governance structure.[8]

Contractability

An action is contractable if third parties are willing and able to deter any deviations from prescribed behaviour.[9] Non-contractability could occur for any of the following reasons:

1 Third parties cannot verify compliance.
2 Third parties cannot impose adequate penalties for deviation (e.g. it is too costly to find and punish violators, or violators have limited personal wealth).
3 Third parties lack personal incentives to carry out costly enforcement activities.
4 Third parties are unwilling to penalize violators for legal or moral reasons (promises to provide lifelong personal service will not be enforced, for example).

It may also prove difficult to transfer certain benefit or cost streams from one agent to another through contracts. Examples include the psychic value of working with congenial colleagues, or the psychic disutility of effort.

When contracting is costly, the parties involved may prefer to have some potentially contractable actions determined in the future through a managerial authority structure. This adds flexibility, but can lead to distortions if the agents who wield authority fail to internalize the full costs their decisions impose on other agents. An authority structure is viable if its provisions can be enforced by third parties in the usual way, or if enforcement is possible through private ordering (discussed next).

Governance structures

Williamson (1987) describes TCE as the 'comparative contracting perspective', and the spirit of TCE is clearly to view governance structures as contractual arrangements.[10] However, TCE also stresses private ordering (Williamson, 1985, pp. 164–6): that is, the use of private enforcement procedures that do not depend upon the courts. These include arbitration, reputational effects, threats to terminate a business relationship and hostage exchange.

Economists, from radicals to property rights theorists, agree that private enforcement procedures play an important role in market economies. However, if perfectly effective forms of private ordering could be devised, first-best outcomes would be feasible and the choice among governance structures would lose interest. Governance structures matter precisely because private ordering is only an imperfect substitute for costless third party enforcement.[11]

Two potential difficulties associated with private ordering warrant special comment.

Credibility. Writers using the TCE approach routinely appeal to termination threats as a private enforcement technique, often without recognizing that retaliation of this sort imposes costs on the enforcer as well. Precisely because the enforcement scheme involved is a private one, the enforcer has no binding obligation to impose the punishment. It is therefore vital to show that private agents have an incentive to carry out any required punishment once a violation has occurred. In game-theoretic jargon, termination threats need to be credible or subgame perfect.[12]

Multiple equilibria. Private enforcement procedures often give rise to many different perfect equilibria (Carmichael, 1990; Dow, 1991a). It cannot be assumed that efficient equilibria necessarily arise. Even in fairly simple coordination games, laboratory subjects can settle on Pareto-dominated equilibria (Van Huyck et al., 1991).

Transaction costs

TCE postulates that the transaction cost associated with a governance structure is a scalar quantity. We are thus concerned with the aggregate pay-off flowing to a coalition, not with the way in which this collective gain is distributed. This approach implies that utility aggregation is a meaningful procedure. When transferable utility cannot be assumed, TCE's research agenda collapses because there is no longer any scalar-valued objective function that can be used to evaluate and compare organizational forms. (Whether TCE could be resurrected using the strict Pareto efficiency criterion remains unclear.) In any case, the assumption of transferable utility limits preferences in substantive ways (for example, it implies risk neutrality and therefore the maximization of expected wealth by individuals or groups).

Efficiency

TCE claims that efficient governance structures are adopted. As discussed in the introduction, I treat this assertion as an empirical hypothesis rather than a concealed definition of 'efficiency' or 'transaction cost'. Doing so implies that there is some independent way of assessing the efficiency of governance structures, without slipping into a circular argument where the existence of a structure is seen as evidence in favour of its efficiency.

Transaction costs are rarely measured directly. Instead, one must use deductive reasoning about the likely efficiency properties of alternative governance structures, given a description of the transaction involved. The choice between market exchange and hierarchy in section 2.1 is one example. There is nothing methodologically illegimitate about this procedure, as long as it yields testable hypotheses.[13]

2.3 Bounded Rationality and Evolutionary Mechanisms

Bounded rationality raises special difficulties for the TCE efficiency claim and deserves separate discussion. The main role of bounded rationality in TCE is to rule out comprehensive *ex ante* contracting (Williamson, 1991, pp. 92–3), where the parties anticipate every possible state of the world and agree in advance on a course of action appropriate to that state. The need for this is clear: if complete contracts were feasible, first-best results could be achieved and governance structures would become irrelevant. Comprehensive contracting could of course be ruled out in other ways: high enforcement costs would suffice. But if TCE were to give up the bounded rationality postulate and permit full-blown expected utility maximization, its analytic framework would be indistinguishable from the mechanism design literature (Williamson, 1985, pp. 50–2). For this reason, bounded rationality is central to TCE's status as a distinctive research programme.

Unfortunately, granting the bounded rationality assumption raises other problems. If agents cannot anticipate and plan for all future contingencies, it follows that they cannot compute the transaction cost associated with each governance structure, since these costs depend precisely on the magnitude of the distortions occurring in various future states of the world. This calls into question the capacity of economic agents to identify or implement efficient governance structures *ex ante*.[14]

Two responses are available at this point. First, one could grant the potential conflict between bounded rationality and the efficiency claim. This would lead one to look for inefficiencies resulting from bounded rationality on the part of organizational designers. North (1990), for example, takes this approach in his discussion of institutional change.

An alternative response is to defend the efficiency claim by arguing that evolutionary selection processes bestow differential *ex post* rewards upon efficient and inefficient structures. Those structures having lower realized transaction costs (or higher net social benefits) will thrive at the expense of less advantageous organizational forms, and will dominate in the long run.[15]

In response to earlier charges of functionalism (Dow, 1987), Williamson (1991, pp. 104–8) has developed a detailed evolutionary hypothesis to account for the spread of multi-divisional structures among large corporations. This is surely progress, but two points need to be made. First, the 'function' served by M-form organization in the Williamson hypothesis is increased profit or present value, which can diverge from net social benefit (e.g. if employees capture quasi-rents). More significantly, Williamson's evolutionary hypothesis applies only to the specific phenomenon it is designed to explain. There is still no general presumption that efficiency claims can be rationalized through an appeal to evolutionary mechanisms.

It is especially important to recognize that an evolutionary formulation of TCE does not by itself deflect the appropriability critique. According to the appropriability approach, governance structures are viable only if they provide adequate inducements to all essential participants. When selection forces operate at the level of individual pay-offs (for example, if input suppliers migrate among governance structures in response to *ex post* pay-off realizations), evolutionary processes will not typically overcome problems of side-payment infeasibility. Selection unambiguously favours structures that maximize aggregate surplus only when side-payments can be used to make such structures Pareto-dominant. If participation bribes are infeasible, a structure maximizing total surplus may be selected against because it proves unattractive to some inputs. The nature of selection forces is thus an empirical question, and cannot be settled *a priori* (see section 5.3 below).

2.4   Standard Contracts as Public Goods

Private organizational arrangements are adopted against the backdrop of prevailing legal and property institutions. At best, these private choices are efficient only in relation to existing institutional rules (North, 1990). Since institutions are public goods, collective actions that alter the institutional framework may enable private agents to devise better governance structures. While this point is rather obvious, its implications for TCE have not received adequate attention.

I will limit my comments to the role of 'default options' as devices for completing contracts. When the parties to a contract have not agreed upon a comprehensive list of rights and duties in advance, and a conflict arises, the courts look to a large body of statutory and common law for guidance. An incomplete contract is 'completed' by applying conventional rights and duties to that specific type of contract (Clark, 1985, p. 60). As Masten puts it,

> many basic terms and conditions are likely to be common across transactions. To minimize the costly duplication of identical provisions in individual contracts, the law provides a set of standard doctrines and

remedies to deal with recurring contractual events. . . . Reliance on common law doctrines . . . permits transactors to choose that combination of legal 'defaults' or 'presets' that most closely approximates the ideal arrangement simply by identifying the class of transactions that the parties intended. (Masten, 1991, p. 206)

These 'standard contracts' defined by the legal system reduce the cost of negotiating and enforcing agreements. But one can expect agents to have conflicting preferences about the provisions of such standard contracts, depending on the kinds of defaults they routinely find useful and the cost of devising special-purpose alternatives where necessary. Standard contracts are therefore public goods, imposing costs on some and providing benefits to others (Clark, 1985, pp. 66–7).

The provisions of standard contracts evolve over time in response to legislation and court decisions. For example, the 'standard' employment contract is an authority relationship where employees are required to obey their employers, and either party can cancel the contract at will (Masten, 1991).[16] Despite this, the courts are increasingly sympathetic to wrongful discharge suits brought by disgruntled former employees. The conventional content of the marriage contract has also evolved in recent years (e.g. in the areas of domestic violence and rules for property division in case of divorce).

The point of this discussion is that the alleged efficiency of private organizational choices cannot be used by TCE adherents to argue against modifications in background institutions. Since it can be costly for private agents to construct special-purpose agreements, organizational choices depend to a large degree upon the existing menu of standard contracts. But standard contracts are public goods, and hence their content must be decided through some mechanism for collective action. One cannot leap carelessly from an assumption of individual rationality to conclusions about the efficiency of the institutional framework itself. Such leaps generally yield either tautologies or non sequiturs.[17]

3   APPROPRIABILITY I: NON-CONTRACTABLE INVESTMENTS

As discussed above, TCE holds that governance structures are explained by their capacity to enhance the collective gains from production and exchange. The *ex post* distribution of these gains is immaterial, since each party's reservation utility can always be covered through side-payments if necessary. Here I will argue to the contrary that the distribution of quasi-rent is frequently decisive for the viability of governance structures.

3.1   Non-contractable Investments: a Simple Model

I begin with an abstract presentation of the argument, after which empirical evidence will be discussed. I assume throughout that agents are sophisticated enough to exploit all possibilities for bargaining, information distortion or shirking arising under each governance structure, and know that others will do the same.

Let a particular governance structure be denoted by $\omega \in \Omega$ where Ω is the set of all feasible structure. Each structure requires the participation of n agents (worker, manager, owner, etc.). We denote the set of agents participating in a governance structure by $N \equiv \{1 \ldots n\}$. The *ex post* pay-off of agent i in structure ω at output price p is $\pi_i(p, \omega)$, where these pay-offs are increasing functions of price. The *ex ante* reservation utility of each agent is normalized at zero.

We assume that each agent must undertake a non-contractable investment in physical or human capital before transactions get underway.[18] Agent i's investment cost, which is non-recoverable or sunk *ex post*, is $Y_i \geqslant 0$. I assume these costs are independent of the governance structure used to organize the transaction.

Structure ω is *viable* at the output price p if all required agents want to participate in this structure *ex ante*, so that an entrepreneur interested in setting up such a structure would find it possible to recruit input suppliers. Formally, ω is viable if $\pi_i(p, \omega) \geqslant Y_i$ for all $i \in N$, since then all agents will have net pay-offs at least equal to their reservation utilities. Under free entry, the structure which stays viable at the lowest output price prevails in the long run, because entry by this structure forces the price of output down to a level where rival structures are no longer attractive to some input suppliers.[19]

Let $\bar{p}(\omega)$ be the lowest output price at which the structure ω is viable. That is,

$$\bar{p}(\omega) \equiv \min \{p \geqslant 0 : \pi_i(p, \omega) \geqslant Y_i \quad \text{for all } i \in N\}$$

The set of equilibrium governance structures E is given by

$$E \equiv \{\omega_e \in \Omega : \bar{p}(\omega_e) \leqslant \bar{p}(\omega) \quad \text{for all } \omega \in \Omega\}$$

Free entry by any structure ω_e in the set E makes it impossible for structures *not* in this set to attract some input suppliers. The equilibrium price of output is accordingly $p_e = \bar{p}(\omega_e)$.

We now want to determine whether an equilibrium structure must maximize aggregate surplus at the price p_e. Pick some ω_e in the equilibrium set E. We want to know whether there could be an alternative structure ω^* not in E with the property

$$\sum_{i \in N} \pi_i(p_e, \omega_e) < \sum_{i \in N} \pi_i(p_e, \omega^*)$$

If so, then by the Kaldor–Hicks efficiency criterion, structure ω^* is socially preferred to the equilibrium structure ω_e at price p_e (since investment costs are identical for the two structures).

It is easy to see that this inequality can hold. In fact, ω^* can be socially preferred to ω_e at all prices, without being viable at any price. To see why, consider the extreme case where some agent j has a zero *ex post* pay-off in the preferred structure ω^* so that $\pi_j(p, \omega^*) = 0$ for all output prices. For example, ω^* could involve an authority structure where j is always forced down to his or her reservation pay-off *ex post*. If $Y_j > 0$ (agent j contributes a specialized asset) then there is no output price at which ω^* is viable, since input suppliers of type j are never attracted to this structure. However, there could well be prices at which the inferior structure ω_e is viable. For instance, this structure might give j a positive share of a smaller quasi-rent, so the j's set-up cost would be covered at some prices.

Whenever an equilibrium structure is inefficient, the agents who would gain from a socially preferred structure ω^* would like to bribe the losers in order to secure their acceptance of ω^*. In the case described above, the remaining agents $i \neq j$ would like to bribe an agent of type j to incur the set-up cost Y_j since the returns from this investment are appropriated (either in whole or in part) by j's coalition partners.

What is required is a participation bribe. There are three general ways of coping with the situation.

1   Other agents could pay j directly to incur the sunk cost Y_j. However, if third parties cannot verify the characteristics of j's investment, j might not perform satisfactorily. On the other hand, the other agents might try to escape their payment obligation by falsely alleging poor performance.

2   Agent j could invest unilaterally and request complementary agents or teams to bid for the use of the resulting asset. This reduces the need for third party verification, since other agents can inspect the asset themselves before they submit bids. But adverse selection problems still arise if j knows more about the asset than the potential bidders do. Moreover, if j's asset is specialized by design to the needs of particular coalition partners, it is usually impossible to solicit competitive bids. Without competitive bidding, j has no assurance of recovering the full sunk cost Y_j.

3   The remaining agents $i \neq j$ could try to eliminate j from the transaction. This is not always possible, however. For example, technological requirements may call for a worker of type j who has certain transaction-specific knowledge or skills. It then becomes impossible for the remainder of the production coalition to acquire the relevant asset (the specific human capital) without somehow inducing a worker of type j

to participate. Likewise, when a specific physical asset is essential and is not owned by $i \neq j$, the coalition must persuade some outside owner (or a potential producer of the asset) to step forward.

3.2   An Example: Capitalist and Labour-managed Firms

Elsewhere (Dow, 1992b) I have developed a formal model which applies these ideas to the choice between capitalist firms (KMFs) and labour-managed firms (LMFs). In the KMF, capital hires labour: asset owners are residual claimants, bargain with workers over the wage rate and choose the firm's output level. In the LMF, labour hires capital: workers are residual claimants, bargain with external owners over the rental fee paid for the use of physical assets and choose output. In each case investments in physical assets are sunk, while labour is general-purpose.

Under these conditions it can be shown that capitalist firms normally arise in equilibrium, even if labour-managed firms would give a larger surplus. In the LMF all quasi-rent goes to workers *ex post*, since asset owners are driven down to their reservation pay-offs when workers choose output. This makes it impossible for capitalists to recover their sunk investment expenditures. But asset owners do appropriate some quasi-rent in a capitalist firm (since workers are unspecialized, they do not need to recoup any sunk costs). Capitalist firms are therefore viable and emerge in equilibrium. This result goes through even if aggregate surplus is smaller in the capitalist firm, as long as investors cannot be bribed *ex ante* to participate in the LMF (that is, investments in physical assets are non-contractable). In this model, capitalist firms prevail for reasons of appropriability, not efficiency.

Like TCE, the appropriability approach generates refutable implications. A central prediction from the analysis reported above is that capitalist firms typically prevail when production requires large investments in specialized physical assets, but labour is unspecialized. Conversely, labour-managed firms emerge when production involves idiosyncratic human capital but physical assets are general-purpose. This prediction is consistent with the actual distribution of capitalist and labour-managed firms in Western economies (see Dow, 1992b, for details). The principal exception involves worker take-overs of capital-intensive firms in declining industries. But this case is also compatible with the theory, because here investments in physical assets have already been made and it is unnecessary to attract new capital suppliers.

3.3   Some Evidence on the Infeasibility of Participation Bribes

Econometric evidence reveals that workers obtain substantial rents in many industries. The explanation is controversial: some writers favour an efficiency wage mechanism (Katz, 1986; Dickens and Katz, 1987; Krueger and Summers, 1988), while others stress insider–outsider effects in the wage bargaining process (Lindbeck and Snower, 1988).

Under either story, we have a puzzle: why are employers in competitive labour markets unable or unwilling to extract *ex ante* compensation for these rents, for instance by requiring workers to bid for jobs? Several reasons have been suggested, including firm-side moral hazard problems (Dow, 1991b), worker liquidity constraints, and legal or sociological factors (Dickens et al., 1989). Employers may also offer rents in order to attract particularly talented workers. If so, it would be self-defeating to deprive employees of these rents *ex ante* (Weiss, 1990). Whatever the actual explanation, here it suffices to observe that employers rarely do charge entry fees (except in the form of rising wage profiles over time), even when they seem to have strong incentives to do so. This suggests that workers do not usually pay participation bribes to their employers.[20]

A related piece of evidence concerns the effect of worker rent extraction on investment decisions. If unionization tends to increase the share of quasi-rent appropriated by workers, and employers do not secure *ex ante* compensation for this diversion, we should observe a negative effect of unionization on investment and firm growth, since worker quasi-rent appropriation resembles a tax on investment returns. *Ex ante* participation bribes from workers would function as a refund on this tax, and should reduce the effect of unionization on investment, other things equal. The data indicate that unionization depresses investment (Addison and Hirsch, 1989), and hence support the hypothesis that *ex ante* compensation in the labour market is partial at best.[21]

A rather different example involves oil field unitization. Wiggins and Libecap (1985) show that large economic gains could be obtained by reorganizing small oil producers under the rubric of unitary ownership, since common pool effects are internalized and incentives for excessive extraction are eliminated. Even so, negotiations to achieve unitization often break down. Wiggins and Libecap argue that these breakdowns result from informational asymmetries concerning the value of individual leases. This is a particulaly vivid instance of *ex ante* side-payment failure.

4 APPROPRIABILITY II: UNREPRESENTED AGENTS

Section 3 discussed organizational failures resulting from *ex post* sharing of the returns to non-contractable investments. Here I develop a related argument: some agents who are affected by a choice among governance structures may not be represented when such choices are made. This creates an externality problem.

Three situations of this sort will be considered.

1   Future organizational participants will capture rents upon joining the production coalition, but it is impossible to extract offsetting present compensation from these agents.
2   Some agents make irreversible precommitments in order to establish a favourable bargaining environment before their eventual bargaining partners arrive on the scene.
3   Agents are involuntarily deprived of existing quasi-rents through a reorganization that is implemented unilaterally by the members of a subcoalition.

I discuss each case in turn.

4.1   Future Organizational Participants

Factor suppliers often appropriate a stream of rents upon joining the firm. For example, workers or managers may enjoy informational rents because employers face an adverse selection problem (Weiss, 1990), or because it is impossible to contract on effort (Shapiro and Stiglitz, 1984; Bowles, 1985). Workers may also appropriate quasi-rent ex post through wage bargaining (Dow, 1985, 1992b). For the reasons discussed in section 3.2, it is frequently difficult for employers to recapture these rents *ex ante*, even in an otherwise competitive labour market.

This fact has systematic consequences for the choice among organizational forms. If there is some exogenous labour turnover, the rents to be appropriated by future workers or managers are part of the social benefit stream generated by the firm, but play little or no role in the private calculations of the agents who set up governance structures in the present. Since returns going to future coalition members are undervalued, the organizational forms actually adopted are likely to be inefficient.

An illustrative example concerns the investment behaviour of the labour-managed firm. In an earlier article (Dow, 1987), I suggested that LMFs might be disadvantaged relative to capitalist rivals for appropriability reasons, despite an advantage on the criterion of net social benefit. I have subsequently amplified this argument (Dow, 1992c) using a formal model of KMF and LMF investment behaviour. It will be helpful at this point to give a brief summary of the conclusions derived from this model.

The LMF could enjoy a static efficiency advantage over the KMF for several reasons, including: (a) greater work incentives or lower monitoring costs (Dong and Dow, 1991; Dow, 1991b); (b) more sharing of private information between workers and managers; (c) less technological and organizational rigidity; or (d) a tendency by LMF managers to internalize worker costs that are ignored by KMF managers (Dow, 1992b,c), so that opportunistic abuses of authority are curbed. Assume some set of these factors applies.

Now consider the investment decisions made by current LMF members. We assume that current members are unable to charge new members an entry fee that fully reflects the present value of the quasi-rent stream these members will enjoy upon entering the firm. This depresses LMF investment incentives by reducing the size of the participation bribes paid by future members. On the other hand, assume that there is a competitive stock market that correctly capitalizes the dividend stream generated by capitalist firms. Then there are parameter values such that:

1 The LMF is socially preferred to the KMF on both static and dynamic Kaldor–Hicks efficiency measures.
2 The KMF grows more rapidly than the LMF.
3 Private agents have perverse incentives to convert LMFs into KMFs, despite a net reduction in the social benefits derived from current and future production.

More generally, it can be shown that whenever the LMF wins the evolutionary race in the long run, it is also socially preferred. The converse, however, is not true: KMFs can win an evolutionary contest against LMFs even when they are socially inferior.

This result reflects the fact that the KMF and LMF are both second-best organizational forms. The KMF suffers from its low static productivity, while the LMF underinvests because it gives insufficient weight to returns captured by future worker-members. Since its liabilities are dynamic rather than static, the LMF often loses a dynamic competition against the KMF, even if its static productivity advantage outweighs its dynamic liabilities from a social (Kaldor–Hicks) point of view.

4.2 Unilateral Precommitment

Another situation involving unrepresented agents arises when one organizational participant (usually a capital supplier) can precommit to assets or production techniques in order to create a favourable *ex post* bargaining environment.[22] To take one example, suppose workers will acquire private information by participating in the production process, and this will allow workers to capture rents after being hired. A capitalist investor will treat these labour rents as a cost item, and hence will precommit to physical facilities that limit the value of the information to be gained by workers once production begins (Dow, 1989).

Such *ex ante* commitments are socially costly if they reduce the aggregate surplus generated through production, but they will prove privately attractive to investors if enough quasi-rent can be shifted from workers to owners. Inefficiencies can be avoided in this situation only if the capitalist internalizes quasi-rents flowing to future workers. The obvious solution, asking incoming workers to bid competitively for jobs, may be ruled out by moral hazard considerations (Dow, 1991b). Similar difficulties emerge whenever firms can unilaterally impose process innovations that limit worker bargaining power, in a setting where workers cannot bribe owners to refrain from such innovations (Dow, 1985).

4.3 Breaking Implicit Contracts

A final instance where the problem of unrepresented agents arises involves transformations of ongoing governance structures in ways that exclude some current rent recipients. When groups who want to revise a governance structure ignore rents presently flowing to others, there is a systematic undervaluation of the status quo. Unless all rent recipients have a veto, or costless bribes can be arranged, the resulting reorganization may violate a Kaldor–Hicks efficiency test.

To pose the problem more formally, suppose that a coalition $N \equiv \{1 \ldots n\}$ has already adopted a governance structure ω_0 where total surplus is $v(N; \omega_0)$. Governance structures determine not only total benefits, but also the distribution of these benefits among individual agents. Letting $x_i(\omega_0)$ be the pay-off flowing to agent i under structure ω_0 we have

$$\sum_{i \in N} x_i(\omega_0) = v(N; \omega_0)$$

where we assume $x_i(\omega_0) > 0$ for all $i \in N$ (everyone has a positive quasi-rent stream). Reservation pay-offs are normalized at zero.

Now suppose there is an alternative governance structure $\hat{\omega}$ which provides a smaller aggregate surplus:

$$v(N; \omega_0) > v(N; \hat{\omega})$$

However, there is a subcoalition S that prefers $\hat{\omega}$ in the sense that if S separates from the original coalition N, its members can achieve larger gains by implementing the structure $\hat{\omega}$. Thus,

$$v(S; \hat{\omega}) = \sum_{i \in S} x_i(\hat{\omega}) > \sum_{i \in S} x_i(\omega_0) = v(S; \omega_0)$$

If the alternative structure $\hat{\omega}$ is adopted, all members of N *not* in the coalition S are deprived of their quasi-rents. That is, we assume $x_i(\hat{\omega}) = 0$ for i not in S.

Clearly the subcoalition S has an incentive to replace the existing governance structure ω_0 with a new governance structure $\hat{\omega}$. This move is inefficient since ω_0 is socially preferred. The problem is that the reorganization can be prevented only if the members of $\bar{S} \equiv N - S$ (the complement of S) can bribe S not to defect. In principle, the members of $\bar{S}$ would be willing to offer an aggregate bribe up to

$$\sum_{i \in S} x_i(\omega_0)$$

to avoid a break-up. Because ω_0 is socially superior, this bribe would be large enough to keep S from defecting.

Unfortunately, there may not be any way of negotiating such bribes in practice. The members of the subcoalition S will often know more about their pay-offs under the new structure than the members of $\bar{S}$, creating problems of asymmetric information. It may also be impossible for the members of S to make credible exit threats without actually leaving, since verbal declarations are likely to be viewed merely as a bluff to extort unwarranted bribes. Moreover, if third parties cannot verify the payment of bribes, there is nothing to keep the members of S from pocketing an initial bribe, and then extorting additional payments later.

There is a good deal of evidence that quasi-rent recipients can strongly resist side-payment demands, even in circumstances where the consequences of refusal ultimately prove quite severe. For example, demands for wage concessions are sometimes rejected by unions even when the firm eventually goes into bankruptcy, and workers lose their jobs. Rather than attributing this outcome to worker irrationality, it is more reasonable to conclude that the employer's claims of financial distress, although true, are not believed, since management has an incentive to lie when times are good (Kennan, 1986). More generally, the occurrence of prolonged strikes shows that distributional conflict over a shared pie can impose substantial costs on both sides when some information is privately held (Kennan and Wilson, 1989).

Stakeholders can also be deprived of quasi-rent streams in the process of corporate reorganization. Hostile take-overs, for example, can lead to a breach of existing implicit contracts with employees or suppliers (Shleifer and Summers, 1988). This breach may result in the transfer of wealth from stakeholders to the new owners of the firm through lay-offs, termination of pension plans or a reduction in union wage premiums. Such transfers appear to account for a significant (although not dominant) fraction of the target-firm take-over premium in cases where a take-over is hostile (Pontiff et al., 1990; Rosett, 1990).

A related example involves attempts by management to escape employee claims on quasi-rent by relocating production. Worker skills are often not only firm-specific but location-specific, because it is costly to disrupt family and community ties. The size of the quasi-rents appropriated by workers can be seriously underestimated when these mobility costs are ignored.[23] Social losses resulting from unilateral relocation decisions may thus be overlooked. Of course, there is an incentive for workers or the local community to avoid these losses by bribing the firm to stay (or buying it out directly), but such efforts can be thwarted by informational or free-rider problems (Ben-Ner and Jun, 1990).

These examples illustrate a more general point: it is often hard for a large, diverse subcoalition (such as the workforce of a firm) to bribe other organizational actors. The negotiation, monitoring and enforcement of such deals are public goods from the viewpoint of subcoalition members, and hence are subject to all the usual difficulties of free-ridership and preference revelation. Since worker interests are frequently more diverse than those of shareholders, participation bribes will normally be more difficult to arrange between a firm and its workforce, as compared with bribes paid by one shareholder group to another.[24]

5 CONCLUSION: THE RELEVANCE OF TRANSACTION COST ECONOMICS

There can be no doubt that TCE has contributed some major theoretical insights, and has significant empirical successes to its credit (particularly in the area of vertical integration; see Joskow, 1991). But TCE also systematically ignores certain forms of organizational failure. These blind spots derive from TCE's insistence that efficiency is the 'main case' (Williamson, 1987) and its associated preoccupation with the social rather than the individual level of analysis.

Production coalitions sometimes pursue joint interests, but at other times fail to restrain the rent-seeking propensities of individual members or subcoalitions. To ask whether efficiency or appropriability is the 'main case' amounts to asking whether the glass is half full or half empty. A more useful research agenda is to identify cases where aggregate efficiency criteria provide a satisfactory first-order explanation of the facts, as opposed to those cases where participation bribes are restricted and appropriability considerations take centre stage.

5.1 The Successes of TCE

The most influential attempts to formalize transaction cost reasoning are concerned with patterns of physical asset ownership (Grossman and Hart,

1986; Hart and Moore, 1990). It is also fair to say that the main empirical successes of TCE involve the issue of vertical integration.[25]

The nature of these theoretical and empirical successes is not a coincidence. *Ex ante* compensation schemes are easiest to implement when transferring ownership rights to physical assets. The only potential obstacle is that of asset valuation, which may require that adverse selection or other informational problems be overcome. Even problems of this sort are diminished if suppliers and customers have been dealing with one another repeatedly over a period of years, and therefore understand the characteristics of the assets involved. Repeated interaction also minimizes the bounded rationality problems that might impede an assessment of the transaction cost savings to be obtained through integration.

5.2   The Limitations of TCE

TCE has had less success in addressing problems of workplace organization and human capital, despite some notable attempts.[26] In particular, Williamson's writings in this area have stimulated much criticism and controversy.[27] This may be in part because of the greater political sensitivity of the issues involved, as compared to vertical integration. There are also some deeper qualitative differences: vertical integration involves relations between two hierarchical firms, while the employment relationship represents the chief building block for hierarchy itself (see chapter 12). Here, however, I want to emphasize a different point: appropriability problems are highly prominent for many labour market transactions, and for this reason TCE's efficiency hypothesis loses persuasive force.

Consider the following stylized facts about labour markets, workplace organization and the employment relationship:

1   Investments in worker skills are often not only sunk, but also non-contractable (due in part to difficulties of third party verification).
2   Because employers cannot own their workers, the potential for avoiding opportunistic bargaining through integrated asset ownership is rather limited (Putterman, 1988).[28]
3   Because incumbent employees often have private information about themselves or the production process, and can be quite costly to replace, labour rents are pervasive. Such rents are viewed as a cost item by employers (Dow, 1988b, 1989).
4   Side-payment schemes, such as requiring workers to bid *ex ante* for jobs, encounter special difficulties in the labour market. These obstacles involve not only firm-side moral hazard (Dow, 1991b) and worker liquidity constraints, but also legal restrictions and sociological effects on morale (Dickens et al., 1989).

5   There is a strong asymmetry between suppliers of capital and labour
     with regard to precommitment strategies. It is often fairly easy for
     capital suppliers to commit irreversibly to certain physical assets (or to
     put it differently, capital suppliers usually find it costly to modify their
     assets *ex post*). Workers face much greater difficulties in committing
     themselves not to alter their skills (Dow, 1985, 1989).

These factors suggest that the governance of labour relations will be
dominated by appropriability considerations. An 'unremitting emphasis
on efficiency' misses much of what is interesting about the organization of
work.

5.3   Efficiency and Appropriability: an Evolutionary Perspective

For its efficiency claims to go through, TCE requires that total social
surplus operates as the main criterion for the spread or extinction of
governance structures. As noted in section 2.3, if selection operates at the
individual level (input suppliers move among governance structures in
response to personal pay-off realizations), TCE's efficiency hypothesis
requires that there be costless side-payments among individual factor
suppliers.

I will close with a related observation. Some innovations make it easier
to overcome collective action problems, and help coalitions to realize
efficiency gains. Other innovations make strategic behaviour more
attractive (or more difficult to police). Within the framework of TCE, it is
impossible to discuss the second sort of innovation, because the analysis
proceeds entirely at the social level (at least insofar as *ex ante* organizational choices are concerned). But if selection forces actually reflect
individual or subcoalition pay-offs, there is no reason to ignore innovations that facilitate rent-seeking behaviour. It is only a matter of faith to
believe that desirable innovations will always outrun socially counter-
productive ones. Because the very same individual pay-off functions come
into play in either case, we can expect people to exert approximately the
same level of effort and ingenuity in searching out innovations of
each type.

The appropriability approach encourages a more systematic exploration of evolutionary mechanisms. If side-payments are feasible at
the social level, selection for socially beneficial innovations will be
strengthened (although selection will still reward rent-seeking innovations
within the interstices of current contractual arrangements). If side-
payments are feasible within subcoalitions but not across them, then
selection will operate on the strategies pursued by subcoalitions (without
extinguishing the attempts of individuals to free-ride in creative new

ways). Finally, if side-payments are completely infeasible, selection forces will favour fully non-cooperative behaviour (Dow, 1988c).

The feasibility of side-payments or participation bribes is thus intimately bound up with the level of aggregation at which evolutionary forces operate. TCE assumes without proof (or even sustained argument) that such forces operate at the social level. But the nature of selection mechanisms is a matter for empirical and theoretical investigation. In a sense, TCE is a distinctive special case of the appropriability approach, one that applies when *ex ante* side-payments are unproblematic. To the extent that this assumption does not grossly misrepresent reality, TCE may be a tolerable simplification. But we should not lose sight of the general case, which requires a theory of organizational structure built up from the foundation of individual pay-offs. Among other aims, a research programme emphasizing appropriability issues will help to identify the empirical boundaries within which TCE can usefully be applied.

NOTES

1 Williamson carefully avoids unqualified optimality claims. In place of a bold assertion that transaction costs will be minimized, he more cautiously maintains that organizational forms 'economize' on such costs. This distinction between strict optimization and economizing is not fundamental here. My critique is not concerned with optimization *per se*, but rather with TCE's reliance on aggregate pay-off measures.

2 TCE could equally well be asked to explain how it is that efficient results are achieved (Dow, 1987). It is not enough to show that people *want* to overcome collective action problems. One must also show that it is *feasible* to do so. In reality, some collective action problems are solved while others are not. The empirical problem is to find some way of distinguishing between the two cases.

3 As Coase (1991a, p. 48) notes, authors are usually charged with tautology only when their propositions are clearly right. However, the efficiency claims of TCE are meant to express empirical rather than logical truth. It is therefore vital for TCE to incorporate some non-tautological assertions, as Williamson (1991) well appreciates.

4 This is the conventional TCE argument about opportunistic *ex post* bargaining popularized by Williamson (1975, pp. 26–8; 1985, pp. 75–7) and Klein et al. (1978). For a good elaboration, see Klein (1991). A second source of distortions under independent ownership involves 'residual ownership rights' (Grossman and Hart, 1986; Hart and Moore, 1990). The most concise version of this approach appears in Hart (1991). Hart shows that independent asset ownership has costs if an asset owner can use non-contracted residual control rights to appropriate part of the profit stream from the asset. Even if the remaining (verifiable) part of the profit stream is

assigned entirely to the user of the asset, this diversion dulls the incentive of the user to supply effort. A third transaction cost derived from independent asset ownership is the cost of persuading contractors to reveal private information (Lewis and Sappington, 1991). For an instructive comparison between the Grossman–Hart 'incentive' approach and Williamson's own 'process' view, see Williamson (1991, pp. 98–104).

5   The transaction costs of hierarchy also include distortions resulting from self-interested abuses of authority. In an earlier work (Dow, 1987) I pointed out that authority will be abused if those who possess it do not fully internalize the costs their decisions impose on subordinate agents. I also emphasized that authority cannot be used selectively to achieve efficiency gains, since agents would not necessarily hold back from self-interested intervention at other times. Finally, I observed that the impossibility of such selective intervention limits firm size. Because all of these points have now been taken on board (Williamson, 1991, pp. 101–3), I will declare victory on this collection of issues.

6   A compact version of the TCE vertical integration story can be found in Williamson (1991, p. 111, note 14).

7   The rigid distinction drawn here between contractable and non-contractable actions is a bit artificial. In practice there are positive but finite costs of contract enforcement, so that a particular action might be worth contracting upon in one context, but not in another.

8   A fundamental limitation of TCE is that it attempts to model production activities as if they were conceptually identical to market exchange. The terminology of 'transactions' and 'contracting' can be seriously misleading as an intellectual framework for the study of production activities within the firm. (Coase himself now believes his classic 1937 article on the nature of the firm spent an excessive amount of time on market contracting, and too little on the administrative task of managing the firm; Coase, 1991b, pp. 65–8.) Flannigan (1992) argues that TCE's preoccupation with market exchange accounts for its use of vertical integration as a paradigm problem. A more production-oriented approach would instead stress issues of coordination and conflict between suppliers of complementary inputs. The paradigmatic problem in this latter perspective is to explain the existing distribution of control rights among factor suppliers (e.g. why capital typically hires labour rather than the reverse). Models of this type include Dow (1992b, c). Brief summaries of these papers appear in sections 3.2 and 4.1 respectively.

9   I adopt the narrow definition of contract used by Masten (1991, p. 198): 'a formal, legal commitment to which each party gives express approval and to which a particular body of law applies.' The phrase 'implicit contract' is ambiguous. To lawyers, an implicit contract is one whose terms are legally enforceable, even though not stated overtly. To economists, an implicit contract is usually an arrangement that can be enforced privately, without reliance on the court system. For a discussion of related issues, see Kronman (1985).

10 Organization theory is not exhausted by the study of formal contractual arrangements, since many different patterns of informal behaviour can be

consistent with a given contractual framework. Indeed, organizational structure can be defined alternatively as a stable pattern of behavioural interaction, repeated probabilistically through time (Dow, 1988a, 1990).

11   In particular, reputation effects are often casually treated as if they were a perfect substitute for binding contractual agreements. The limitations of reputation as an enforcement device are highlighted by Klein (1991, p. 216).

12   A case in point is the Klein and Leffler (1981) theory of product quality assurance. In their analysis, firms which opportunistically degrade quality are punished through the defection of consumers to rival firms. This termination threat may not be credible if consumers incur a cost when switching firms (e.g. due to product differentiation). The same problem arises in spades for long-term supply relations in intermediate product markets. Threats by an employer to fire shirking workers may likewise be non-credible when it is expensive to replace incumbent employees (Dow, 1991a).

13   Ideally, TCE will take the risk of predicting phenomena yet to be observed, and do so correctly. This requirement seems to have been met for vertical integration (Joskow, 1991).

14   In one of his few direct comments on this issue, Williamson (1985, p. 38) asserts that 'the ramifications of alternative contracts are intuited if not fully thought through'. This is a shaky basis on which to erect an entire research programme. In the context of an earlier debate, Williamson (1987) asks whether I subscribe to Herbert Simon's definition of bounded rationality as behaviour that is 'intendedly rational, but only limitedly so'. I have no quarrel with this definition, but it is a bit of a red herring. Any definition of bounded rationality which rules out comprehensive planning for all future contingencies will also, strictly speaking, rule out *ex ante* computation of transaction costs. The implication of Williamson's query is that because 'intendedly rational' agents are motivated to economize on transaction costs, they will somehow arrive at reasonable estimates of the true (but unknown) costs. The motivation is clear, but the estimation procedure remains murky.

15   Winter (1991, pp. 189–93) provides a compact discussion of the relationship between TCE and evolutionary economics. Other presentations include Langlois (1986) and Dow (1987).

16   Finkin (1986) shows that the courts have historically given great weight to customary employer practices in determining whether certain implicit terms of the employment contract are legally enforceable.

17   For a sample of the analytic mischief caused by such leaps, see Eggertsson (1990, pp. 20–5). Some authors hold that the common law evolves toward greater economic efficiency over time (Priest, 1977). Others have advanced similar claims about the structure of property rights (see the remarks on the 'naive theory of property rights' in Eggertsson, 1990, chapter 8). Such claims take us far beyond the present topic, but are problematic to say the least. Clark (1985) comments sceptically on efficiency claims concerning corporate law.

18   Non-contractability of *ex ante* investments is also a theme of Grossman and Hart (1986) and Hart and Moore (1990), but the emphasis of these authors differs. Their point is that governance structures (specifically, the pattern of

physical asset ownership) will be crafted to minimize the distortions resulting from non-contractable investments. Hart and Moore explicitly note that their analysis presupposes frictionless *ex ante* bargaining among input suppliers.

19 Grossman and Hart (1986) and Hart and Moore (1990) work with models where non-contractable investments are represented by a continuum. Here, such investments are indivisible: they are either undertaken, or not.

20 If workers capture rents *ex post*, labour markets are *ex ante* competitive and participation bribes are costless, then these bribes should rise to a level where the market clears. However, there is direct evidence that some labour markets do not clear. For instance, job application data indicate that minimum wage workers and prospective employees of unionized firms queue for jobs (Holzer et al., 1991).

21 Other explanations for these findings could be given. For example, unionization might depress investment by reducing productivity. Most authors, however, argue for a positive union productivity effect. The existence and nature of this effect are controversial (see Addison and Hirsch, 1989).

22 Strategic precommitment is a familiar issue in the context of market structure (Tirole, 1989, chapter 8), but has received little attention in studies of organizational form.

23 Consider a well-paid employee of Highly Specific Enterprises who lives in River City. If Highly Specific relocates to Brazil, the worker has two options: (a) move to the distant city of Oceanside to obtain equally well paid employment; or (b) stay in River City and flip hamburgers. If cutting off social ties is costless, the employee is currently getting very little quasi-rent (only the cost of hiring a moving van and going to Oceanside). But if there are high intangible costs of dissolving family and community connections, the worker's next best alternative might be to remain in River City and flip hamburgers. In this case, the worker enjoys a large quasi-rent from employment at Highly Specific.

24 Klein (1991, pp. 219–20) argues that large worker teams which collectively possess essential firm-specific human capital might be unable to hold up an employer opportunistically, because it is too costly for large coalitions to collude. If such a team cannot collude to hold up an employer, it seems unlikely that it could collectively bribe an employer to refrain from unilateral reorganization, in cases where the quasi-rent currently flowing to the team is jeopardized. Relatedly, Hansmann (1990) suggests that the collective action problems arising within large, diverse worker groups are the most important factor impeding the further spread of labour-managed firms in Western economies. For evidence that these problems are empirically important in LMFs, see Benham and Keefer (1991).

25 TCE's hypothesis about multi-divisional organization has also survived some empirical testing (Armour and Teece, 1978). Williamson (1991) emphasizes take-over mechanisms as a core element of this hypothesis. To this extent, multi-divisional organization is another instance where governance structures arise through transfers of asset ownership, and the argument in the next paragraph of the text applies here as well.

26 See Williamson (1975, chapter 4, 1980).
27 Williamson (1991, p. 96) remarks that 'The study of labor organization . . . turns out to have numerous parallels with, rather than be sharply different from, the study of intermediate product markets . . . contrary opinion notwithstanding.' A great deal of contrary opinion has nevertheless piled up: see Putterman (1981, 1984), Jones (1982, 1983) and Dow (1987). Replies to these criticisms appear in Williamson (1981, 1983a,b 1987). Other relevant discussions include Willman (1982) and Szostak (1989).
28 Klein (1991) argues that 'ownership' of a large team which collectively embodies specific human capital is feasible, in the sense that the employment contracts which hold the team together can be transferred from one firm to another through market transactions. The supply of capital and labour inputs could also be integrated through the collective ownership of physical assets by workers themselves (Dow, 1992c).

REFERENCES

Addison, J. and Hirsch, B. (1989) Union effects on productivity, profits, and growth: has the long run arrived? *Journal of Labor Economics*, 7, 72–105.

Armour, H. and Teece, D. (1978) Organizational structure and economic performance: a test of the multidivisional hypothesis. *Bell Journal of Economics*, 9, 106–22.

Benham, L. and Keefer, P. (1991) Voting in firms: the role of agenda control, size, and voter homogeneity. *Economic Inquiry*, 29, 706–19.

Ben-Ner, A. and Jun, B. (1990) Buy-out in a bargaining game with asymmetric information. University of Minnesota and Korea University, unpublished manuscript.

Bowles, S. (1985) The production process in a competitive economy. *American Economic Review*, 75, 16–36.

Carmichael, H.L. (1990) Efficiency wage models of unemployment – one view. *Economic Inquiry*, 28, 269–95.

Clark, R. (1985) Agency costs versus fiduciary duties. In J. Pratt and R. Zeckhauser (eds), *Principals and Agents: the Structure of Business*. Boston, MA: Harvard Business School Press.

Coase, R. (1991a) The nature of the firm: meaning. In O. Williamson and S. Winter (eds), *The Nature of the Firm*. New York: Oxford University Press.

Coase, R. (1991b) The nature of the firm: influence. In O. Williamson and S. Winter (eds), *The Nature of the Firm,* New York: Oxford University Press.

Dickens, W. and Katz, L. (1987) Inter-industry wage differences and industry characteristics. In K. Lang and J. Leonard (eds),

Unemployment and the Structure of Labor Markets. Oxford: Basil Blackwell.

Dickens, W., Katz, L., Lang, K. and Summers, L. (1989) Employee crime and the monitoring puzzle. *Journal of Labor Economics*, 7, 331–47.

Dong, X.-Y. and Dow, G. (1991) Mutual monitoring in production teams: theory and evidence from Chinese agriculture. Department of Economics Research Paper 91-19, University of Alberta.

Dow, G. (1985) Internal bargaining and strategic innovation in the theory of the firm. *Journal of Economic Behavior and Organization*, 6, 301–20.

Dow, G. (1987) The function of authority in transaction cost economics. *Journal of Economic Behavior and Organization*, 8, 13–38.

Dow, G. (1988a) Configurational and coactivational views of organizational structure. *Academy of Management Review*, 13, 53–64.

Dow, G. (1988b) Information, production decisions, and intra-firm bargaining. *International Economic Review*, 29, 57–79.

Dow, G. (1988c) The evolution of organizational form: selection, efficiency, and the new institutional economics. *Economic Analysis and Worker's Management*, 22, 139–67.

Dow, G. (1989) Knowledge is power: informational precommitment in the capitalist firm. *European Journal of Political Economy*, 5, 161–76.

Dow, G. (1990) The organization as an adaptive network. *Journal of Economic Behavior and Organization*, 14, 159–85.

Dow, G. (1991a) Firing threats and effort conventions in efficiency wage theory. Department of Economics, University of Alberta, unpublished manuscript.

Dow, G. (1991b) Selling jobs: moral hazard in capitalist and labor-managed firms. Department of Economics, University of Alberta, unpublished manuscript.

Dow, G. (1992a) Review of O. Williamson and S. Winter (eds), The Nature of the Firm. *Business History Review*.

Dow, G. (1992b) Why capital hires labor: a bargaining perspective. Department of Economics, University of Alberta, unpublished manuscript.

Dow, G. (1992c) Democracy versus appropriability: can labor-managed firms flourish in a capitalist world? In S. Bowles, H. Gintis and B. Gustafsson (eds), *Democracy and Markets: Problems of Participation and Efficiency*. New York: Cambridge University Press.

Eggertsson, T. (1990) *Economic Behavior and Institutions*. New York: Cambridge University Press.

Finkin, M. (1986) The bureaucratization of work: employer policies and contract law. *Wisconsin Law Review*, 733–53.

Flannigan, R. (1992) The nature of the firm. University of Saskatchewan Law School, unpublished manuscript.

Grossman, S. and Hart, O. (1986) The costs and benefits of ownership: a theory of vertical and lateral integration. *Journal of Political Economy*, 94, 691–719.

Hansmann, H. (1990) When does worker ownership work? ESOPs, law firms, codetermination, and economic democracy. *Yale Law Journal*, 99, 1749–816.

Hart, O. (1991) Incomplete contracts and the theory of the firm. In O. Williamson and S. Winter (eds). *The Nature of the Firm*. New York: Oxford University Press.

Hart, O. and Moore, J. (1990) Property rights and the nature of the firm. *Journal of Political Economy*, 98, 1119–58.

Holzer, H., Katz, L. and Krueger, A. (1991) Job queues and wages. *Quarterly Journal of Economics*, 106, 739–68.

Jones, S. R. H. (1982) The organization of work: a historical dimension. *Journal of Economic Behavior and Organization*, 3, 117–37.

Jones, S. R. H. (1983) Technology and the organization of work: a reply. *Journal of Economic Behavior and Organization*, 4, 63–6.

Joskow, P. (1991) Asset specificity and the structure of vertical relationships: empirical evidence. In O. Williamson and S. Winter (eds), *The Nature of the Firm*. New York: Oxford University Press.

Katz, L. (1986) Efficiency wage theories: a partial evaluation. In S. Fischer (ed.), *NBER Macroeconomics Annual*. Cambridge, MA: MIT Press, 235–89.

Kennan, J. (1986) The economics of strikes. In O. Ashenfelter and R. Layard (eds), *Handbook of Labor Economics*, vol. 2. New York: Elsevier Science Publishing.

Kennan, J. and Wilson, R. (1989) Strategic bargaining models and interpretation of strike data. *Journal of Applied Econometrics*, 4, S87–S130.

Klein, B. (1991) Vertical integration as organizational ownership: the Fisher Body–General Motors relationship revisited. In O. Williamson and S. Winter (eds), *The Nature of the Firm*. New York: Oxford University Press.

Klein, B., Crawford, R. and Alchian, A. (1978) Vertical integration, appropriable rents, and the competitive contracting process. *Journal of Law and Economics*, , 21, 297–326.

Klein, B. and Leffler, K. (1981) The role of market forces in assuring contractual performance. *Journal of Political Economy*, 89, 615–41.

Kronman, A. (1985) Contract law and the state of nature. *Journal of Law, Economics, and Organization*, 1, 5–32.

Krueger, A. and Summers, L. (1988) Efficiency wages and the inter-industry wage structure. *Econometrica*, 56, 259–93.

Langlois, R. (1986) Rationality, institutions, and explanation. In R. Langlois (ed.), *Economics as a Process*. New York: Cambridge University Press.

Lewis, T. and Sappington, D. (1991) Technological change and the boundaries of the firm. *American Economic Review*, 81, 887–900.

Lindbeck, A. and Snower, D. (1988) *The Insider–Outsider Theory of Employment and Unemployment*. Cambridge, MA: MIT Press.

Masten, S. (1991) A legal basis for the firm. In O. Williamson and S. Winter (eds), *The Nature of the Firm*. New York: Oxford University Press.

North, D. (1990) *Institutions, Institutional Change and Economic Performance*. New York: Cambridge University Press.

Pontiff, J., Shleifer, A. and Weisbach, M. (1990) Reversions of excess pension assets after takeovers. *Rand Journal of Economics*, 21, 600–13.

Priest, G. (1977) The common law process and the selection of efficient rules. *Journal of Legal Studies*, 6, 65–82.

Putterman, L. (1981) The organization of work: comment. *Journal of Economic Behavior and Organization*, 2, 273–9.

Putterman, L. (1984) On some recent explanations of why capital hires labor. *Economic Inquiry*, 22, 171–87.

Putterman, L. (1988) The firm as association versus the firm as commodity. *Economics and Philosophy*, 4, 243–66.

Rosett, J. (1990) Do union wealth concessions explain takeover premiums? *Journal of Financial Economics*, 27, 263–82.

Shapiro, C. and Stiglitz, J. (1984) Equilibrium unemployment as a worker discipline device. *American Economic Review*, 74, 433–44.

Shleifer, A. and Summers, L. (1988) Breach of trust in hostile takeovers. In A. Auerbach (ed.), *Corporate Takeovers: Causes and Consequences*. Chicago: University of Chicago Press.

Szostak, R. (1989) The organization of work: the emergence of the factory revisited. *Journal of Economic Behavior and Organization*, 11, 343–58.

Tirole, J. (1989) *The Theory of Industrial Organization*. Cambridge, MA: MIT Press.

Van Huyck, J., Battalio, R. and Beil, R. (1991) Strategic uncertainty, equilibrium selection, and coordination failure in average opinion games. *Quarterly Journal of Economics*, 106, 885–910.

Weiss, A. (1990) *Efficiency Wages*. Princeton, NJ: Princeton University Press.

Wiggins, S. and Libecap, G. (1985) Oil field unitization. *American Economic Review*, 75, 368–85.

Williamson, O. (1975) *Markets and Hierarchies*. New York: Free Press.

Williamson, O. (1980) The organization of work. *Journal of Economic Behavior and Organization*, 1, 5–38.

Williamson, O. (1981) The organization of work: reply. *Journal of Economic Behavior and Organization*, 2, 281–3.

Williamson, O. (1983a) Technology and the organization of work: a reply to Jones. *Journal of Economic Behavior and Organization*, 4, 57–62.

Williamson, O. (1983b) Technology and the organization of work: a rejoinder. *Journal of Economic Behavior and Organization*, 4, 67–8.

Williamson, O. (1985) *The Economic Institutions of Capitalism*. New York: Free Press.

Williamson, O. (1987) Transaction cost economics: the comparative contracting perspective. *Journal of Economic Behavior and Organization*, 8, 617–25.

Williamson, O. (1991) The logic of economic organization. In O. Williamson and S. Winter (eds), *The Nature of the Firm*. New York: Oxford University Press.

Williamson, O. and Ouchi, W. (1981) The markets and hierarchies program of research: origins, implications, prospects. In A. Van de Ven and W. Joyce (eds), *Perspectives on Organization Design and Behavior*. New York: Wiley-Interscience.

Williamson, O. and Winter, S. (eds) (1991) *The Nature of the Firm: Origins, Evolution, and Development*. New York: Oxford University Press.

Willman, P. (1982) Opportunism in labour contracting. *Journal of Economic Behavior and Organization*, 3, 83–98.

Winter, S. (1991) On Coase, competence, and the corporation. In O. Williamson and S. Winter (eds), *The Nature of the Firm*. New York: Oxford University Press.

7

Power and Efficiency in the Firm: Understanding the Employment Relationship

PAUL MARGINSON

1 INTRODUCTION

The question of why productive activity should be organized within firms has stimulated considerable debate between proponents of two broad paradigms. New institutionalists, notably Williamson (1975, 1980, 1981), have tried to demonstrate that the evolution of the firm from the putting-out system to the large modern corporation has taken place primarily for efficiency reasons. In contrast radical authors, such as Marglin (1974) and Edwards (1979), have stressed the search for superior means of management control over labour as the underlying dynamic explaining the evolution of the firm. McPherson (1983) and Putterman (1986) provide useful reviews of some of the relevant literature. Both approaches signify an important departure from the standard neoclassical theory of the firm, in which the production of outputs from inputs is treated as a purely technical relationship. This is because forms of work organization are considered to affect the transformation of inputs into outputs.

This chapter is concerned with the characterization and analysis of the employment relationship offered by the competing, efficiency and power, perspectives of the firm. Building on existing criticisms in the literature, the aim is to demonstrate that considerations of power and control, as well as those of efficiency, are essential to an adequate theorization of the firm and the relations between management and labour within it. The efficiency claims of the new institutionalists are subjected to scrutiny.

I am most grateful for the helpful comments of Keith Cowling, Paul Edwards, Jean Hartley, Peter Nolan and Christos Pitelis on this and earlier versions of the chapter. Valuable comments also came from the participants at the Sixteenth EARIE Conference in Budapest, September 1989.

Although a number of scholars have contributed to the refinement of the 'efficient institutions' approach, the argument focuses on the work of Oliver Williamson. This is because Williamson is centrally identified with the development of the approach, and in his many writings he has comprehensively covered the issues with which this chapter is concerned.

The chapter starts by summarizing the main features of the efficient institutions approach. Four central propositions are identified. In the following section these are questioned, existing criticism is discussed and counter propositions are developed. An alternative approach to the firm, resting on a recognition of the importance of power as well as efficiency considerations, is then sketched. A further section identifies some inadequacies of existing writings from a power perspective and discusses why the exercise of power cannot be adequately modelled through coercive means alone, before some conclusions are drawn.

2 THE EFFICIENT INSTITUTIONS PARADIGM

Williamson (1975) outlines a theory of the firm based on transactions costs minimization. Where information is imperfect and costly, economic coordination can no longer be costlessly achieved through the market as envisaged in the standard neoclassical model of perfect competition. Following Coase (1937), Williamson argues that the coordination of economic activity through administrative units (firms) rather than markets can be explained in terms of the costs incurred in transacting in markets. If organizations reduce the costs of transacting below those obtaining in the market then they are considered to be more efficient. Transaction costs are seen to stem from the combination of certain environmental factors with certain attributes of human behaviour. Williamson identifies uncertainty/complexity and bilateral or small numbers exchange relations as the pertinent environmental factors in which two assumed attributes of human behaviour become important for economic outcomes. These assumptions are crucial to the approach. First, human agents are assumed to be boundedly rational, which recognizes that there are computational limits to human capabilities in processing information (Simon, 1955). Bounded rationality contrasts with the usual assumption of global rationality, which implies human capacity to process an infinite quantity of information. Second, human agents are assumed to be self-interested or opportunistic. Thus they will pursue individualistic or sectional, as distinct from organizational, goals.

In the context of the employment relation, the existence of uncertainty over the precise work tasks required to be performed during any particular period, when combined with bounded rationality, makes the negotiation of a complex contract covering all potential contingencies extremely costly, if not impossible. Hence, Williamson argues, the contract between employers and workers will necessarily be incomplete. Moreover, the propensity of workers to behave opportunistically necessitates the conclusion of this incomplete contract within an organization, the firm, where employers have power, within limits, to allocate workers to tasks, specify effort levels and monitor behaviour. Costs incurred when organizing production through market transactions, such as embezzlement and cheating, are minimized and an improvement in efficiency is consequently achieved. The resulting authority relation is assumed to be in the interest of both employers and workers, because organizational performance is enhanced through the curbing of self-interested behaviour.

The employment of workers within an organization is, however, itself associated with certain transactions costs. These stem from problems of asset specificity, which is the degree to which skills and know-how are specific to the firm and hence not tradable on the open market. Where workers have firm-specific skills that are not immediately replaceable, a situation of small numbers exchange relations pertains and there is scope for opportunistic behaviour. Workers may use the bargaining power deriving from their possession of firm-specific skills to obtain an undue share of the returns accruing to internal organization. Williamson et al. (1975) argue that such problems can be overcome by the creation of a collective organization, involving both employers and workers, aimed at generating an atmosphere of trust, a common frame of reference and goal congruence between management and workers. In this context they cite the development of the bureaucratic mode of employment relation in contemporary large corporations, characterized by a structured internal labour market with low ports of entry, internal job ladders, on-the-job training, associated promotion opportunities and deferred compensation.[1]

In the creation of a collective organization, union recognition and collective bargaining are seen by Williamson et al. as important, although not essential, facilitators. Unions assist in elevating organizational goals above opportunistic or sectional ones. The argument draws on the application of Hirschman's (1970) exit-voice model to trade unions by Freeman (1976), and is made more explicit by Williamson (1984). Workers are likely to develop a collective voice through a union in preference to individualized means of expressing dissatisfaction, such as quitting, only when they have a strong interest in maintaining a continuing employment relationship, by dint of possessing firm-specific skills. Where workers do not possess such skills, they are assumed to have less interest in a continuing relationship with a particular employer, and therefore less interest in joining a union. For their part, employers in firms characterized by high degrees of asset specificity will be interested in promoting a union because of its role in minimizing sectional or self-interested behaviour, and its orientation towards organizational goals. Workers and employers in firms characterized by firm-specific skills have, according to Williamson, a mutual interest in developing collective organization.

The foregoing argument utilizes the concept of transactions costs to develop a comparative perspective to the question of whether markets or firms are more efficient at coordinating economic activity. Which is the more efficient form depends on the nature of the transaction involved. Specifically, the employment relation is more likely to be internalized in an organization where the production process exhibits a high degree of asset specificity, where uncertainty about precise tasks to be performed is greater or where the process is more complex. In a further development of this comparative framework, Williamson (1980) has also attempted to demonstrate that efficiency considerations prevail when examining the organization of production in an historical perspective.

Williamson's (1980) method is to compare the transactions costs properties of alternative modes of organizing work, holding technology constant. The efficiency properties of historically earlier forms of work organization, such as putting-out, are rated as poor. Embezzlement and cheating were endemic to the system, which also required large inventories to be held. Eventually, putting-out was supplanted by modes of work organization possessing superior efficiency properties in transactions costs terms. The first step was inside contracting, followed by the hierarchical capitalist firm where labour is directly employed. However, as noted above, the direct employment of workers is itself associated with transactions costs arising out of asset specificity. These problems are supposedly mitigated by the emergence of the bureaucratic form of work organization in the large corporation. Williamson concludes that the evolution of the firm is the result of the search for ever more efficient forms of employment organization. Moreover, since later forms of internal organization, which vest more power in the managers of firms, through strengthened hierarchy, are also shown to be more efficient, Williamson contends that considerations of power are secondary.

This outline of the main features of the efficient institutions framework employed by Williamson to explain the organization of productive activity within the firm, and more particularly the employment relationship, embodies a number of key propositions. First, hierarchy is viewed as being in the mutual interest of both workers and employers. Second, workers can act opportunistically, and by implication possess bargaining power, only insofar as they command firm-specific skills. Relatedly, trade unions are expected to arise for efficiency reasons, in circumstances where both workers and employers have an interest in a continuing employment relation. Third, the problems of opportunism inherent in the labour contract are seen as being no different in kind from those which exist in any other contractual relationship. Fourth, to paraphrase Marx, efficiency acts as the motor of history.

3 EFFICIENCY, HIERARCHY AND DOMINANCE

Each of these key propositions of the efficient institutions approach is open to question. First, authority within the employment relationship may be used in the interests of one party rather than both. Second, workers derive bargaining power from sources other than their possession of firm-specific skills. Allied to this, union organization need not rest on the existence of firm-specific skills. Third, the peculiarities of the labour contract cannot be reduced to the problem of opportunistic behaviour. Fourth, efficiency is not the only consideration driving the historical evolution of forms of work organization. These lines of argument are developed and then drawn together in the five subsections below.

3.1 Hierarchy and the Mutual Interest

According to the efficient institutions paradigm the role of hierarchy in the capitalist firm is to ensure the prevalence of common goals over sectional or individual goals. Because self-interested behaviour is curbed to the benefit of broader community or organizational goals, hierarchy is viewed as being in the mutual interests of both employers and workers. This perspective on the authority relation is shared, to differing extents, by a number of writers. At one extreme, Jensen and Meckling (1976) deny the existence of an authority relation within the firm, preferring to view the firm as a special kind of market bringing together a coalition of interests. Alchian and Demsetz (1972) argue that workers will voluntarily submit themselves to authority in order to solve the problem of metering worker effort, and thereby minimize the incentive for individuals to shirk under team production. For Williamson et al. (1975), the legitimacy of the authority relation lies in a process of voluntary exchange between workers and employers. Workers cede limited authority to management over the direction of tasks and the specification of effort levels, in return for guarantees relating to wages, conditions and security of employment. Aoki (1984) takes a similar view. The joint rule-making process that characterizes collective bargaining 'is an exchange process between the acceptance of the authoritarian nature of an employment relationship and a democratic participation in drawing up the rules through which such authority is exercised' (p. 130).

Bowles (1985) characterizes these models as 'neo-Hobbesian' because they focus on the archetypal Hobbesian problem of reconciling self-interested behaviour with the common good. Conflict exists within the firm, but it is conflict between self-interest and the common good. The explanation of the functional nature of hierarchy within the firm 'bears a close resemblance to the original Hobbesian rationale for the state as a socially necessary form of coercion' (Bowles, 1985, p. 16). Workers submit themselves voluntarily to the employer's authority in a manner analogous to the voluntary acceptance by individual citizens of the state's authority. Given this view of authority, it should not matter 'whether capital hires labour or the other way around' (Samuelson, 1957, p. 894).

Samuelson's famous aphorism, however, applies to a world where there are perfect markets for both labour and capital. In this case transactions costs will be zero, economic activity will always be coordinated through markets and questions of power in the market do not arise. However, as Williamson (1980) himself recognizes, the forms of employment relationship considered by writers adopting an efficient institutions approach are specifically predicated on the existence of factor immobilities, for both labour and capital, and market imperfections. As a result, transactions costs are positive and the possibility arises that these may be minimized by coordinating economic activity through an organization rather than through the market. Moreover, in a situation where both physical and human capital are firm-specific, bargaining power will accrue to both employers and workers. Employers' bargaining power stems from the fact that workers' skills are firm-specific and therefore not tradable on the open market. Workers' bargaining power derives from the fact that their skills are costly to replace. Such questions of power have not been satisfactorily handled by Williamson and others.

Several writers have pointed to an underlying asymmetry in the application of the behavioural assumption of opportunism. Williamson (1980, p. 7) has claimed that 'except as incumbent workers enjoy advantages over outsiders (by reason presumably of firm specific experience) there would be no need for supervision and discipline beyond that imposed by the market'. Under this formulation workers are assumed to act opportunistically, while employers are assumed to act in accordance with an (undefined) community interest. Only employers are faced by a problem of bounded rationality. As Willman (1983) notes, this is a weak basis on which to erect an efficiency justification of hierarchy. One has only to be consistent in the assumptions made, by also allowing for employers to be opportunistic and workers to be boundedly rational, to see the tenuous foundation of Williamson's argument. Take, for example, internal labour markets. These are incompatible with competitive hiring, firing and wage setting. Williamson et al. (1975) underline the efficiency benefits stemming from the effectiveness of such an arrangement in curbing workers' ability to exercise their bargaining power in an opportunistic fashion. But they are silent on the scope internal labour markets provide for employer opportunism. FitzRoy and Kraft (1987) note that where workers possess firm-specific skills their labour market mobility is impeded. They are therefore susceptible to 'managerial pressure' aimed at eliciting additional effort. The restraints on worker mobility 'give the firm a measure of power over its employees' (McPherson, 1983, p. 363).

Where the existence of power is admitted by Williamson, it is argued that mechanisms exist by which employers or workers are constrained from using their power. Thus, Williamson (1984, pp. 99–100) concedes that an asymmetry exists between employers and workers in relations characterized by firm-specific skills, in that employers have informational advantages and possess more extensive resources than the typical employee. However, Williamson argues that employers exploiting this advantage will acquire a reputation for cheating and find it difficult to attract workers into the firm in the future. Workers are assumed to exercise some power over the firm in this respect. Consequently employers are constrained from exploiting their power through reputation effects. Implicitly one source of power is assumed to be exactly offset by another source.[2]

The implicit assumption that bargaining power within the firm is equally distributed is crucial to Williamson's argument that considerations of power can be set aside.[3] But it is a highly questionable one on which to proceed. Consider again firm-specific skills. By dint of their firm-specific skills workers may possess a degree of bargaining power, but as Enderwick (1984) notes, workers will also have experienced loss of power deriving from the market for skills external to the firm. There is no *a priori* reason why the latter should exactly offset the former. More generally, 'it is hard to imagine plausible theoretical models in which firms can capture the efficiency benefits of these [internal labour market] practices while being entirely blocked from exploiting their power' (McPherson, 1983, p. 363).

That both employees and workers have power resources at their disposal is recognized in some recent game-theoretic treatments of the firm (Cable, 1986; Leibenstein, 1987; Dow, 1988). Employers and workers are seen to derive power from the fact that it is costly for either party to terminate the employment relationship in the presence of factor immobilities. Under such circumstances both parties have the scope to act in an opportunistic fashion and neither party has complete control over decisions. Outcomes are therefore uncertain, being dependent on the interaction of strategic choices by the parties and by the bargaining power at their disposal. The latter is conditioned by such factors as the state of the labour market, work group solidarity and norms and the firm specificity of skills and capital equipment.

Thus far the discussion has concentrated on the need to treat workers and employers in a behaviourally symmetric fashion. But the consequences of opportunism by employers can have much more widespread ramifications. These lie in the possibility that authority itself can be used in an opportunistic fashion. As Dow (1987) observes, authority provides a tool, decision by fiat, that is tailor-made for the unilateral pursuit of self-interest. This is the more so where those able to impose decisions by fiat also possess informational advantages, such as those enjoyed by employers as compared to workers. Williamson himself admits of such a possibility, albeit under 'extreme circumstances':

> Internal organization is thus able to adapt more effectively than can inter-firm trading to changing market and technical circumstances. Not only do employment contracts contemplate such flexibility by providing for 'zones of acceptance' within which orders will be implemented without resistance, but orders that exceed the scope of the authority relation can be implemented in extreme circumstances. (Williamson, 1985, p. 249, italics added)

But because authority relations create the 'structural preconditions' (Dow, 1987, p. 21) under which employer opportunism can flourish, it is reasonable to presume that such abuses of authority are likely to occur under normal as well as extreme circumstances.

Furthermore, employers are likely to display a preference for hierarchical forms of work organization, within which authority can be more readily exercised. This can be demonstrated by comparing the properties of differing modes of organization. If authority were purely an efficiency phenomenon then there would be no difference in the degree of hierarchy employed in the capitalist firm from that employed in a workers' cooperative. Putterman (1982) shows that in terms of organizational efficiency there is excessive monitoring and supervision in capitalist as compared to worker-controlled firms. Bowles (1985) demonstrates that a preference for hierarchy results in socially inefficient forms of work organization being selected by employers (see Cable, 1987, and Dow, 1988, for a game-theoretic treatment of the same issue). Distinguishing between the capacity to work purchased by the employer and the actual labour input, Bowles focuses on the conflict of interest between employers and workers over workers' effort levels. His method is to supplement the traditional production function with a third term representing worker effort. It is assumed that employers are able to compel workers to act in ways that they would not themselves choose, but that the exercise of this authority is costly. This cost takes two forms: the use of supervision and the payment of a wage premium above the market rate. Assuming decreasing returns to both these elements generates a unique profit-maximizing point, which is at a lower level of output than if no such costs arose. The form of internal organization preferred by capitalist employers is thus shown to be socially inefficient.

Historical evidence demonstrates well that employers are likely to select forms of work organization that most effectively enable them to serve their own interests. Pollard (1965), Thompson (1967) and Marglin (1974) all illustrate how the institution of hierarchy through the factory system had its origins in a search by employers for a more effective means of coercing workers to work. Factory organization was associated with working more days of the week, longer hours of the day and more intensively. Marglin argues that early factories employed the same techniques as those utilized in putting-out, but provided the employer with a more effective means of control over workers' choice between productive time and leisure time. Employers will also prefer technologies that maintain or enhance their authority. Landes (1986), in his response to Marglin, while arguing that factory production remained at a cost disadvantage to domestic industry until power-driven machines were available, concurs that technological choice is dictated by returns in money *and* power. Edwards (1979) notes that machine-pacing technologies were considered by employers to have particularly desirable properties in securing control over workers. And Ozanne (1967) documents how, in the 1880s, new, untested and untried, machines were brought into the plant he studied to break the power of a group of workers controlling a crucial production operation. In sum, both theory and history indicate that choices of technology and work organization which most effectively enable employers to pursue their own interests may not be the most efficient.

An analogy with the state is again suggestive. North (1981) argues that contractual theories of the state explain the initial gains to be made from the formation of the state, but fail to account for the subsequent behaviour of groups within the state attempting to pursue their own interests. In contrast, predatory or exploitative theories of the state ignore the initial gains from contracting but provide an explanation of the rent-extracting activities of groups gaining control of the state. In general, North argues that there is a tension between the attempts of ruling groups to maximize the rent accruing to them, and the efforts of all parties to reduce the costs of transactions associated with rent collection and the provision of state services. Thus, 'Efficient property rights may lead to higher income in the state but lower tax revenues for the ruler because of transactions costs (monitoring, metering and collecting taxes) as compared to those of a more inefficient set of property rights' (North, 1981,

p. 28), in which case a less efficient set of property rights can be expected to prevail. Ruling groups will maximize their own income, and only subject to that will they devise rules to lower transactions costs and secure improvements in social efficiency.

Like ruling groups, employers are in a position to use authority to further their own interests. Unlike ruling groups, employers do not possess a monopoly of violence. They are also concerned to tap the creativity of their workforce, as well as to secure control. Thus the exercise of employer authority is more likely to take forms other than direct coercion (see the discussion in section 4). It might be argued that employers also differ from ruling groups in that they are more effectively constrained from using authority to pursue their own interests by competitive pressures. This would be the case if workers were able to raise their own capital and establish firms organized along less hierarchical lines that were more efficient.[4] However, as Putterman (1982, 1984) argues, the institutions of capitalist society militate against workers raising their own capital to take them outside of the sphere of employer prerogative. Providers of equity finance in conventional institutions expect to secure some voting or other supervisory control over firm policy. Cooperatives are therefore likely to have to pay an additional premium to secure equity without granting voting or other supervisory rights that would fundamentally compromise their purpose. In her study, Thornley (1981) highlights this and other problems faced by existing cooperatives in the UK in raising capital. For these reasons, employers are unlikely to be faced by externally binding constraints.

In sum, the efficient institutions proposition that hierarchy is in the mutual interest of employers and workers is flawed because it fails to take adequate account of power considerations. Drawing on the arguments above, the following proposition is preferred:

> Employers select that means of work organization consistent with the objectives of maximizing their own return and maintaining or strengthening their own authority.

The usefulness of this proposition is shown by the distinct light it throws on the question of participative forms of work organization. Where the organization of production and employment is determined jointly between employers and workers it has been shown that benefits can arise in overall organizational efficiency (McCain, 1980; Leibenstein, 1982; Cable, 1987; Dow, 1988). If, however, the choice of production and organization variables is unilaterally taken by management then modes of organization may well be selected that correspond to the maximum private return for employers, but that are socially less efficient (Bowles, 1985; Cable, 1987; Dow, 1988). Yet participative forms of work organization are infrequently seen to emerge in capitalist societies. As noted above, the institutions of capitalist society militate against workers raising their own capital to take them outside of the sphere of employer prerogative. Participative forms are only likely to be adopted either where workers are able to exercise sufficient countervailing power to make the costs to employers of exercising their prerogative prohibitively high, or where the state intervenes legally to require joint determination of aspects of production organization, as is the case in Germany.[5]

3.2 Firm-specific Skills, Bargaining Power and Unionism

A second proposition is that workers possess bargaining power only insofar as they possess firm-specific skills (Williamson et al., 1975; Williamson, 1980, p. 7). The social dimension of these firm-specific skills is emphasized by Aoki (1984), who treats them as collective goods, not individually appropriable, resting on work customs which are transferred through social processes. 'On-the-job socialization' is itself firm-specific, and is the basis on which workers are able to extract a share of the rent deriving from internal organization. Further, as was noted in section 2, it is argued that firm-specific skills are at the root of union organization (Williamson, 1984).

The claim that workers' bargaining power is contingent on their development of firm-specific skills denies the possibility that there may be other bases of bargaining power. It will be argued that once these other bases are taken into account, it becomes impossible to subsume the reasons for, and history of, trade union organization within an efficient institutions approach.

An important category of skills that are not firm-specific in character is those, such as craft and technical skills, which are transferable across markets. Workers derive bargaining power from possessing these market skills (Enderwick, 1984); specifically from the fact that such skills are relatively scarce, being costly and time-consuming to acquire. Workers acquiring firm-specific skills may suffer a loss of market bargaining power as equivalent employment opportunities outside of the firm disappear. But, echoing the argument of the previous section, there is no reason why the loss of market bargaining power should be exactly offset by workplace bargaining power associated with firm-specific skills.

Even where workers possess neither firm-specific nor market skills they may still possess bargaining power. Goldberg (1980, p. 262) argues that 'workers acting in concert' can act opportunistically whether skilled or not. Workers possess a degree of bargaining power by dint of their ability to work in a perfunctory manner and thereby impair performance. Hence employers need to encourage workers to perform certain tasks and expand certain levels of effort, even where firm-specific skills are minimal. Goldberg argues that a principal means of doing so is deferred compensation, and in this context cites Henry Ford's $5 day as a prime example (see also Raff and Somers, 1987). Goldberg concludes that the existence of a continuing employment relationship, as well as institutional features associated with structured internal labour markets, such as age–earnings profiles (see Lazear, 1981), can be explained without recourse to firm-specific skills.

Implicit in Goldberg's argument is the notion that workers can derive bargaining power from the mere act of combination. By 'acting in concert', workers with few skills of either a market or firm-specific nature can make themselves costly to replace. Friedman (1977) and Ozanne (1967) provide evidence of this process in their respective studies of the UK car industry and a large US agricultural equipment manufacturer. The history of workers' organization in the docks in both countries, originating as it did among an unskilled and casual workforce, provides a further example. The point is important. Power does not arise automatically from the possession of certain skills. Although the acquisition of skills may enhance bargaining power, its realization is contingent on some form of independent organization by workers. Such organization can take the form of trade union organization, but not necessarily so.[6] Organization is a precondition for the effective deployment of bargaining power, as Shorter and Tilly (1974) demonstrate in their historical study of strikes in France, for example. Moreover, action cannot be read off directly from organization, as a further factor intervenes: mobilization (Klandermans, 1984, 1986). Thus bargaining power depends on organization and mobilization as well as intrinsic factors such as the possession of firm-specific or market skills. Firm-specific skills are neither necessary nor sufficient for bargaining power to exist.

Williamson (1984) predicts that unions will develop early in industries with a high degree of firm-specific skills (e.g. railways) and late in those industries where skills are differentiated (e.g. farm labouring). He is silent on the question of union organization based on market skills. Yet the possession of market skills has provided a successful basis around which workers have developed trade union organization. Historically, in both the USA and the UK, the early growth of unionism was based on market, not firm-specific, skills (Hyman, 1975; Edwards, 1979). An example is the printing industry, where union organization around market skills across several industrial countries dates way back into the nineteenth century. Moreover, this form of union organization does not hinge on a continuing employment relation. Many workers organized into unions in printing continued to be employed on a casual basis. This was equally true of the docks in the UK. A major objective of trade unions in these sectors was to secure a permanent employment relationship. To the extent that they were successful in this objective, and contrary to Williamson's (1984) postulate, union organization preceded, and was not a consequence of, the establishment of a continuing employment relation.

At best, then, Williamson's explanation is partial. He appears to concede this in a revision of his earlier writing where a more modest claim is made to explain the development of a particular type of union, known as 'company unions' (Williamson, 1985, p. 255). This type of union, which organized workers on the basis of their employer rather than their occupation, made its appearance in the United States following the successful 'open shop' campaigns waged by large employers in the early 1900s (Sisson, 1987). In general, union organization cannot be considered as being endogenous to a particular type of employment relation, nor contingent on the development of firm-specific skills.

Although Goldberg (1980) develops a more satisfactory approach to workers' bargaining power, his analysis remains within a framework in which the primary concern is with opportunistic behaviour by workers. By showing that workers are able to exercise power irrespective of whether they possess firm-specific skills, Goldberg implies that the scope for such opportunistc behaviour is enhanced. Union organization, under this view, still serves to restrain opportunistic behaviour. But why should employers concerned to develop collective organization in order to restrain opportunistic behaviour (Williamson et al., 1975) choose unionism as the preferred form? While unions can provide a 'voice' for workers, their presence is not essential to the 'voice' effect. Some prominent non-union firms employ extensive consultation procedures, suggestion schemes and participative arrangements in order to forestall union organization by providing substitute 'voice' channels. In the USA in particular, large employers have had a long-standing preference for collective arrangements of a non-union character. Kochan et al. (1986) provide recent evidence.

A very different perspective on unionism arises once account is taken of the possibility that employers act opportunistically. FitzRoy and Kraft (1987), for example, argue that in order to protect themselves from the consequences of employer opportunism workers organize themselves into trade unions. Under this view, union organization arises as a means by which workers exercise countervailing bargaining power within an employment relationship where employers can utilize authority to pursue their own interests. Ozanne's (1967) study of the large US machinery manufacturer International Harvester provides evidence. He shows how it was only during periods when the company was wholly or partially unionized that improvements in working hours and wages occurred and resistance to effort intensification was successful. Other periods were characterized by effort intensification and wage stagnation.

Once trade unions are seen as exercising countervailing power within the employment relationship a further possibility arises: that employers will be concerned to shape union organization into forms that minimize any threat to their authority. (Indeed, as noted above, employers may go further and attempt to eliminate trade union organization altogether.) Employers can shape union organization in many ways. In the UK, Brown (1981) suggests, in some circumstances employers have promoted facilities for shop stewards, including provision for full-time shop stewards, preferring to deal with a union organization that is internally, or firm, based, rather than externally based. Recently, successive incoming employers to the UK, most notably Nissan, have demonstrated a clear preference for a particular type of unionism: single union and 'no strike' (Wickens, 1987). Employers on 'greenfield' sites have also sought to select which union, if any, their future employees will belong to (Bassett, 1986).

In the USA, Ozanne (1967) shows, the companies' owners were continually active in trying to mould the shape of union organization. Their tactics varied from attempts to break the power of craft union organization by the introduction of replacement machines, to the establishment of a yellow, or company, union. Moreover, the effects of company unionism as opposed to independent unionism are indicated by the fact that during the period when the former existed, and with it a 'voice' mechanism, pay and conditions of work were unaffected as compared to periods with no union organization.

In short, the shape of trade union organization itself does not arise out of some efficiency blueprint, but is a product of conflict between employers and workers. Contrary to the efficient institutions propositions, firm-specific skills are neither necessary nor sufficient for workers' bargaining power to exist. Nor is trade union organization contingent on the development of firm-specific skills. The following proposition summarizes the argument of this section:

> The exercise of bargaining power by workers rests on the formation of countervailing organizations (including trade unions) against the use of authority by employers. Employers will try to minimize the threat to their authority posed by workers' (trade union) organization.

3.3   Is the Labour Contract Like Any Other Contract?

The efficient institutions paradigm treats the labour contract as being no different from any other contract. The same environmental phenomena, uncertainty and small numbers exchange relations in the presence of asset specificity, and the same behavioural assumptions, bounded rationality and opportunism, are employed to 'explain' the employment relationship as are used in the analysis of other contractual and organizational relationships. Thus: 'Such apparently unrelated phenomena as the employment relation, aspects of regulation, certain nonstandard contracting practices, corporate governance, and even family organization are variations on a theme' (Williamson, 1985, p. 13).

Goldberg (1980), while differing from Williamson as to whether firm-specific skills are an essential precondition of a continuing employment relation, takes a similar position on the nature of the labour contract. Referring to the distinction between the capacity to work purchased by the employer (labour-power) and actual work performed (labour), Goldberg comments: 'The employment relationship is not, as the radicals suggest, unique in this regard. Most exchange relations will entail, in varying degrees, the type of gap between promise and execution implicit in the labour–labour-power distinction' (p. 253). In support of his contention, Goldberg identifies four aspects of transactions – bounded rationality, opportunism, absence of outside enforcement of contracts and that exchange relations have a history – which lead to this kind of distinction occurring in contractual relations. Goldberg continues:

> Parties cannot always count on getting precisely what they bargained for, be they employer–employee, franchisor–franchisee, steel producer–fabricator, or even husband–wife. Indeed, it *always* pays for a party not to perform its part of an agreement if that non-performance does not decrease the probability that the other parties will fulfil their obligations and if it suffers no loss . . . as a consequence of non-performance. (Goldberg, 1980, p. 253, italics in original)

Opportunism and the problem of measurement (bounded rationality) are seen by Williamson and Goldberg to lie at the heart of the problem. If there were no problem of measuring actual work performed, workers could be paid by the piece and opportunism would not matter. But it is argued that because problems of work measurement exist workers are paid by time and scope for opportunistic behaviour arises in terms of their levels of effort. Opportunistic behaviour occurs when one party cheats on the contract specified in the market. The contract between franchisor and franchisee, for example, attempts to specify comprehensively the terms under which the franchisee supplies goods and services and the basis and amount of royalties paid to the franchisor. If the parties do not get 'precisely what they bargained for' it is not because they mutually agreed to leave a part of the contract unspecified, but because one or both parties have cheated on the terms of the contract.

Unlike in other contractual arrangements, aspects of the labour contract are deliberately left unspecified. Bargaining over precise allocation of tasks and effort levels takes place *after* the conclusion of the contract in the market: 'in the case of labour, the market transaction is not the only transaction that is relevant. Even after the contract terms are agreed, the employer has to deal with economic agents who still have their own interest (and indeed a conflict of interest) at stake, which is not the case with the purchase of other inputs' (Malcolmson, 1984, p. 120).

As well as there being scope for opportunistic behaviour in relation to what is contractually agreed, conflict can take place between employers and workers within the process of production as to precise tasks to be performed and effort levels to be supplied. More generally, the rationale of the employment relationship in the capitalist firm can be seen as the production of goods and services at a profit to the employer. Additional value is generated in production through securing actual work performed whose value is in excess of the price of labour inputs. This is not a question of cheating or opportunism, because the employer's right to direct workers to tasks and to specify effort levels is, within limits, contractually agreed before production commences. It is in this sense that Marx (1974) maintained that labour and capital engaged as equals in the realm of exchange, but confronted each other as unequals within production.[7]

It is this aspect of the employment relationship that is at the root of the distinction between the capacity to work purchased by employers and actual work performed. For other factors of production, such as capital equipment or raw materials, no such distinction arises. Given quantities of raw materials or capital equipment purchased will have a fixed relationship with productive output. But for labour, the relationship between the capacity to work purchased and actual work performed is variable and unspecifiable before production commences. The transformation of the capacity to work into actual work performed will depend on the employer's ability to direct workers to tasks, and to secure worker effort. Both employer and worker have an interest in leaving these unspecified, the employer in order to secure task allocation and levels of effort commensurate with profitable production, the worker in order to secure control over the pace and content of his or her work. These interests inherently conflict.

In contradistinction to Williamson's (1985) and Goldberg's (1980) contention that the labour contract is in essence like any other contract, the above arguments can be summarized in the following proposition:

The labour contract is unlike other contracts because the possibility exists that the value of actual work performed will exceed that of the capacity to work purchased not because of any opportunistic behaviour, but because the contract provides that, within limits, workers will submit to employer authority over the allocation of tasks and the specification of effort levels.

The advantage of this proposition can be further demonstrated by considering what would happen if opportunistic behaviour were to occur under a situation where contract fulfilment could be measured and *ex post* settling up enforced. Under a commercial contract the party engaging in opportunistic behaviour would incur a loss, through the payment of a penalty (see Fama, 1980, for an application in the case of managerial opportunism). Within the employment contract this would occur if, for example, the employer failed to pay the agreed rate. But if the employer devises a form of work organization that achieves higher effort levels or a more efficacious allocation of tasks, with the result that more work is performed, no cheating has occurred and there is no *ex post* settling up. This also explains why payment by time should ever occur. It does so precisely because the relationship between labour input and work performed is not pre-specified. The capacity to work is purchased by the employer and not a specific quantity of labour output.

3.4 Historical Evolution of the Firm

Williamson (1980) claims that efficiency considerations have dominated the evolution of modes of employing labour. More limited claims about the extent to which efficiency considerations underlie the evolution of forms of work organization have been made by others, and these are considered below. Williamson's concern was to refute Marglin's (1974) proposition that the evolution of the capitalist hierarchical mode of employing labour can best be understood from a perspective that emphasizes employers' aims of exercising control over workers. Williamson's claim has been questioned on methodological grounds (Dow, 1987). The construction of, and conclusions from, his historical comparative exercise, aimed at demonstrating that efficiency considerations will win out in the end, are also open to objection.

Showing that one form of work organization has desirable efficiency properties as compared to another says nothing about the causal process by which it arose. In this section, concern focuses on whether a particular form of work organization emerged because it had superior efficiency properties to historically earlier forms. Williamson (1980) formulates the hypothesis in its strongest possible form: 'the best evidence that power (labour control) is driving organizational outcomes would be a demonstration that less efficient modes that serve to concentrate power displace more efficient modes in which power is more evenly distributed' (p. 20). Note, however, that showing that, out of two alternative forms of work organization with equivalent efficiency properties in transactions costs terms, the one selected served to maximize employers' private returns by enhancing their authority, would be sufficient to demonstrate the relevance of power considerations.

Dow (1987) considers three types of causal process that might be employed to demonstrate that a particular mode of employing labour arose for efficiency reasons. These involve arguments built on intentionality, adaptive learning and competitive market pressures. Dow finds each line of argument unsatisfactory. First, intentionality is questionable because of the bounded rationality assumption employed in the efficient institutions approach. 'If agents cannot cope with contracts featuring complex contingencies, it is doubtful that they can select in advance an efficient decision making procedure to use in adapting to future circumstances' (Dow, 1987, p. 27). Moreover, small numbers exchange relations and the scope for employer opportunism in the selection of modes of work organization also pose problems for an efficiency explanation.

In a rejoinder, Williamson (1987) claims that intentionality can still be appealed to because bounded rationality constitutes limited rationality and not irrationality. This seems akin to a claim for adaptive learning, which is the second type of causal process that Dow considers. Dow notes that organizational routines, far from being adaptive, exhibit considerable inertia. In addition, where imperfect information is combined with the possibility that information is used for opportunistic ends (information impactedness) an efficient outcome is unlikely. For these reasons convergence on an efficient outcome through adaptive learning or myopic adjustment cannot be presumed.

Third, competitive processes might be appealed to. Dow notes that such a 'hidden hand' mechanism would be consistent with problems of bounded rationality. Williamson (1985) himself finds an argument based on the 'efficacy of competition to preserve a sort between more and less efficient modes and to shift resources in favour of the former' to be 'plausible' (p. 22), but concedes that a more fully developed theory of the selection process is required. However, competitive processes need not result in efficient outcomes. For example, large corporations have expended considerable resources in competing for monopoly power (Cowling et al., 1980). And Chandler (1977) charts how the competitive strategies of large companies were successfully aimed at securing greater control over their competitive environments. The efficiency of particular outcomes has to be demonstrated and not presumed.

A further problem of method concerns the definition of efficiency employed. An increase in technological efficiency is usually taken to mean an increase in output for given inputs, or the production of the same output with given inputs. (Economic efficiency takes account of relative price effects as well, and the two definitions may not always coincide.) Importantly for the argument here, employers can cost minimize and gain more for less without there being a corresponding increase in technological efficiency. Indeed it is possible that a production system that gives more for less, i.e. is more profitable, may be less efficient in technological terms than another, less profitable, system. To see why, recall the discussion of the previous subsection on the peculiarity of labour as an input. By securing greater effort from workers, employers can increase output and revenues, but the cost of labour inputs remains unchanged.

Thus, a strengthening of the authority relation, such as occurred with the shift from the putting-out system to factory production (Marglin, 1974; Williamson, 1980), could result in more output from the same capacity of labour purchased. But to the extent that the increase in output is secured through employers' ability to extract more labour effort from a given workforce, then labour input has increased as well. Thus while costs may have been minimized and profits increased, the efficiency implications of strengthening the authority relation are indeterminate – both outputs and inputs have increased. On this question Marglin (1974) and Landes (1986) would appear to be in agreement. Landes argues that what mattered in the evolution of the factory system was not technological efficiency *per se* but 'cost efficiency and predictability (enforceability) of output' (p. 594). Landes continues:

> there is an inherent logic to technological change, which is governed by the law (condition) of minimization of inputs; or conversely, of maximization of output. The aim is to get the most for least. This is not to say that innovations that satisfy that condition are intrinsically good or 'better' – to use Marglin's word. They just pay more – in money and power, depending on the economic and social system. (Landes, 1986, p. 620)

There are no claims to technological efficiency here, only to cost minimization and increased profits.

Williamson's (1980) own attempt to demonstrate that efficiency considerations explain the evolution of forms of work organization sidesteps the issue of technological efficiency by holding technology constant. The overall argument and conclusions of the exercise, whereby alternative forms of work organization are compared in terms of their transactions cost attributes, have been outlined in section 2. In the comparison, one form of cooperative organization, based on communal ownership and communal reward, emerges as having good efficiency properties in transactions cost terms, on a par with those of the capitalist bureaucratic mode. According to Williamson, however, it is weak on leadership and monitoring properties. But this rating is a direct result of Williamson's definition of cooperative, requiring rotation of tasks including leadership and monitoring – a requirement that in his analysis generates inefficiencies in transactions cost terms. In practice, however, producer cooperatives have been observed to have a permanent division of tasks, including monitoring (Putterman, 1984). (Moreover, while rotation may be transactionally inefficient in Williamson's static sense, it may provide a process of learning that results in dynamic efficiency gains.) A centralized monitoring structure does not, of itself, rule out worker control as Williamson assumes. It is not the existence of hierarchy that defines an organization as capitalist, but the use of hierarchy by one economic agent to exercise command over other economic agents.

Williamson's low rating of its leadership and monitoring properties notwithstanding, the communal ownership–communal reward form of cooperative compares favourably in his rating exercise with the bureaucratic hierarchical mode, characteristic of the contemporary large firm, in efficiency terms. If this is the case, why do we observe the latter to be so widespread, while cooperatives are relatively rare? Williamson is silent on this question. A dimension of analysis is missing, explaining why one form of efficient organization should develop and not another. Putterman (1982) and Dow (1987) cite appropriation considerations as being important. Within a cooperative the benefits of internal organization as compared to market coordination accrue equally to all the members of the firm. In contrast, within a capitalist firm it is possible for the employer to secure all, or a disproportionate share, of the benefits deriving from internal organization. In societies where there is an uneven distribution of wealth and power, the incentive for individual entrepreneurs to establish a capitalist firm is greater because returns to internal organization within a cooperative have to be shared. Appropriability considerations are, of course, central to Marglin's (1974) argument about the emergence of the factory system. It was precisely the power to appropriate the returns from the organization of production in the factory that, Marglin argues, spurred capitalist employers to embrace that system.

The relevance of power considerations to the evolution of the firm is further demonstrated by studies which show that workers have not passively accepted the transition of the employment relationship from putting-out through to the internal labour market of the large corporation; at times they have resisted. Montgomery (1979) describes how, at the turn of the century in the USA, an upsurge in worker agitation for cooperative ideals coincided with the attempts of large firms to impose new systems of direct control and supervision in place of delegated systems akin to inside contracting. Lazonick (1979) shows how the persistence of inside contracting in the UK cotton industry, long after its US counterpart had adopted direct systems of control, was related to the organized strength of key operatives in production.

A more limited claim to the efficiency of existing modes of organizing work, which would appear to recognize the force of such points, is made by Goldberg (1980): 'An efficient institution is one that survives in a particular context. The efficacy of a particular arrangement will depend upon the ability of the parties to exert legal or extra-legal power' (p. 268). At one level this defines the efficiency of a particular form of work organization in terms of its capacity to survive, a line of argument long familiar to economists (Friedman, 1953). Reservations about the ability of competitive processes to select an efficient outcome in the presence of market imperfections and information impactedness have already been outlined above.

None the less, Goldberg draws specific attention to the power that employers and workers are able to exercise, and to 'context'. The latter presumably includes not only the legal framework within which the employment relation operates, but also the educational system, the financial system, the political context and the family. These are unlikely to operate in a neutral fashion. For example, Bowles and Gintis (1976) show how the schooling system in the United States has been fashioned to reflect the dominant, capitalist, mode of organizing work. The financial system in the USA and the UK has been shown to militate against the development of cooperatives because equity is provided on less favourable terms where some measure of control through voting or other supervisory rights is not available (Thornley, 1981; Putterman, 1982, 1984). And political intervention has been crucial in the United States in affecting the ability of workers to exercise countervailing power through trade union organization. Given the opportunities open to employers and workers to exercise power, discussed in section 3.2, together with the additional opportunity to influence the context in which power is exercised, it is hard to see how efficiency considerations can win out in any global or historical sense. Indeed, Goldberg's argument would seem to have much in common with North's (1981) proposition that efficiency considerations are contingent on the primary concern of a ruling group to maintain its state power.

Contrary to Williamson's claim that efficiency considerations are primary, this section has underlined the salience of power considerations to a satisfactory explanation of the evolution of forms of work organization. The following proposition summarizes the argument:

The historical evolution of the firm reflects a series of choices by employers over technology and work organization which served to maximize their own

private return; there is no presumption that these choices were technologically or organizationally efficient.

3.5 Employer Control and the Firm

The argument of the preceding subsections can now be drawn together.
By paying proper attention to the power aspects of relationships between
employers and workers, the propositions developed throw a distinct light
on the nature of the firm.

Central to an adequate theorization of the firm is the proposition that
employers and workers have an inherent conflict of interest over the
utilization of the worker's capacity to work after the labour contract has
been concluded. Employers are motivated by the acquisition of profit,
which necessitates cost minimization and control over the production
process, including workers' effort and task adaptability. Workers are
motivated by the need to attain an adequate standard of living, and to
exert control over the pace and content of their work. Employers do
not purchase a specified quantity of work performed through a precise
contract, but control over workers' capacity to produce through an
incomplete contract. Scope for conflict thus exists not only over the terms
of the incomplete contract, but subsequently over the precise labour that
workers are required to perform.

Employers are able to use the authority which the incomplete nature
of the labour contract vests in them to try and secure an outcome to this
conflict that is favourable to their interests. Forms of technology and
work organization can be selected by employers that best enable them
to exploit workers' capacity to work, thereby maximizing their private
return. But the outcome will not necessarily be socially efficient. Indeed
this is only likely to occur where workers are in a position, through their
own organization or through legislative support, to select technology
and work organization jointly with employers. Workers, for their part,
develop their own forms of organization in order to exercise countervailing
power against the use of authority by employers. In turn, employers will
try to shape the form of workers' organization, including trade unions, in
order to minimize the challenge to their dominance. The exercise of
power depends on extrinsic factors, organization and mobilization of
resources, as well as intrinsic factors, the possession of certain skills or
the ability to hire and fire. The wider context, the legal, political and
socio-economic systems, is also an important influence on the exercise of
power. Outcomes, in terms of those parts of the labour contract which
are left unspecified, are therefore indeterminate.

Such an approach has features in common with the 'control' models of
the firm proposed by writers such as Marglin (1974) and Edwards (1979),

and formalized by Bowles (1985). The next section considers the adequacy of these models in their analysis of the employment relationship.

4   POWER APPROACHES TO THE FIRM AND THE LIMITS TO COERCION

Power or 'control' models of the firm have emphasized the coercive nature of employer authority (Marglin, 1974; Edwards, 1979; Bowles, 1985). The essence of the authority relation is seen to lie in the ability of the employer to force workers to do things which they would not otherwise do. In Bowles's formal model, which was outlined in section 3.1, labour effort is secured through coercive means either directly or indirectly. Direct coercion is exercised through supervision and monitoring, indirect coercion by the ability to impose a cost on workers for non-compliance with employer directives. By paying a premium above the market wage, the employer can make job loss, and the threat of it, costly to the worker.[8] Marglin similarly emphasizes the role of indirect coercion arising from the consequences of being thrown out of work as well as the direct coercion of the supervisory and monitoring systems developed in the early factories.

In contrast, as described in the previous section, writers taking an efficient institutions approach have emphasized the consensual nature of the authority relation (Alchian and Demsetz, 1972; Williamson et al., 1975; Aoki, 1984). Workers' voluntary submission to authority is seen to be in the interests of *both* employers and workers in so far as organizational goals are thereby elevated above sectional ones. The inadequacies of this view of authority have already been spelled out. In this section it is argued that it is not enough to simply counterpose coercion to consensus, as writers taking a power approach have tended to do. To focus on the coercive aspect of the employment relationship alone is to ignore that employers secure effort from workers by other means, and their reasons for doing so. The aim is to develop an account of the interplay of coercion and consensus within the employment relationship.

The starting point is a recognition that the exercise of employer authority is contractually agreed, and acceptable, only within limits. Workers are voluntary agents who retain rights, most importantly to quit the employment relationship. In this sense workers differ from slaves and serfs, who can be compelled to submit to authority. The fact that authority relations in the capitalist firm 'arise endogenously via the bargains struck among initially autonomous agents, rather than through crude coercion' (Dow, 1987, p. 16) places initial limits on the exercise of employer authority. But these are not the only limits to the use of coercion in the employment relationship. Following the argument in section 3.3, workers enter the employment relationship with their own set of interests, which conflict with those of the employer. Post-contract, the employer is still faced with the problem of securing labour effort and task adaptability.

Crucially, employers may be concerned to harness workers' adaptability and creativity, as well as to direct them to tasks. Thus a distinction exists between what has been termed perfunctory and commensurate performance by workers. Perfunctory performance is associated with low levels of effort and task adaptability, commensurate performance with high task adaptability and effort levels. Friedman (1977) argues that labour enters the employment relationship in a contradictory manner. Labour is at the same time both flexible in the tasks to which it can be applied and resistant to intensification of effort and direction of tasks. Employers need to enlist the creative potential of labour as well as overcoming its recalcitrance. Coercion may well overcome workers' recalcitrance, as is the case in Bowles's model, but it is unlikely to harness workers' flexibility and creativity. Coercive means can secure perfunctory, but not commensurate, performance from workers. Employers must to some degree seek a cooperative relation with workers in order to harness their creative and productive powers. Workers also have an interest in working effectively. This is because the viability of the firm has implications for their own future employment security and pecuniary rewards (Cressey and MacInnes, 1980).

The circumstances under which employers are able to secure commensurate, rather than perfunctory, performance from their workers have been the concern of a diverse literature. In psychology, an extensive literature is concerned with individuals' motivation. The several theories developed break down into two basic directions of analysis (Nicholson, 1981): theories concerned with mobilizing energy or effort and theories concerned with the direction of effort – the values, goals and purposes for which energy is expended. In economics, various literatures have pointed to the importance of institutional arrangements in securing commensurate performance. From their standpoint of concern with worker opportunism, Williamson et al. (1975) identify perfunctory performance with the pursuit of opportunistic or sectional interests in individualized work settings. Commensurate performance, on the other hand, is seen to result from the creation of a collective organization within which common interests are elevated above sectional ones. In the growing literature on participation, concerned with opportunism by employers as well as workers, it is argued that commensurate performance is more likely to result where decisions on aspects of work organization are taken jointly rather than unilaterally by the employer (Cable and Fitzroy, 1980; McCain, 1980; Fitzroy and Kraft, 1987). In similar vein, Freeman (1976) argues that unions can have performance-enhancing effects through giving workers a voice within the firm.

A different perspective is offered by efficiency wage theories, whose central insight is that employers are able to elicit greater effort from workers by the payment of a wage above the market rate. It is presumed that employers pay a higher wage because it results in higher profits. Thus, employers will pay an 'efficiency' wage where the costs of doing so are less than those incurred through monitoring workers' effort (Stiglitz, 1984; Raff and Somers, 1987). The claim to efficiency is questionable as, recalling the discussion of section 3.3, higher profits do not guarantee that an increase in efficiency has occurred.[9] Such problems notwithstanding, the central insight of the approach is an important one, and is not contingent on the claim to efficiency.

One variant of the efficiency wage approach underlies the work of Bowles (1985) and Goldberg (1980) discussed above. If there are pecuniary costs to losing a job, workers will be induced to work harder. A second variant emphasizes the importance of workers' norms about what constitutes a fair day's work (Akerlof, 1982). In return for a wage in excess of that obtainable elsewhere, workers are prepared to work at levels of effort and adaptability in excess of minimum, or perfunctory, work standards. A similar idea underpins Annable's (1984) efficiency wage model of the firm. Employers are able to secure effort through the payment of a wage premium. The wage premium is determined by reference to a wage norm, which is defined as the 'workers' standard of fair treatment and is rooted in custom and tradition' (Annable, 1984, p. 8).

The use of concepts such as norms and conventions in the analysis of worker effort draws heavily on sociological and psychological models of human behaviour. Sociologists have questioned the assumption employed in economic models that workers are necessarily averse to effort (Cressey and MacInnes, 1980). Studies have suggested that rather than seeking 'not to work', workers attempt to control the pace and content of their work (see, for example, Baldamus, 1961; Lupton, 1963; Roy, 1969). They do this by enforcing norms or conventions about the amount of effort to be expended. Effort is seen as a relative concept, most notably in its relation to pay. Behavioural approaches to effort stress the range of means by which employers can elicit effort from workers (Mintzberg, 1983). These range from direct supervision, where effort is secured by issuing instructions to workers and monitoring their actions, to reliance on norms and conventions. The latter extends to professionalization, where workers have internalized values about how work should be performed and effort levels, requiring no direct supervision. Socialization occurs prior to employment through the training required to perform the work. This contrasts with socialization on the job, associated with the enforcement of effort norms and conventions, referred to above. Mintzberg notes that most employers simultaneously adopt several approaches to eliciting effort from their workforces, according to such things as the differing nature of the tasks being performed and the extent of prior training.[10]

The argument of this section points to the importance of a complex range of influences by which labour effort is secured, of which the coercive means emphasized by critics such as Marglin (1974) and Bowles (1985) are only one. In their analysis of how employers secure effort and adaptability from workers these 'control' models offer only a partial explanation. It has been suggested that institutional and normative factors are also important in securing labour effort. An emphasis on coercion to the exclusion of other factors ignores employers' need to enlist the creativity of workers, or that workers have their own conventions about levels of effort to be expended. Importantly, the strategies for securing labour effort pursued by employers may vary according to the position of workers in the production process, or external circumstances. Employers may be more concerned to harness the creativity of some groups of workers than of others. What Friedman (1977) has termed 'responsible autonomy' strategies are characterized by a degree of work group self-management aimed at enlisting workers' creativity, and contrast with 'direct control' strategies, which are more overtly coercive.

5 CONCLUSIONS

This chapter has argued that issues of power are inherent to the type of economic problem addressed by efficient institutions theories, characterized as they are by factor immobilities and market imperfections. According to its own assumption of self-interested behaviour, the efficient institutions approach should anticipate that employers will use the authority vested in them by the incomplete nature of the labour contract to pursue their own interests, in which case employers may select forms of work organization that maximize their own private returns and are consistent with maintaining or enhancing their authority. It follows that claims to the efficiency of the resultant forms of work organization can no longer be sustained. It has been further argued that workers' bargaining power cannot be reduced to a derivative condition dependent on the possession of firm-specific skills. Workers will try to counter employer authority through their own autonomous forms of organization, and in turn employers will try to shape worker organization so as to minimize the threat to their authority.

Power or control models of the firm provide a more satisfactory account of the nature and consequence of the exercise of employer authority. But in doing so they lay too much emphasis on the role of coercion. Little attention is paid to the needs of employers to secure commensurate as distinct from perfunctory performance from employees. In contrast, the efficient institutions literature displays a greater sensitivity to the importance of institutions and 'atmosphere' (Williamson, 1975) in eliciting commensurate rather than perfunctory performance from workers.

This reflects a strength of the efficient institutions approach, namely its sensitivity to the potential contribution of other disciplinary approaches to the analysis of economic problems. The associated concepts of bounded rationality on the part of human agents and complexity and uncertainty in the environment are explicitly drawn from organization studies. But a corresponding weakness lies in its attempt to incorporate such insights as stylized facts into a framework that in other respects has much in common with traditional neoclassical economics. Thus, despite the important collective aspect of the employment relationship, the analysis is largely conducted in terms of the individualistic concept of opportunism. Little attention is paid to concepts that might bind workers to each other or to their employers, such as norms or conventions, or work groups together, such as solidarity.

Like neoclassical economics, the efficient institutions approach also claims that its concepts are of general applicability. It is argued that the concepts of transactions costs, asset specificity and opportunism can be equally fruitfully applied to a wide range of economic problems. Such a claim to generality can deny the specificity of a particular relationship, with consequent limitations for a proper understanding of it. This was argued to be so in the case of the labour contract. Writers such as Williamson (1985) and Goldberg (1980) claim that the labour contract is just like any other. To the contrary, it was shown that the labour contract differs from others, because aspects of the contract are mutually left open, to be decided later at the discretion of the employer. Subsequent conflict over effort levels and precise tasks to be performed is conceptually different from acting opportunistically, or cheating, over contractually agreed terms.

Perhaps economics is least comfortable when dealing with issues of power (Rothschild, 1971). It is well known that situations of bilateral monopoly and small numbers are conducive to the exercise of power. These situations characterize the types of employment relationship with which the efficient institutions approach is concerned. Among those economists recognizing the importance of power within the firm, emphasis has been placed on the use of coercion. Regard needs to be paid to the limits on the exercise of coercion to secure worker effort, and to the importance of normative factors. More broadly, the role of non-coercive means of maintaining power, including socialization and legitimation, requires attention. A more adequate treatment of power within economics is essential to further developments in the theory of the firm.

NOTES

1 In relation to the latter, Lazear (1981) has demonstrated that age–earnings profiles which pay workers according to seniority have superior incentive properties in terms of work effort.
2 Elsewhere, it is claimed that the bureaucratic mode of employment relation will curb managerial opportunism, such as arbitary behaviour by supervisors, as well as worker opportunism (Williamson, 1987). However, this leaves open how opportunism by top management is constrained.
3 Again, there are parallels with contractual theories of the state, which assume an equal distribution among groups and individuals within society of the potential to pursue sectional interest through coercive or violent means (North, 1981). Considerations of power in the role exercised by the state are thereby abstracted from, in order to focus on its integrative and coordinating functions.
4 Such would also be the case in the presence of perfect markets for either capital (Jensen and Meckling, 1976) or managers (Fama, 1980). In practice, asset specificity is likely to create considerable asymmetries in the information available to insiders, the managers of the firm, and agents on the external market, rendering these markets highly imperfect.
5 In a study of the productivity effects of participation in the Federal Republic of Germany, Cable and Fitzroy (1980) found that firms with participatory arrangements displayed higher productivity than those without such arrangements. They were also more profitable. This is indicative of the social benefits that may accrue from cooperative forms of work organization.
6 The case of British dockworkers demonstrates that workers' organization need not specifically be trade union organization (Phillips and Whiteside, 1985).
7 The marriage contract might be seen as embodying a similar distinction between an initial exchange between equals that provides one party, the man, with authority over the other. Exploring the extent of such similiarity would require an analysis of patriarchal relations (Walby, 1986) beyond the scope of this study. It is the presence of a power dimension in each of the employment and marriage contracts that renders an analysis based solely on the efficiency properties of these transactions inadequate.
8 Goldberg (1980) employs similar reasoning from an efficiency perspective. Employers discourage behaviour by workers that impairs performance by imposing a cost on non-compliance. In Goldberg's case the cost takes the form of deferred payments, and Goldberg (1980, p. 263) notes that Henry Ford's $5 day was contingent on workers being deemed to perform satisfactorily.

9   For example, by paying the $5 day Ford was able to secure increased worker effort, and thereby increase output revenues and profits. Raff and Somers (1987) cite this as a prime instance of the payment of efficiency wages. Management was successful in getting workers to work harder by making payment of the $5 contingent on satisfactory performance (Meyer, 1981). But to claim that this represents an improvement in efficiency presumes, rather than demonstrates, that workers were fully compensated for working harder.

10 Norms and conventions play a central role in Leibenstein's (1987) analysis of the firm. Utilizing a prisoner's dilemma framework, Leibenstein argues that effort norms, and associated wage norms, are established by convention. By adhering to these conventions employers and workers can avoid the low level outcome of the prisoner's dilemma. Unlike the efficiency wage approach, however, Leibenstein makes no presumption that adherence to conventions will result in an efficient outcome.

   In a further paper, Raff (1988) demonstrates that none of the standard efficiency wage explanations, relating to turnover costs, adverse selection or moral hazard, are plausible explanations for Ford's introduction of the $5 day. He concludes that the $5 day was intended to forestall union organization and buy industrial peace.

REFERENCES

Akerlof, G. A. (1982) Labor contracts as partial gift exchange. *Quarterly Journal of Economics*, 98, 543–69.

Alchian, A. and Demsetz, H. (1972) Production, information costs and economic organization. *American Economic Review*, 62, 777–95.

Annable, J. E. (1984) *The Price of Industrial Labor*. Lexington, MA: Lexington Books.

Aoki, M. (1984) *The Co-operative Game Theory of the Firm*. Oxford: Clarendon Press.

Baldamus, W. (1961) *Efficiency and Effort*. London: Tavistock.

Bassett, P. (1986) *Strike Free: New Industrial Relations in Britain*. London: Macmillan.

Bowles, S. (1985) The production process in a competitive economy: Walrasian, neo-Hobbesian, and Marxian Models. *American Economic Review*, 75, 16–36.

Bowles, S. and Gintis, H. (1976) *Schooling in Capitalist America*. London: Routledge and Kegan Paul.

Brown, W. (ed.) (1981) *The Changing Contours of British Industrial Relations*. Oxford: Blackwell.

Cable, J. (1986) Why is participatory production not the norm? Warwick Economic Research Paper No. 272, University of Warwick, May.

Cable, J. (1987) Control, technology and the social efficiency of traditional production. Warwick Economic Research Paper No. 279, University of Warwick, June.

Cable, J. and FitzRoy, F. (1980) Productive efficiency, incentives and employee participation. *Kyklos*, 33, 100–20.

Chandler, A. D. (1977) *The Visible Hand*. Cambridge, MA: Harvard University Press.

Coase, R. (1937) The nature of the firm. *Economica*, 4, 386–405.

Cowling, K., Stoneman, P., Cubbin, J., Cable, J., Hall, G., Domberger, S. and Dutton, P. (1980) *Mergers and Economic Performance*. Cambridge: Cambridge University Press.

Cressey, P. and MacInnes, J. (1980) Voting for Ford: industrial democracy and the control of labour. *Capital and Class*, 11, 5–37.

Dow, G. K. (1987) The function of authority in transaction cost economics. *Journal of Economic Behavior and Organization*, 8, 13–38.

Dow, G. K. (1988) The evolution of organizational form: selection, efficiency and the new institutional economics. Research Paper 88-02, Department of Economics, University of Alberta, January.

Edwards, R. (1979) *Contested Terrain*. London: Heinemann.

Enderwick, P. (1984) The labour utilisation practices of multinationals and obstacles to multinational collective bargaining. *Journal of Industrial Relations*, 26, 345–64.

Fama, E (1980) Agency problems and the theory of the firm. *Journal of Political Economy*, 88, 288–307.

FitzRoy, F. R. and Kraft, K. (1987) Efficiency and internal organisation: works councils in West German firms. *Economica*, 54, 493–504.

Freeman, R. B. (1976) Individual mobility and union voice in the labour market. *American Economic Review, Papers and Proceedings*, 66, 361–77.

Friedman, A. L. (1977) *Industry and Labour*. London: Macmillan.

Friedman, M. (1953) *Essays in Positive Economics*. Chicago: University of Chicago Press.

Goldberg, V. P. (1980) Bridges over contested terrain. *Journal of Economic Behavior and Organization*, 1, 249–74.

Hirschman, A. O. (1970) *Exit, Voice and Loyalty*. Cambridge, MA: Harvard University Press.

Hyman, R. (1975) *Industrial Relations: a Marxist Introduction*. London: Macmillan.

Jensen, M. and Meckling, W. (1976) Theory of the firm: managerial behaviour, agency costs and ownership. *Journal of Financial Economics*, 3, 305–60.

Klandermans, P. G. (1984) Mobilisation and participation in trade union action: a value expectancy approach. *Journal of Occupational Psychology*, 57, 107–20.

Klandermans, P. G. (1986) Psychology and trade union participation: joining, acting, quitting. *Journal of Occupational Psychology*, 59, 189–204.

Kochan, T. A., Katz, H. and McKersie, R. B. (1986) *The Transformation of American Industrial Relations*. New York: Basic Books.

Landes, D. S. (1986) What do bosses really do? *Journal of Economic History*, 46, 585–623.

Lazear, E. P. (1981) Agency, earnings profiles, productivity and hours restrictions. *American Economic Review*, 71, 606–20.

Lazonick, W. H. (1979) Industrial relations and technical change: the case of the self-acting mule. *Cambridge Journal of Economics*, 3, 231–62.

Leibenstein, H. (1982) The prisoners' dilemma in the invisible hand: an analysis of intrafirm productivity. *American Economic Review, Papers and Proceedings*, 72, 92–7.

Leibenstein, H. (1987) *Inside the Firm: the Inefficiencies of Hierarchy*. Cambridge, MA: Harvard University Press.

Lupton, T. (1963) *On the Shop Floor*. Oxford: Pergamon.

McCain, R. A. (1980) A theory of co-determination. *Zeitschrift für National-Oekonomie*, 40, 65–90.

McPherson, M. (1983) Efficiency and liberty in the productive enterprise: recent work in the economics of work organization. *Philosophy and Public Affairs*, 12, 354–68.

Malcolmson, J. E. (1984) Efficient labour organization: incentives, power and the transactions cost approach. In F. Stephen (ed.), *Firms, Organization and Labour*. London: Macmillan.

Marglin, S. A. (1974) What do bosses do? *Review of Radical Political Economics*, 6, 60–112.

Marx, K. (1974) *Capital*, volume 1. London: Lawrence and Wishart.

Meyer, S. (1981) *The Five-Dollar Day: Labor Management and Social Control in the Ford Motor Company, 1908–21*. Albany: State University of New York Press.

Mintzberg, H. (1983) *Structure in Fives: Designing Effective Organizations*. Englewood Cliffs, NJ: Prentice-Hall.

Montgomery, D. (1979) *Workers' Control in America*. Cambridge: Cambridge University Press.

Nicholson, N. (1981) Motivation: a test case for the integration of psychology and industrial relations. In A. W. J. Thomson and M. Warner (eds), *The Behavioural Sciences and Industrial Relations*. Aldershot: Gower.

North, D. C. (1981) *Structure and Change in Economic History*. New York: Norton.

Ozanne, R. (1967) *A Century of Labor–Management Relations*. Madison:

University of Wisconsin Press.

Phillips, G. and Whiteside, N. (1985) *Casual Labour: the Unemployment Question in the Port Transport Industry 1890–1970*. Oxford: Clarendon Press.

Pollard, S. (1965) *The Genesis of Modern Management*. London: Edward Arnold.

Putterman, L. (1982) Some behavioral perspectives on the dominance of hierarchical over democractic forms of enterprise. *Journal of Economic Behavior and Organization*, 3, 139–60.

Putterman, L. (1984) On some recent explanations of why capital hires labor. *Economic Inquiry*, 22, 171–87.

Putterman, L. (ed.) (1986) *The Economic Nature of the Firm*. Cambridge: Cambridge University Press.

Raff, D. M. G. (1988) Wage determination theory and the five dollar day at Ford. *Journal of Economic History*, 48, 387–99.

Raff, D. M. G. and Somers, L. H. (1987) Did Henry Ford pay efficiency wages? *Journal of Labor Economics*, 5, 557–86.

Rothschild, K. (ed.) (1971) *Power in Economics*. Harmondsworth: Penguin.

Roy, D. (1969) Making-out: a workers' counter-system of control of work sanction and relationships. In T. Burns (ed.), *Industrial Man*. Harmondsworth: Penguin.

Samuelson, P. (1957) Wage and interest: a modern discussion of Marxian economic models. *American Economic Review*, 47, 884–912.

Shorter, E. and Tilly, C. (1974) *Strikes in France, 1830–1968*. Cambridge: Cambridge University Press.

Simon, H. A. (1955) A behavioural model of rational choice. *Quarterly Journal of Economics*, 69, 99–118.

Sisson, K. (1987) *The Management of Collective Bargaining: an International Comparison*. Oxford: Blackwell.

Stiglitz, J. E. (1984) Theories of wage rigidity. National Bureau of Economic Research Working Paper No. 1442.

Thompson, E. P. (1967) Time, work discipline and industrial capitalism. *Past and Present*, 38, 56–97.

Thornley, J. (1981) *Workers' Co-operatives: Jobs and Dreams*. London: Heinemann.

Walby, S. (1986) *Patriarchy at Work*. Cambridge: Polity Press.

Wickens, P. (1987) *The Road to Nissan*. Basingstoke: Macmillan.

Williamson, O. E. (1975) *Markets and Hierarchies*. New York: Free Press.

Williamson, O. E. (1980) The organization of work: a comparative institutional assessment. *Journal of Economic Behavior and Organization*, 1, 5–38.

Williamson, O. E. (1981) The modern corporation, origins, evolution, attributes. *Journal of Economic Literature*, 19, 1537–68.

Williamson, O. E. (1984) Efficient labour organization. In F. Stephen (ed.), *Firms, Organization and Labour*. London: Macmillan.

Williamson, O. E. (1985) *The Economic Institutions of Capitalism*. New York: Free Press.

Williamson, O. E. (1987) Transaction cost economics: the comparative contracting perspective. *Journal of Economic Behavior and Organization*, 8, 617–25.

Williamson, O. E., Wachter, M. L. and Harris, J. E. (1975) Understanding the employment relation: the analysis of idiosyncratic change. *Bell Journal of Economics*, 6, 250–78.

Willman, P. (1983) The organisational failures framework and industrial sociology. In A. Francis, J. Turk and P. Willman (eds), *Power, Efficiency and Institutions*. London: Heinemann.

8

Transaction Costs . . . and Revenues

MICHAEL DIETRICH

1 INTRODUCTION

The basic idea behind this contribution is that transaction cost economics is based on partial reasoning. Put briefly, and using Kornai's (1971) terminology, the framework relies on the control aspect of resource allocation and ignores the use dimension. Either it must be argued that the use aspects of resource allocation do not change with different governance structures, which of course can be assumed, but in so doing attention is diverted away from useful areas of analysis. Or it must be acknowledged that transaction cost reasoning is only potentially half a theory of an analysis of governance structures. It follows that the framework should be broadened to accommodate both control and use aspects of economic organization. This chapter suggests a way in which this may be achieved, and in particular links the choice of governance structures to differential abilities to generate revenue rather than transaction cost efficiencies.[1] In broadening the analysis the analytical centre of gravity will be shifted significantly.

In brief the argument can be presented as follows.[2] Transaction cost economics is based on pre-given units, or technologically separable activities. When an exchange takes place between these units transaction costs will be incurred, in much the same way as friction exists in the physical world. Therefore efficiency consideration and competition imply that different governance structures evolve to minimize these costs of organizing resource allocation. But equally, governance structures can evolve to facilitate transformation in the units themselves. Their sizes or

The comments of Marco Bellandi, Geoff Hodgson, Tariq Riaz and Christos Pitelis on earlier versions of this chapter have led to significant improvements in the arguments presented. Their time and efforts are greatly appreciated and duly acknowledged.

shapes may change, the latter describing for a firm product–market characteristics. In a more dynamic context, different governance structures may have implications for the speed or direction of growth. These changes in the units can be referred to as the benefits of resource allocation (Dietrich, 1991), and are based on the use to which resources are put – summarized in this chapter as revenue-generating ability. This broadening of the analysis implies that if governance structures exist because of benefit advantages (at least for some organizational actors), the attendant costs may or may not change. If transaction costs do change with different governance structures they may increase, to exploit potential benefits. An obvious implication of such a possibility is that the evolution of governance structures cannot just rely on transaction cost economizing.

It is important to recognize that (implicitly) assuming unchanged governance structure benefits is not done just because of expositional convenience; it is an analytical requirement to maintain the logical conherence of the analysis. As Dow points out:

> in comparing costs across governance structures, it is essential that the relevant transaction be specified independently of the governance structure which is superimposed upon it. Otherwise, the claim that 'transaction X is organised under governance structure Y' would express not an empirical truth, but only a concealed tautology. If the attributes of a transaction do not remain invariant when one governance structure is replaced by another, the transaction costs involved are meaningless. (Dow, 1987, p. 18)

To claim that the attributes of a transaction must not change when governance structures are compared is equivalent to saying that the benefits to be derived are unchanged. An advantage of the approach taken here is that it is not necessary to make the gross assumption of invariance of benefits.

The rest of this chapter is organized as follows. In the next section a framework is developed that recognizes both the costs and benefits of governance structures. Following this, organizational benefits are explored in more detail and the implications for transaction cost reasoning discussed. It is argued that transaction cost economics must be based in a wider framework that acknowledges the importance of idiosyncratic organizational dynamics and the centrality of power as well as efficiency. Finally some conclusions are drawn.

2 COSTS, BENEFITS AND THE EXISTENCE OF FIRMS

There are two building blocks to the framework to be developed in this section. The first involves characterizing the firm in general as an arena to transform inputs into outputs for use by other legally independent economic units. The central feature is, therefore, the management of a production and/or distribution process (see Fourie, 1989). This involves recognition of both use and exchange values (Marx, 1976). Intra-firm management must recognize the former; market processes are dominated by the latter. Hence costs of resource allocation can be identified as transaction and organization costs (Kay, 1984) for respectively markets and firms.

The second building block is to follow standard procedure and define transaction costs (organization costs will be considered shortly) in terms of three factors: search and information costs, bargaining and decision costs, and policing and enforcement costs. But if we restrict ourselves to firms rather than final consumers, these factors can be recast in terms of the management and related costs associated with the construction and enforcement of contracts. To simplify we can assume that such costs occur over two time periods. In the short run the overall stock of managerial resources is given. Thus the only way to increase managerial input into any one contracting activity is to divert resources away from other activities. In the long run the overall stock of managerial and complementary resources can be increased.[3]

Using these assumptions it is possible to define a short-run relationship between management input per unit time into any one contracting activity determining contract output. The latter can be defined in terms of two 'joint products': responsibilities and prices. Thus greater management effort produces a more detailed specification and policing of responsibilities and/or more advantageous prices (higher/lower for outputs/inputs). Ignoring, for the moment, complexities associated with organizational dynamics, it is possible to depict any one short-run contracting process as in figure 8.1. The diminishing returns involved here would seem to be appropriate because of bounds on information collection and processing capabilities. To maintain the simplicity of the diagram, however, we have to assume that all contracting and internal organization efforts are separable. If this is not the case, increased efforts in any one area, achieved at the expense of effort in another, will have general systemic effects on managerial activity. Approximate separability will exist if managerial and other inputs are specialized and hence direct links between them are limited.

While increased management time input in any one activity is likely to have an effect as traced by figure 8.1, its static nature should not be over-emphasized. Increased (decreased) effort per unit time will shift the curve up (down). This endogenization of effort implies that technical efficiency levels are a function of organizational relationships, as discussed in more detail below, rather than being an optimality norm. In the long run, when

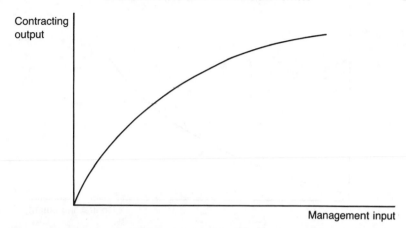

Figure 8.1 Short-run relationship between management input and contract characteristics.

the stock of managerial assets can grow (or decline), a set of curves such as that in figure 8.1 can be mapped out defining the nature of any contracting scale economies. In addition, however, more subtle effects are likely to be important. Additions to a management team will change organizational dynamics (Penrose, 1959; Nelson and Winter, 1982), an effect that is likely to be greater at higher levels of the organizational hierarchy. Therefore, long-run expansion (or contraction) does not just involve returns to scale imposed on to an otherwise unchanged contracting process. Shifting organizational dynamics can impede or facilitate any scale effects, and in addition can affect the trade-off between management input and bounds on information collection and processing. Finally, more obvious technological change can affect figure 8.1. For example, the exploitation of advances in information technology can enhance the information collection and processing abilities of an organization.

Using standard microeconomic techniques the short-run relationships between inputs and outputs can be transformed into the associated transaction costs. The main theoretical issue here is the valuation of input prices, given that the overall stock of management is fixed in the short run. The resource cost of extra management input into any one activity is the opportunity cost of the management in terms of lost contracting (and organizational) activity. Hence it is appropriate to price managerial input in terms of an increasing opportunity cost function.

Thus figure 8.2 can be defined, C_m being the transaction costs of a particular market-based activity. This diagram has an intuitive appeal because when more advantageous prices result from search activity

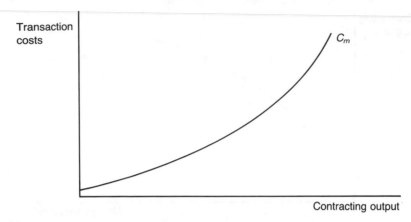

Figure 8.2   Transaction costs of a market-based activity.

or negotiation, and/or as a more precise negotiation or policing of responsibilities is undertaken, transaction costs concomitantly rise. It is obvious that C_m will shift in response to the factors discussed above, which reflect the dynamics of organizational activity.

The costs of internal organization can be modelled in an analogous way to that just specified, except that managerial input results in the specification or policing of intra-firm responsibilities. A diagram equivalent to figure 8.2 that describes the organization costs of a particular intra-firm activity can therefore be derived. Using this framework we can restate the fundamental theorem of transaction cost economics explaining the existence of firms: it may be possible to economize on the costs of resource allocation by using partial contracts and managerial direction for labour inputs or internalization within unified ownership for non-human inputs. This theorem can be depicted as in figure 8.3.

In this diagram the costs of resource allocation incurred by the partial (for labour inputs) or complete internalization of one particular activity are described as C_f, involving lower fixed costs or increased efficiency levels than C_m, or C'_f, involving long-run cost advantages. In short, the tangents to C_m and C_f or C'_f in figure 8.3 indicate average cost savings from intra-firm rather than market relationships. If a Williamsonian (1985) analysis is adopted, it follows that the extent of these costs savings will be a function of asset specificity, frequency of use and uncertainty. In a different transaction cost tradition, that developed to understand internalization of multinational companies, Hennart (1991) suggests that the extent of any difference between transaction and organization costs will depend on the costs of monitoring performance within a hier-

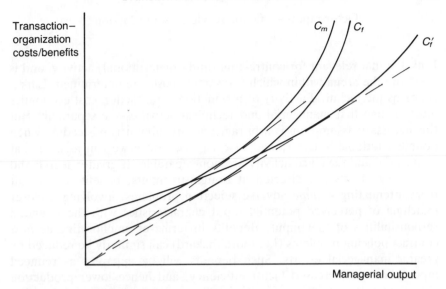

Figure 8.3   The fundamental theorem of transaction cost economics.

archy, cultural differences between superior and subordinate units, and managerial skills.

When transaction cost economics is presented as in figure 8.3, an obvious problem becomes clear: it is only potentially half a theory because any benefits from resource allocation are omitted from the analysis. Ignoring, for the moment, the important issue of benefits for whom, we can understand their general nature by specifying the connections between production–distribution activities and economic governance. To disentangle the different effects we can separate distribution from production and contracting from internal management effort. Concentrating first on distribution contracts, greater information searching, bargaining and contract policing efforts can result in higher output prices or greater sales volumes. The resulting increased revenues imply that managerial effort endogenizes market characteristics.

The analysis of input contracts is more complex. Penrose's (1959) and Leibenstein's (1966) analyses show that output is produced by factor services that are derivable from factor inputs. But there is not a simple one-to-one mapping from inputs to services (as implicitly assumed in orthodox theory); rather the connection is determined by contracting (and organizational) activity. The following simple flow diagram illustrates the issues involved:

factor inputs → factor services → production.
1   2

Link 1 is that relevant for contracting (and organizational) activity, and is therefore the arena within which transaction costs are determined. Link 2 concerns the technical activity of production. Transaction cost economics must assume that managerial and technical activities are separable. But this necessary assumption is arbitrary and arguably it is misleading when bounded rationality is assumed to exist. Therefore we can assume that managerial and technical activity are non-separable. If greater search and bargaining efforts are directed at bought-in inputs, benefits can result from attenuating *ex ante* adverse selection problems, involving a closer matching of perceived potential input characteristics with the intended responsibilities of that input. Benefits in terms of ameliorating *ex post* contract policing problems (i.e. moral hazard) can similarly be reduced by greater managerial efforts. Such benefits will be apparent as reduced input prices or increased factor efficiency, and hence lower production (i.e. marginal) costs, which in turn implies maintaining/increasing market share and performance.

The links between intra-firm resource allocation and organizational benefits revolve around the same *ex ante* and *ex post* decision-making problems. Curiously we can use Williamson's (1975, 1985) arguments that intra-firm organization can facilitate adaptation to environmental change for the following reasons: opportunistic behaviour is less likely within a firm; disputes can be settled by top management; convergent expectations can facilitate planning; and access to relevant information will reduce haggling. While these factors will allow organizational cost savings by, for example, allowing responsibility specification and policing at lower cost, at the same time greater efforts in these areas will lead to greater revenues and/or lower production costs because organizational and technical activity are non-separable. The only way that such benefits can be ruled out is to make a perfect information assumption, which is inconsistent with transaction cost analysis.

It is now possible to specify the benefits derivable from different governance structures. Increased managerial activity will change production costs and revenues, not just transaction–organization costs. Therefore, in figure 8.4 $C_{m/f}$ describes the transaction–organization costs (assumed identical) for one particular activity while B_m describes the excess of revenue over costs other than those described by C_m, i.e. for that particular market based activity. B_f is defined equivalently when the same activity is internalized (note that B_m may be above B_f). As we move around B_f (or B_m) the increased managerial activity results in increased revenues and/or lower production costs. Arguably such benefits would

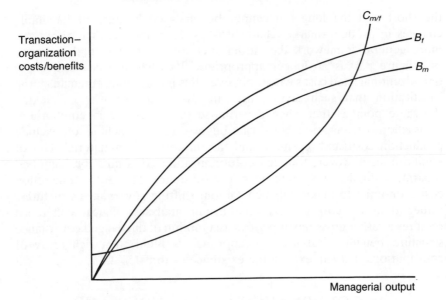

Figure 8.4   Governance structure benefits and the existence of firms.

occur at a diminishing rate; hence the concavity of the curves. At low levels of managerial effort increased input into any one contracting or organizational process will be at the expense of 'small' reductions in other activities. But given the convexity of organizational effort, successive additions to managerial input into any one activity will be more than countered by efficiency reductions elsewhere, thus dragging down gross profitability.

Using figure 8.4 we can now reinterpret transaction cost economics. Comparisons of governance structures based solely on transaction costs must assume unchanged product–market characteristics (i.e. organizational benefits) to avoid tautological reasoning. Unchanged benefits imply:

1 That the B_f and B_m curves coincide.
2 That comparisons of governance structures must occur at a given level of management effort. In the latter changes, organizational benefits change by a movement around the curve(s).

Points 1 and 2 indicate the strict conditions upon which transaction cost economics must be based. These (implicit) assumptions imply that transaction cost economics is an organizational comparative static general equilibrium framework. In short, governance structure dynamics in both the short and the long run cannot be analysed because of inevitable changes in product–market characteristics. It is obvious that within this more general framework the earlier mentioned 'fundamental theorem' (see figure 8.3) is no longer appropriate. Its relevance is restricted to organizational fixed cost savings, but even this ignores long-run managerial substitution that such savings may involve. Another way of making the same point is that when governance structures are in equilibrium, transaction–organization costs can be assessed to include or exclude production costs and revenues, and the difference is immaterial. Out of equilibrium, however, transaction–organization costs must be identified separately for the analysis to have any substance. Hence for transaction cost economics to make statements about shifting governance structures, rather than *ex post* general equilibrium analyses, logical coherence requires a rather gross *ceteris paribus* assumption of unchanged governance structure benefits. But such an approach is blind to a rich array of contributions that can explain the existence of firms.

3   GOVERNANCE STRUCTURES AND REVENUE GENERATION

It is clear from figure 8.4 that while the buying in of the service in question is possible because B_f lies above C_f (in part), greater returns will be derivable from internalization. The greater returns are not due to transaction cost savings but rather to increased benefits. In general terms, this difference between B_f and B_m will be a function of two factors: skill idiosyncracy and the exploitation of monopoly advantages.[4] These two factors will be discussed in turn.

3.1   Governance Structures and Skill Idiosyncracy

The extent of skill idiosyncracy is related to the nature of knowledge. Knowledge can be described on a continuum from transferable to embedded (Badaracco, 1991). The former is characterized in terms of being readily codifiable and consequently communicable. Embedded knowledge is based on social relationships. Equivalently, Michael Polanyi (1967) suggests that knowledge is idiosyncratic and tacit when it cannot be fully expressed and codified. Such knowledge, however, may be shared to a significant degree by individuals who have a common experience. Similarly, Nelson and Winter (1982) stress the importance of skills that are developed through continued use in stable conditions.

In effect, expertise or embedded–tacit knowledge represents a sunk cost for a firm. For new skill development the extent of this cost depends on the complexity of the skill(s) and the similarity with the current knowledge base of the individual(s) concerned. Therefore the feasibility of skill development is a function of the costs involved and competitive pressures that might limit the time available for acquisition. It follows that when knowledge and skills are idiosyncratic, or embedded–tacit, net revenues and profitability are higher with in-house use rather than market-based activity. More generally, rents from asset use cannot be readily obtained by sale of its service(s), and therefore profitable exploitation must involve direct use. Richardson (1972) has developed an equivalent argument when he suggests that a firm will group activities based on a common body of skills or expertise. Activities that are necessary but outside this core will be bought in.

An example may be useful to illuminate this argument. A manufacturer of computer-aided engineering equipment can either contract out fitting and installation or use in-house employees. An advantage of internalization is that higher quality standards can be more easily achieved and maintained. If the fitting of the equipment is externalized the labour force used need not possess the specific skills required, as the contractors may work for a number of companies. Higher quality has obvious market benefits in terms of extra turnover. In addition, benefits may exist in terms of promoting the company as a high quality supplier. If effective, this product differentiation can result in a higher mark-up of price over cost. Such monopoly benefits will be discussed below.

The relatively greater profitability of internal organization involved with this example results from extra net revenues; contracting–organization costs may or may not differ. The complexity of these various effects is alluded to by Williamson when he discusses vertical integration between producers and distributors:

> The normal presumption that exchange between producers of differentiated goods and distribution stages will be efficiently mediated by autonomous contracting is progressively weakened as demand externalities increase . . .
> The externalities of concern are those that arise in conjunction with the *unintended* debasement of quality for a branded good or service, for instance when one retailer's poor service in installation or repair injures a product's reputation for performance and limits the sales of other retailers. When contractual safeguards are too costly transactions become internalized with a firm. (Williamson, 1981, pp. 1549–50, emphasis added)

Clearly benefit as well as cost factors are involved in Williamson's example. In addition, given the existence of the debasement-of-quality problem, both greater contractual safeguards and internalization will involve higher transaction–organization costs. These complexities can only be ignored by assuming complete, *ex ante* recognition of all contracting–organizational contingencies, which is clearly inconsistent with Williamson's approach. Furthermore, the overhead and other costs of internal organization may imply higher transaction–organization costs that are more than countered by the greater benefits derivable. In short, the sole attention given to *ex post* relative governance structure costs, as in the last sentence of the above quotation, is incomplete given the reasoning upon which it is based. This discussion raises matters that will be taken up again later. For the moment two issues will be considered: how transaction cost theorists ignore the possibility of differential benefits, and the relative importance of cost and benefit factors.

The Williamsonian tradition fails to acknowledge the issues raised here for two reasons. First, it is clear that the benefits discussed only exist if bounded rationality is evident. This concept is based on the idea that individuals have limited computational capacity (Simon, 1957, 1965), which in turn implies that any non-trivial problem is too complex to be understood in its entirety. Note that this is different from standard uncertainty, which exists when cause–effect relationships and consequently possible outcomes can be understood, as defined by existing information, but objective probabilities of occurrence cannot be specified because of the novelty of events. In the absense of complexity, all available information can be used in its entirety, which implies unproblematic, if limited, understanding of reality. In such a situation disagreements are based on different information input and the beliefs this engenders. With complexity, however, individuals must make sense of their world; hence differences of understanding, even with identical information, can exist.

Arguably Williamson, while claiming to use bounded rationality in his analysis, does so in an incomplete way that accommodates standard uncertainty but not complexity. The following quotations are illustrative:

> Consider . . . the situation where . . . opportunism is assumed to be absent, which implies that the word of an agent is as good as his bond. Although gaps will appear in these contracts, because of bounded rationality, they do not pose execution hazards if the parties take recourse to a self-enforcing general clause. Each party to the contract simply pledges at the outset to execute the contract efficiently (in a joint profit-maximizing manner) and to seek only fair returns at contract renewal intervals. Strategic behavior is thereby denied. (Williamson, 1985, p. 31)

> Plainly, were it not for opportunism, all behavior could be rule governed. This need not, moreover, require comprehensive preplanning. Unanticipated events could be dealt with by general rules, whereby the parties agree to be bound by actions of a joint profit-maximizing kind. Thus problems during contract execution could be avoided by *ex ante* insistence upon a general clause of the following kind: I agree candidly to disclose all relevant information and thereafter to propose and cooperate in joint profit-maximizing courses of action. (Williamson, 1985, p. 4)

In the first quotation bounded rationality is recognized, but reference is made to joint maximizing behaviour. But given complexity, there is no reason to assume that individual perceptions and objectives will allow the definition of a unique maximizing strategy. Similarly, it is claimed that only fair returns will be demanded. But how can objectively fair returns be defined when bounded rationality exists? In the second quotation the general clause refers to the disclosure of all relevant information and maximizing behaviour. Once again: where is bounded rationality?

The implication of these comments is clear. Bounded rationality is used in a way that is not consistent with its original meaning, with the result that the analysis can be chanelled in directions that preclude recognizing organizational benefits that are based on, among other things, limited ability to disclose information. But even if bounded rationality is used in ways consistent with its original meaning it is always possible to assume that organizational benefits do not exist. Consider the following passage, in which Williamson discusses different forms of work organization:

> The workers employed under each mode [of organization] are a random sample of the technically qualified population of which they are a part. . . . Thus although certain work modes may be competitively viable if they are staffed with workers with *special* attributes, that is foreclosed by . . . [this] stipulation wherein all modes are assessed with respect to a common work-force. (Williamson, 1985, pp. 214–15, emphasis in original)

This constraining of the analysis is not limited to the Williamsonian transaction cost tradition. The equivalent, internalization, analysis of multinational companies suffers from the same problem, as is recognized by Cantwell (1991, p. 47): 'the benefits of internalization tend to be greater where each participating affiliate begins with strong ownership advantages, owing to the potential for economies of scope, technological complementarities, and so forth.' In addition, Cantwell claims: 'Even when considering [internalization and] oligopolistic interdependence in the form of an exchange of threats, Casson (1987) assumes constant long-run market shares, or in other words fixed and exogenous ownership advantages' (p. 49). Differential ownership advantages can be based on idiosyncratic organizational characteristics, and hence organizational benefits, that can only be ignored within a transaction cost framework if they are assumed fixed and exogenous.

Cantwell continues his discussion by suggesting a broadening of the internalization framework to accommodate an active role for managerial strategy rather than viewing the firm as a passive reactor to exogenous circumstances. This may appear a useful way of assessing the relative importance of cost and benefit factors. It is now recognized that effective strategic management systems must acknowledge the centrality of corporate culture (Johnson and Scholes, 1988) or idiosyncratic organizational characteristics. Furthermore, such characteristics are important discriminators of consistently good/bad performance (Peters and Waterman, 1982; Clutterbuck and Goldsmith, 1984; Whipp et al., 1989). Prahalad and Hamel (1990) claim that corporate success depends on what they call 'core competence', which is 'the collective learning in the organization, especially how to coordinate diverse production skills and integrate multiple streams of technologies . . . [and] it is also about the organization of work and the delivery of value' (p. 82). In other words, the development of a particular core competence implies internalization because the use of market-based relationships, and the resulting rupturing of internal networks, reduces the ability to deliver value. Contracting–organization costs have no part in this explanation. To this extent benefit factors may be correspondingly more important in explaining the development and evolution of governance structures.

While such a conclusion is suggestive, cost and benefit factors cannot be assessed in such a simple comparative way. Transaction–organization costs assume unchanged organizational characteristics and hence, as argued earlier, are comparative static. On the other hand benefits from idiosyncratic organization are dynamic because they describe differential abilities to adjust to, exploit and mould environmental developments in ways based on shifting internal comparative advantages. It follows that a simple comparison of static and dynamic factors involves a simultaneous use of differing perspectives. A consistent analysis might suggest that *given* a strategic orientation, efficient governance structures become relevant. But even this is an oversimplification because the analysis of business policy suggests that effective strategic management is a continuous process. Hence current expenditures should always be undertaken to develop future capabilities, and in this respect it is not obvious what (transaction) cost minimization means (Dietrich, 1990). From a static perspective some current expenditures are discretionary but still dynamically essential.

We can therefore draw the provisional conclusion that governance structures may be explained in transaction cost terms in situations that are intrinsically characterized by minimal strategic restructuring and/or when firms emphasize static efficiencies at the expense of dynamic opportunities. Alternatively we must accommodate the complexity that governance structures may develop for future, not just current, use. The latter possibility implies either using a standard intertemporal neoclassical optimizing framework with no bounded rationality, or subordinating transaction cost reasoning in ways suggested here. But this suggestion that transaction cost analysis is only appropriate in a static world is merely provisional, because the benefits of governance structures also involve monopoly power.

3.2 Governance Structures and Monopoly Power

A comparison of the Williamsonian and multinational company (internalization) transaction cost traditions indicates an interesting difference with regard to the analysis of monopoly power. Williamson (for example, 1985) recognizes the possibility but plays down its importance. On the other hand, internalization theorists (for example, Casson, 1985) recognize the centrality of monopoly power but collapse the analysis into a transaction cost framework. It will be suggested here that while the latter approach is an improvement on the former, problems are still evident.

The ability to collapse monopoly power into contracting efficiency is based on the (implicit) assumption of exogeneity of monopoly advantages. This means that transaction–organization costs redistribute given aggregate profits. The analysis is consequently centred on bargaining and policing issues between contracting parties over these aggregate returns – the appropriate organizational form being the one technically most efficient in terms of the bargaining and policing costs involved. Hence power is reduced to efficiency. What is not considered, however, is the possibility that different arrangements may endogenize monopoly advantages, as it is assumed that market imperfections are exogenous or natural (Yamin and Nixson, 1988). It follows that in a non-zero sum world the organizational problem is not just the distribution of given profits but the creation of greater profit potential. To put the same point another way: the existence and objectives of firms are non-separable (Pitelis, 1991).

Central to a more general analysis of governance structures and monopoly power is the organizational equivalent of the distinction between pecuniary and technical economies, a distinction that transaction cost theorists appear not to recognize.[5] Standard microeconomic theory defines pecuniary economies as those resulting from price changes; technical economies, on the other hand, derive from changes in input–output relationships. Transaction cost arguments are concerned with mutual advantages (Pareto improvements) that are derivable when particular governance structures reduce transaction costs, and hence (implicitly) only apply to technical gains.

To introduce the possibility of pecuniary advantage we must distinguish between *ex ante* (dynamic) and *ex post* (static) effects. The former accommodates the possibility of creative activity, with the resulting endogenization of transaction characteristics and, at least potentially, monopoly advantages. Therefore a pecuniary advantage is possible that represents a transfer between parties and hence does not involve mutual benefits. In terms of the framework set out above, pecuniary transfers represent a governance structure benefit for those in effective control of the transaction, rather than a cost. The ability to realize these (private) gains depends on relative monopoly power and bargaining ability. *Ex post*, i.e. when transaction characteristics are given, we return, at least in principle, to orthodox transaction cost analysis. But the same complications exist here as were suggested in the previous subsection. It is not analytically appropriate to separate dynamic and static factors. Hence, while the distinction between technical and pecuniary economies is clear in theory, in practice the two effects cannot be disentangled. It follows that a failure to integrate monopoly power into the analysis of governance structures is, at least potentially, a major problem. This shortcoming can be removed by concentrating on governance structure benefits as well as costs.

A useful place to develop these points is the much discussed transition from the putting-out system to the factory. This illustrates in a stark way a number of key issues of relevance here. The putting-out system existed as an important means of organizing production from the sixteenth to the eighteenth centuries (Salaman, 1981). Its basic characteristic was domestic-based production coordinated by a central entrepreneur. The latter provides finance, raw materials etc., and has claim over the output produced. The central advantage of this system, compared to the handicraft production that preceded it, was the possible development of a division of labour. But disadvantages were also evident. Embezzlement, cheating and quality control problems were endemic to putting-out, and in addition large inventories were required to absorb and adapt to change. Against this background Williamson (1980, 1985) suggests that putting-out gave way to the factory system because of the latter's superior efficiency properties in terms of transaction costs.

To analyse this claim we can start from the proposition that for embezzlement etc. to be feasible, rather than just a one-off theft, an information asymmetry must exist to the domestic workers' advantage. *Ex ante* the entrepreneur would have one of two possible solutions to this problem: first, to undertake closer monitoring of the domestic workers; second, to shift to factory-based production. Either of these strategies would involve a reduction in the information asymmetry that allows the embezzlement. It is clear, however, that the first possibility involves transaction–organization cost increases rather than savings. In terms of figure 8.4 the extra monitoring is shown by a movement around $C_{m/f}$. With the second possibility the organizational overheads necessary for the detailed control to reduce embezzlement and cheating are likely to have increased with the shift from putting-out to factory; hence, everything else being equal, combined transaction and organization costs will go up, not fall. It will be rational to incur these costs only if they are less than any extra revenues from being able to use the previously stolen materials. The real gain to the entrepreneur, of reducing the information asymmetry, is therefore a transfer from the domestic workers, who would clearly be worse off (Francis, 1983). The fact that the workers break contractual, or legal, obligations is irrelevant to this conclusion.

Everything else is not equal, however. *Ex post*, i.e. once the information asymmetry has been reduced to tolerable (for the entrepreneur) levels, transaction cost savings may be evident. For example, if we assume that the entrepreneur undertakes closer monitoring of domestic workers, a shift to a factory may involve savings in terms of inventory and quality control economies. This is a real gain because the same management output can be achieved with fewer resources: it follows that mutual financial gain is possible.

A number of conclusions may be drawn from this analysis. First, both costs and benefits of resource allocation will have increased with the shift from putting-out to factory, but the latter to a greater extent than the former. Second, transaction cost reasoning, by itself, is only relevant to the *ex post* situation when the embezzlement problem has been removed. In effect, this limited relevance implies that all contract construction and policing problems have been sucessfully resolved, which is only possible in a comparative static framework. If dynamic considerations are introduced, and shifts in governance structures analysed, bounded rationality renders this framework problematic for reasons already discussed.

The final conclusion that can be drawn from the above is central to the Williamsonian project. He argues that the evolution of governance structures responds to efficiency differences; questions of power are not relevant. But the distinction between technical contracting–organizational efficiency gains and transfers between parties is based on the distinction between efficiency and power. Consequently, Williamson's explanation of the demise of the putting-out system is incomplete. As Marglin (1974) suggests, this demise was based on the ability of capitalists to extract greater surpluses, which represent transfers from labour to capital, because of the augmented power of the latter. In a later work Marglin (1984) suggests that this power is derived from differential control, or a monopoly over knowledge of production activities. In more technical language, the factory shifted the basis of the information asymmetry between workers and entrepreneurs–capitalists in favour of the latter, thus facilitating the extraction of a latent surplus, i.e. greater benefits to capitalists. More generally, such intra-firm transfers are the result of senior management opportunism (Dow, 1987; Willman, 1983). This power differential hinges on the dependency of one party on another: it must not be possible to move away from a relationship that is working ·to one's disadvantage. Fitzroy and Kraft (1985, 1987) point out that the possession of firm-specific skills will impede labour market mobility and hence exacerbate this managerial opportunism problem because of the increased dependency of workers on the firm. Williamson's (1975) view that bilateral monopoly, resulting from workers developing firm-specific skills, only presents a problem for management because of worker opportunism consequently not only is one-sided, but also sidesteps this important link between the exercise of power and the development of governance structures.

The relevance of the issues raised here is not restricted to the rise of the factory system or intra-organizational bargaining. An illuminating example is that of the development of multinational corporations (MNCs). A unifying characteristic of the application of transaction cost theory to MNCs is the importance of proprietary knowledge (Casson, 1987), the reasoning being as follows. A firm may develop a new technology, monopoly returns to which are necessary to recover costs and hence allow future innovative activity. The central problem for the firm is that competition reduces rents because the marginal cost of using technology is lower than its development. A number of means exist to suppress competition (Casson 1979, 1985). A market-sharing agreement or cartel may be formed. A cartel has transaction cost advantages over an arm's length agreement, for example licensing, because the tangible organization means that there is no need to renegotiate contracts as if new when conditions change. On the other hand, cartel members have an incentive to free-ride, and hence policing costs are high. MNC development reduces these policing problems and is therefore reducible to transaction costs rather than monopoly power *per se*.

There would appear to be two problems with this subordination of monopoly power to transaction costs. First, it is possible to reverse the reasoning and claim that without the potential monopoly gain the differential transaction–organization costs would be irrelevant. In short the analysis of governance structures requires both costs and benefits: sole attention given to one of these factors is analytically meaningful only if the other factor is assumed constant, which as argued earlier is not the case. The second problem with the internalization reasoning is that it does not separate pecuniary and technical advantages. The possibility of cheating by cartel members is a pecuniary transfer to the free-rider's advantage. To counter this cheating (some) cartel members have an incentive to merge or undertake foreign direct investment. The advantages involved here, however, can only be obtained at the differential cost of controlling resource allocation internally rather than by cartel or licensing. It is by no means obvious why this cost difference should be negative when the overhead and running costs of international operations are recognized. In addition, if this organization cost difference is assumed to be always negative, why is this given more importance than the non-transaction cost pecuniary advantages of avoiding cheating?

An interesting asymmetry may exist here in that while internalization is explicable in terms of high organizational benefits because of monopoly power and secrecy, which require relatively high transaction–organization costs to allow their exploitation, licensing is likely to exploit lower transaction–organization costs when monopoly benefits are relatively unimportant. This conclusion is consistent with that of Davidson and McFetridge (1982) in their study of 1382 cases of technology transfer by 32 US MNCs. They found that licensing was increased the older was the technology, the more peripheral the innovation was to the core business, the smaller was the R&D investment, and the greater was the innovator's experience in international licensing. The first three of these factors are consistent with the low monopoly benefit and transaction–organization cost thesis. The final factor is consistent with the development of a body of idiosyncratic knowledge in the area of licensing, as discussed above. Hennart (1991, pp. 87–8) discusses Davidson and McFetridge's work and concludes that 'the choice between licensing and FDI can be explained by the relative efficiency of the market for knowledge'. Efficiency is interpreted in terms of transaction costs. The partial nature of such a conclusion is clear.

These two examples, the rise of the factory and MNC development, illustrate the connections between economic power and choice of governance structure. However, it is inappropriate to jump from the use of examples to any claim concerning the relative importance of power and efficiency. But in a way, posing the problem in terms of relative importance is vacuous because it misses the point that power effects are endemic (Yamin and Nixson, 1988).

Earlier, monopoly power was linked to the ability to effect pecuniary transfers from one party to another in a non-zero sum world. An equivalent perspective is provided by Malcolmson (1984). He suggests that questions of power can only be ignored in perfect markets. But this economic utopia is based on three factors: no barriers to entry to facilitate monopoly; universal equilibrium in the sense of general market clearing; and, ironically, no transaction costs. The previously discussed idiosyncratic and dynamic characteristics of firms are sufficient reason to question the appropriateness of the first two factors, and the relevance of the third is obvious. We are therefore left with the inevitable conclusion that questions of power are central to our understanding of governance structures, both inside and outside the firm. Furthermore, such effects coexist with efficiency reasoning. One way of conceptualizing this coexistence is to posit multiple organizational solutions, each with its own power–efficency characteristics. In static terms this collapses into an organizational equivalent of orthodox distribution–efficiency welfare analysis. But dynamically, particular governance structure characteristics will define developmental paths that are not reducible to a uni-dimensional efficiency reasoning[6] because of organizational benefits. In short, the evolution of governance structures is not neutral or inevitable.

4 CONCLUSION

This chapter has attempted to broaden the analysis of choice of governance structure to include the benefits involved as well as the costs. Benefits define, in general terms, the attributes of a transaction. If such attributes are not specified independently, transaction cost economics degenerates into a tautology whenever exchange facilitates changes in the units involved. It has been argued that such changes are endemic rather than the exception because of idiosyncratic firm advantages and monopoly power. The arguments presented have been developed in terms of the rationale for firms – in terms of figure 8.4, B_f was above B_m. This is arbitrary, and it is possible (see Dietrich, 1991) to turn the whole analysis on its head and examine the situation where B_m is greater than B_f. The nature of such a possibility is obvious: inability to replicate another firm's activity, contracting out to gain monopoly advantages etc.

So where does the analysis suggested here leave conventional transaction cost economics? The answer to such a question depends, to some extent, on the particular tradition we are considering. Efforts have been made to distinguish the Williamsonian perspective from that used to understand multinational development. The latter is more developed in its recognition of monopoly advantages. But ignoring such details, transaction cost reasoning in general is based on short-term, static economizing and exogenous or black-box governance structure benefits, and to this extent it would seem to be correct to place it in the neoclassical economics camp (Dietrich, 1990). To endogenize governance structure benefits involves a dynamic perspective that recognizes the importance of differential power. Arguably, dynamics and power are inseparable: nowhere is this more obvious than in the way Williamson (1975) side-steps these issues. Rational senior management behaviour is identified with orthodox profit maximization in his explanation of the transition from U-form to M-form organizational structures, and consequently only worker and middle-level management opportunism is considered relevant. If we move away from static profit maximization, however, and emphasize developmental dynamics, the attendant rationality norm is no longer appropriate and senior management opportunism, or more generally power considerations, become relevant. At root, what is involved here is a methodological difficulty. Orthodox microeconomics has been developed to understand the functioning of markets, for which read the price mechanism. In this analysis governance structures do not exist and are not relevant. But it does not follow that an adequate understanding of governance structures can be developed by simply adding to orthodox microeconomics. If this is done the resulting analysis is clearly a very special case: static and powerless.

NOTES

1   The arguments presented in this chapter focus on the existence and nature of the firm. Hence transaction cost perspectives on issues such as diversification and governance structures between markets and hierarchies (i.e. quasi-integration) are not discussed (see Dietrich, 1991, where some of these matters are addressed). In addition this latter article sets out a more formal presentation of the framework used here.

2   This presentation of the argument was suggested to the author by Marco Bellandi of the University of Florence, Italy.

3   A technical point is that in addition to the assumptions made in the text it simplifies presentation to assume that managerial and complementary non-human inputs occur in fixed proportions in the short run.

4   The analysis presented here is constrained within a monetary framework and hence the possibility of non-monetary benefits is ignored. One such benefit that would appear to be important is a desire for independence from intra-firm authority. Such a factor is potentially an even greater problem for transaction cost economics than the benefits suggested in the text because of its non-monetary nature.

5   An exception here in Hennart (1991). He suggests that the distinction between pecuniary and non-pecuniary externalities is important in explaining foreign direct investment (p. 84). But in the same chapter (pp. 96–8) he collapses both into a transaction cost framework.

6   Dietrich (1992) develops this argument in more detail, and draws out industrial policy implications, by suggesting that organizational dynamics generate path-dependent trajectories rather than self-equilibrating behaviour.

REFERENCES

Badaracco, J. L. Jr (1991) *The Knowledge Link*. Boston, MA: Harvard Business School Press.

Cantwell, J. (1991) A survey of theories of international production. In C. N. Pitelis and R. Sugden (eds), *The Nature of Transnational Firm*. London: Routledge.

Casson, M. (1979) *Alternatives to the Multinational Enterprise*. London: Macmillan.

Casson, M. (1985) Multinational monopolies and international cartels. In P. J. Buckley and M. Casson (eds), *The Economic Theory of the Multinational Enterprise: Selected Papers*. London: Macmillan.

Casson, M. (1987) *The Firm and the Market: Studies in Multinational Enterprise and the Scope of the Firm*. Oxford: Blackwell.

Clutterbuck, D. and Goldsmith, W. (1984) *The Winning Streak*. London: Weidenfeld and Nicholson.

Davidson, W. H. and McFetridge, D. (1982) International technology transactions and the theory of the firm. Working Paper No. 106, Amos Tuck School of Business Administration.

Dietrich, M. (1990) Corporate management and the economics of the firm. *British Review of Economic Issues*, 12(28), 21–35.

Dietrich, M. (1991) Firms, markets and transaction cost economics. *Scottish Journal of Political Economy*, 38(1), 41–57.

Dietrich, M. (1992) The foundations of industrial policy. In K. Cowling and R. Sugden (eds), *Current Issues in Industrial Economic Strategy*. Manchester: Manchester University Press.

Dow, G. K. (1987) The function of authority in transaction cost economics. *Journal of Economic Behaviour and Organization*, 8, 13–38.

Fitzroy, F. R. and Kraft, K. (1985) Unionization, wages and efficiency. *Kyklos*, 38, 537–54.

Fitzroy, F. R. and Kraft, K. (1987) Efficiency and internal organisation: works councils in West German firms. *Economica*, 54, 493–504.

Fourie, F. C. V. N. (1989) The nature of firms and markets: do transactions approaches help? *South African Journal of Economics*, 57(2), 142–160.

Francis, A. (1983) Markets and hierarchies: efficiency or domination? In A. Francis, J. Turk and P. Willman (eds), *Power Efficiency and Institutions*. London: Heinemann.

Hennart, J. F. (1991) The transaction cost theory of the multinational enterprise. In C. N. Pitelis and R. Sugden (eds), *The Nature of Transnational Firm*. London: Routledge.

Johnson, G. and Scholes, K. (1988) *Exploring Corporate Strategy*, 2nd edn. London: Prentice Hall.

Kay, N. M. (1984) *The Emergent Firm: Knowledge, Ignorance and Surprise in Economic Organisation*. London: Macmillan.

Kornai, J. (1971) *Anti-Equilibrium: on Economic Systems Theory and the Tasks of Research*. Amsterdam: North-Holland.

Leibenstein, H. (1966) Allocative efficiency vs 'X efficiency'. *American Economic Review*, 56, 392–415.

Malcolmson, J. M. (1984) Efficient labour organization: incentives, power and the transaction cost approach. In F. H. Stephen (ed.),

Firms, Organization and Labour. London: Macmillan.

Marglin, S. A. (1974) What do bosses do? The origins and functions of hierarchy in capitalist production, part I. *Review of Radical Political Economics*, 6(2), 60–112.

Marglin, S. A. (1984) Knowledge and power. In F. H. Stephen (ed.), *Firms, Organization and Labour*. London: Macmillan.

Marx, K. (1976) *Capital*, volume 1. Harmondsworth: Penguin.

Nelson, R. R. and Winter, S. G. (1982) *An Evolutionary Theory of Economic Change*. Harvard University Press.

Penrose, E. T. (1959) *The Theory of the Growth of the Firm*. Oxford: Basil Blackwell.

Peters, T. S. and Waterman, R. H. (1982) *In Search of Excellence*. New York: Harper and Row.

Pitelis, C. (1991) *Market and Non-market Hierarchies*: *Theory of Institutional Failure*. Oxford: Blackwell.

Polanyi, M. (1967) *The Tacit Dimension*. London: Routledge and Kegan Paul.

Prahalad, C. K. and Hamel, G. (1990) The core competence of the corporation. *Harvard Business Review*, May–June, 79–91.

Richardson, G. B. (1972) The organisation of industry. *Economic Journal*, 82, 883–96.

Salaman, G. (1981) *Class and the Corporation*. London: Fontana.

Simon, H. A. (1957) *Models of Man*. New York: John Wiley and Sons.

Simon, H. A. (1965) *Administrative Behaviour*, 2nd edn. London: Collier-Macmillan.

Whipp, R., Rosenfeld, R. and Pettigrew, A. (1989) Culture and competitiveness: evidence from two mature UK industries. *Journal of Management Studies*, 26(6), 561–85.

Williamson, O. E. (1975) *Markets and Hierarchies: Analysis and Antitrust Implications. A Study in the Economics of Internal Organization*. New York: Free Press.

Williamson, O. E. (1980) The organization of work. *Journal of Economic Behaviour and Organization*, 1, 5–38.

Williamson, O. E. (1981) The modern corporation: origins, evolution, attributes. *Journal of Economic Literature*, 19, 1537–68.

Williamson, O. E. (1985) *The Economic Institutions of Capitalism: Firms, Markets, Relational Contracting*. New York: The Free Press.

Willman, P. (1983) The organisational failures framework and industrial sociology. In A. Francis, J. Turk and P. Willman (eds), *Power, Efficiency and Institutions*. London: Heinemann.

Yamin, M. and Nixson, F. (1988) Transnational corporations and the control of restrictive business practices: theoretical issues and empirical evidence. *International Review of Applied Economics*, January.

9

Transaction Cost Economics and the State

1 INTRODUCTION

1.1 The Gap

Several important implications for the role of the state in the economy flow from transaction cost economics. Yet these implications have been largely ignored in the rapidly growing transaction cost literature. This chapter will identify the resulting gap in the literature and make a small contribution towards filling it. One chapter cannot do the whole job. The gap is too large. Nevertheless, the most important implications will be introduced in bare form, pointing the way for the many future works that need to be done, if the gap is to be filled. Of course, the gap may not be filled at all. Only time will tell if the apparent *laissez-faire* preconceptions of mainstream economics keep researchers away from the many decidedly non-*laissez-faire* implications of transaction cost economics, for that is where the gap has emerged.[1] This chapter addresses the gap in the form of four questions: (a) what is the role of the state in the institutionalization of exchange transactions? (b) What is the role of the state in the adjudication of disputes that arise from exchange transactions? (c) In the provision of public goods, should the state make or buy them? (d) What kind of 'state' should we choose to rely on for institutionalizing exchange transactions, adjudicating disputes and providing public goods?

DePaul University provided generous support. I thank Christos Pitelis for inviting me to contribute to this book and for making helpful comments on an earlier draft. I also wish to thank Oliver E. Williamson for his pathbreaking work in transaction cost economics, for he opened a path that I could follow, even though I have taken the path in a totally different direction and urge others to do the same. Needless to say, the views are my own: Pitelis, Williamson and my university should not be held liable.

Investigating these four questions leads to several decidedly non-*laissez-faire* conclusions. The state plays a determining role in the institutionalization of exchange transactions. The state's definitions and protections of property rights are essential to exchange. Furthermore, the state helps to establish, interpret and enforce a whole series of rules and procedures governing specific exchange processes. Applying transaction cost analysis to the provision of public goods seriously questions the efficiency of contracting out or privatization of public goods and services. In fact, in conceptualizing the role of the state, instead of being seen as intervening in the exchange process, the state should be seen as an important participant in the exchange process. The state is best seen as a transaction cost minimizer, not as an inefficient intervener. Furthermore, two kinds of state serve the role of transaction cost minimizer – the traditional nation state and the rising corporate state. The choice of which state to rely upon as a transaction cost minimizer in different situations is exceedingly important and is fraught with efficiency and equity implications.

1.2 Concepts Needed to Fill the Gap

To fill the gap in the transaction cost literature, three concepts from original institutionalism must be added to the corpus of the new institutionalism. The first concept is that of 'sovereignty', developed by John R. Commons (1924, 1934, 1950). Commons realized that *laissez-faire* was not possible in market economies. Instead, collective action exercised by some form of sovereignty was needed to establish property rights and to adjudicate disputes. Without sovereignty, the continuity of market transactions would break down. Sovereignty is collective action that defines rights, resolves disputes and monitors performance. The second concept is the interstitial nature of market exchange as understood by Thorstein Veblen (1904). Although he did not use the vocabulary of transaction cost economics, Veblen emphasized that the 'market' was a perilous place, plagued by sharp practices, non-performance and deceit. To Veblen, not just a select few types of market transactions involved high transaction costs. Instead, virtually all types of market transactions in a business system involved high transaction costs. The third concept is the evolutionary value of democratic participation as understood by contemporary, radical institutionalists (Tool, 1979, 1986; Dugger, 1989b; Dugger and Waller, 1992). They emphasize the evolutionary character of human relations – humans learn from their culture and adapt to their institutions. The radical institutionalists also emphasize the value of individual participation in a democratic society. If economic institutions are hierarchical in character, then humans will learn to give orders and to take them. But if economic institutions are participatory in character, then humans will learn to participate. Furthermore, if economic institutions are built on the assumptions that humans are lazy and pursue their self-interest with guile, then humans will learn how to shirk and deceive. But if economic institutions are built on the assumptions that humans enjoy work and pursue their self-interest with honesty, then humans will learn how to enjoy work and be honest.

1.3   Definition of the State

The traditional definition of the state comes from Max Weber, who defines it as 'a human community that (successfully) claims the *monopoly of the legitimate use of physical force* within a given territory' (Weber, 1946, p. 78). In economics, particularly transaction cost economics, this definition is unduly narrow. It excludes the fact that firms frequently act like states, not in the exercise of violence but in the exercise of sovereignty none the less. Individual entrepreneurs exercise little sovereignty in their own small firms. But large corporations, particularly multinational ones, can become so powerful that they do exercise power that rivals the sovereignty of the traditional nation state.

Such multinational corporate 'firms' establish 'governance structures' that define rights, resolve disputes and monitor performance.[2] The corporate firm as a 'governance structure' exercises sovereignty, even though it does not claim a monopoly on the use of physical force. For the purpose of explaining economic behaviour, the state is best defined as an agent that exercises sovereignty. This allows us to understand the corporate firm as an alternative to the traditionally defined state. The corporate firm, to the extent it establishes a 'governance structure' that can define rights, settle disputes and monitor performance, truly is an alternative to the state because it truly exercises sovereignty. It exercises more than just authority. It is more than just a hierarchy. When it establishes a governance structure, it becomes a kind of state. So, in transaction cost economics we need to use a definition of the state that comes closer to actual economic practices and we need terms that reflect the fact that the corporate firm and the traditional state are alternative agents of sovereignty – alternative states, so to speak.

Since the traditional state and the large multinational corporation serve as alternative sources of sovereignty, I propose that we downplay the monopoly on violence aspect of the state and define the state as any agent that exercises sovereignty. Furthermore, I propose that we distinguish between the traditional state and the large multinational corporation by referring to the first as the nation state and to the second as the corporate state. This practice will recognize the fact that they both partake of 'stateness'. Doing so is in keeping with the realities of corporate capitalism at the end of the twentieth century.

None the less, the similarity of the nation state and the corporate state should not be taken too far. Both of them do exercise sovereignty. By that I mean they both possess and use authority to tell individuals what to do and to monitor how those individuals do what they are told. The commands of each are considered legitimate by the individuals commanded. Legitimacy gives their commands authority. But for each, authority goes only so far. Their realms are limited. This is because the two states compete for power, with each possessed of different strengths and weaknesses in their struggle to expand their realms. The nation state has the power to tax and to use violence. But the corporate state has the power to withhold information and to withdraw investments. The corporate state needs the security of tenure and the physical safety provided by the nation state. But the nation state needs the investment and the jobs provided by the corporate state. When violence is emphasized, the nation state seems possessed of overwhelming power, compared to the corporate state. But in their competition for power, the nation state is not always the victor, nor are its victories absolute and final, for the economic power of the corporate state makes it a serious and continuous contender. The corporate state is most effective in its competition with the nation state in societies where the nation state is ideologically denied the ability to own the means of production. The corporate state is also most effective when the nation state with which it contends is a small country with a weak economy, desperately in need of the corporate state's investments.

The two states also cooperate. The corporate state provides the nation state with jobs, investments and commodities, while the nation state provides the corporate state with subsidies, protections from economic competitors, security of tenure and an infrastructure that significantly improves corporate performance. That infrastructure is far more than a transportation and communication system. It includes a whole series of public goods and a whole series of laws, rights and procedures that not only facilitate but also establish exchange transactions.

The two states also collude. In my nation state, the United States, the cold war against the Soviet Union provided numerous opportunities for the military arm of the nation state to collude with corporate defence contractors in the use of tax revenues and in the use of police repression to both milk the taxpayers and silence them. Cold war collusion is a form of the more widespread 'corporatism'.

In their cooperation, collusion and competition, their sovereign realms overlap and intersect in fluid patterns of dominance, subservience, mutual benefit and mutual harm.[3] Their sovereignty is always relative, never absolute.

Sovereignty can be inside or outside. It can be exercised from within a dispute or from outside of a dispute. When exercised from within a dispute, the sovereign agent is a party to the dispute itself. When exercised from outside of a dispute, the sovereign agent is not a party to the dispute itself. For example, nation states exercise inside sovereignty *vis-à-vis* each other when the victor in a war dicates the terms of peace to the loser. Nation states exercise outside sovereignty when they settle a dispute between two corporations or between a corporation and a union. The difference between inside and outside sovereignty is important not only in questions of fairness but also in questions of power. The nation state's power *vis-à-vis* the corporate state is enhanced through the nation state's ability to serve as a source of outside sovereignty to the corporation. But the corporate state's power *vis-à-vis* other interests is enhanced by its ability to serve as a source of inside sovereignty in settling disputes with workers, shareholders and consumers.

2 INSTITUTIONALIZING EXCHANGE TRANSACTIONS

2.1 The Artificial Market

Now that the definitional underbrush has been cleared away and important concepts introduced, we can proceed to the important questions, the first one being: what is the role of the state (either the corporate state or the nation state) in the institutionalization of exchange transactions? When exchange transactions are institutionalized, they take place in 'the market'. Economists use the term 'market' much too freely, and almost never bother to explain what it means. A market is a particular institutionalized setting in which a series of exchange transactions take place. That setting provides the market transactors with the benefits of a uniform price, uniform weights and measures, established, public channels of physical exchange, and established, public routines for initiating, executing and adjudicating transactions.[4] Not all exchange transactions take place in markets. Many are isolated exchanges taking place outside 'the market'. Such exchanges are unique events fraught with risk and uncertainty for the transactors in that the exchanges take place without the benefits just mentioned. And that is why markets are established – so the transactors can enjoy these benefits by moving their isolated exchanges into a routinized structure of rules, information flows and secured expectations. When markets are established, who has the power to do so and how they exercise that power determine how the benefits of the market are to be shared by the market participants.

Markets are not natural, not spontaneous (Dugger, 1989a). This is true of even the most rudimentary feature of a market – a common price. The practice of negotiating and making public the uniform price of a market must be institutionalized. The uniform, public price of a market that economic theory takes for granted or assumes to be created by a mythical auctioneer is not a product of spontaneous generation but a product of institutional evolution. It is not natural. Instead, the secret price and the selective rebate are natural. To purge them from exchange transactions and thereby reap the benefit of a public, uniform price, a market must be institutionalized. It must be created by human action. A market is not a fact of nature. A market is a product of human artifice; a market is artificial. To enjoy all the benefits of the market, at least the following five features have to be institutionalized through collective action, through the work of sovereignty. Exactly how these features are institutionalized profoundly alters the distribution of benefits that the market can bestow.

2.2   Institutionalized Features of the Market

Property rights

Whether an exchange takes place in the market or not, before any kind of exchange can take place property rights must be established. Exchange is exchange of property rights. Without them, no exchange takes place. *Property rights are prior to exchange.* Property rights are the foundation of exchange. Property rights are sets of opportunities to use and/or to sell, the rights being recognized and protected by sovereignty. Without sovereignty, there are no property rights. Propery rights can be vested in an individual or in a collectivity. The property rights or sets of opportunities of one party are also the exposures of another party. My right of use or sale can expose you to harm. So the distribution of property rights between parties is a distribution of opportunities and exposures. And that distribution will give rise to disputes, since the party or parties exposed to my right to use or to sell will frequently object to my doing so. To secure my property rights, a sovereign agent must stand ready to protect my opportunity against your objection, or I must be a sovereign agent myself. If I am a sovereign agent – like the old British East India Company – and you are not, then unless I am economically irrational and choose not to pursue my own self-interest, the distribution and protection of property rights will benefit me over you. The way markets work and how the benefits of the market are shared are determined by the way property rights are defined, distributed and protected. Once it is established, the only thing natural about a market is an inevitable *laissez-faire* outcry from those who are benefiting the most from its operation, whenever those who are losing attempt to institute a rearrangement. Such outcries are repeated so many times that we are tempted to believe them. We are tempted to believe that the market should be left alone by the state, even though that would be impossible. Without the state, either the nation state or the corporate state, the property rights that make the market itself possible would not exist.

Just as there is nothing 'natural' about the market, there is nothing 'natural' about property rights either. They do not just come into existence spontaneously. Property rights are the evolving products of centuries of conflict, cooperation, collusion and competition. Throughout that evolution, the sovereignty of the state, either the nation state or the corporate state, has played the leading role of resolving conflict over property rights so that market transactors can get on with their transactions. The exercise of sovereignty keeps the conflict of interests over property rights from going too far; keeps them from destroying the cultural, procedural and legal bonds that hold us together into a going concern.[5]

Uniform price

In mainstream economic theory, a market is characterized by a uniform price and that price is set by a Walrasian auctioneer.[6] But in the actual markets established by human beings, specific channels of information are maintained so that the different market participants can enquire into the quantities being traded and the prices at which the trades take place. Elaborate and expensive networks of 'ticker tapes', price boards, electronic communications and other information channels are maintained for the differential benefit of the market participants. How the information channels work, who has access to them and under what terms access is obtained are all important issues that determine who benefits from timely information and who does not. Furthermore, elaborate rules are established and enforced regarding what is 'inside' information and what is not, who can trade on it and who cannot. The nature of the rules and the way in which they are enforced determine how the benefits of the market are distributed. Since these are all matters of considerable import to the market participants, considerable conflict arises over them. Disputes must be settled by sovereignty, by the exercise of power over the market. The power can be exercised by a party inside the market (a corporate state) or by a party outside the market (a nation state). If these matters are not settled, or are settled in a grossly unfair way, the market will break down as transactors take their trades elsewhere or cease trading.

Furthermore, the power required to settle these matters has little to do with the number of buyers or sellers in the market. The 'market power' referred to here is not a question of monopoly or oligopoly, it is a question of sovereignty.

Standards of weight and measure

The issues joined under this heading extend far beyond the definitions of an ounce, a litre, a foot or a metre. The issues include establishing and monitoring standards of truthful advertising and of truthful labelling, determining the extend of product liability, and even establishing and monitoring the nature of the medium of exchange – money. If we assume that economic agents pursue their self-interest with guile and with bounded rationality, then the power of sovereignty is needed to establish and monitor standards of advertising and labelling, lest advertising and labelling both degenerate into the art of lying. If we assume bounded rationality and self-interest with guile, then sovereignty must establish and enforce the extent of product liability, lest we be overwhelmed with disputes between dishonest buyers claiming harm and irresponsible sellers causing harm. The transaction cost economics of the consumer movement is a significant and vast area that has been largely neglected in the transaction cost literature. Last, and certainly not least, if we assume bounded rationality and self-interest with guile, then sovereignty must establish a uniform medium of exchange possessed of a stable or pre-dictable value. This involves banking legislation, currency reform and international agreement. Markets work most efficiently when the participants know not only what they are buying but also what they are paying.

Channels of physical exchange

The efficient physical movement of goods and information to and from the market is also essential. The great market cities – New York, London and many others – have always played a leading role in the provision of canals, ports, railways and airports to facilitate the physical movement of goods through their markets. Whether it be the movement of workers from home to factory or the movement of goods from buyer to seller, the transportation networks provided or subsidized by the municipal state and by the larger nation state have been crucial to the development of markets. Sovereignty in one form or another has also been crucial to the development of communications networks, the nervous system of the market. This is all obvious. Also obvious is the fact that a communication system and a transportation system are built in some specific place. But the obvious is often ignored in pure theory. Here is another theoretical field in which transaction cost analysis could be expanded considerably. The actual location of a new canal or railway is a subject of major conflict, since running it through one city and not another means considerable benefits for the first and possible ruin for the second. The resolution of such major conflicts regarding the location of essential market infrastructure generally requires the exercise of sovereignty, particularly when we assume that the interests involved in the conflicts will pursue their self-interest with guile and with bounded rationality.

Transaction routines

Market transactions take place within a network of institutionalized routines. Three sets of routines are involved: first, the transaction is initiated; second, it is executed; finally, if need arises, it is adjudicated. Considerable cost can be incurred at each stage, particularly if we assume that the transactors possess only bounded rationality and pursue their interest with guile. At each stage, routine is a powerful transaction cost economizer. The great stock exchanges would be lost without a whole supporting network of routines that have been evolving over many decades. Institutionalized routines reduce uncertainty and reduce the range of options that need to be considered. They push non-essential features into the background and bring essential features into focus. But institutionalized routines also reduce options and allocate opportunities. At the initiation stage of a transaction, routine can determine who is allowed to solicit a trade and who is not. At the execution stage, routine can determine how the trade is done and by whom. At the adjudication stage, routine can determine who adjudicates and how they do so. Since the exact form of a routine can bestow considerable benefit or harm on self-interested parties, and since routines are no longer routine if they are continually disputed, routines must be established, monitored and enforced by sovereignty. To gain the benefit of routine as a cost economizer, the disputes that arise over particular routines must be resolved before the conflict disrupts the routine itself. In other words, the institutionalized system of routines must be protected from too much conflict lest the system break down and the market participants lose the benefits of the routines.

   Markets, then, are elaborate social mechanisms that provide potential transactors with a whole series of institutionalized services. Markets are like public utilities. They represent a large fixed investment needed to provide essential services to members of the transacting public.

And markets must be institutionalized. They do not just 'exist'. Most importantly, the details about specific markets matter a great deal to the participants in those markets so they generate significant disputes. The nature and distribution of property rights are fundamental. Property rights are prior to exchange. But also important are the details regarding how information flows through the market, how standards of weight and measure are set, how and where physical flows of goods and information take place, and how the numerous routines of exchange are institutionalized. All of these details are established through the operation of sovereignty, either that of the nation state or that of the corporate state.

3 ADJUDICATING DISPUTES

3.1 Transaction Costs and Disputes Are Pervasive

The transaction cost literature brings out the costs and the risks of disputes arising when economic agents pursue their self-interest with bounded rationality and with guile. Such agents may fail to perform their side of a contract as expected, imposing significant costs on other agents and giving rise to disputes and to the need for dispute resolution. But only a few kinds of transactions and only a few kinds of costs have been investigated in any depth. The cost to an employer of employee guile (the principal–agent problem) and the cost to an intermediate buyer of supplier guile (the make or buy decision) have been emphasized in the literature while the costs of many other kinds of transactions have been largely neglected.

This neglect is unwarranted, for significant transaction cost is inherent in most transactions, not just in the few transactions that have been emphasized in the literature. Transactions are seldom instantaneous. Rather, they usually involve a sequence of events and performances. Most transactions involve significant risks of non-performance and of unexpected events. Most transactions begin with the buyer first paying the seller. Then, the seller delivers the commodity to the buyer. So, most transactions involve a first mover and a second mover. The second mover acquires an advantage over the first mover and can impose costs on the first mover, particularly if we assume self-interest with guile and bounded rationality. The importance of second mover advantage cannot be over-emphasized. Second mover advantage is present in *all* transactions involving a sequence of performances and events. Since instantaneous, mutual performance is rare, second mover advantage is ubiquitous, making transaction costs ubiquitous as well.

Transaction costs and transaction disputes are far more widespread than the existing literature indicates. So, too, is the need for dispute resolution. A market economy is a disputatious economy. To keep it running smoothly requires the frequent exercise of sovereignty. To emphasize the importance of sovereignty in a market economy, several second mover advantages will be discussed in the following section.

3.2 Second Mover Advantages

In labour transactions

Disputes over who will bear the costs and who will enjoy the benefits of second mover advantages strongly influence the nature of work in capitalist economies. But the disputes are very complex and the issues have been addressed more thoroughly in the Marxist literature than in the transaction cost literature.[7] Let me just sketch out a few of the issues that need to be addressed by transaction cost economics.

If the usual sequence of buying and selling took place in the labour transaction, the worker would have the second mover advantage. The corporate employer would be the first mover because the corporation would first buy the worker's time and the worker would then deliver her time to her employer. As the seller of a commodity, the worker acquires the second mover advantage. The worker can sell her time for the prevailing wage and then shirk her duties, using her second mover advantage and imposing the costs of inefficient performance on her employer. To protect itself, the first-moving corporate employer designs an elaborate managerial hierarchy for monitoring and motivating workers to perform efficiently. This is the usual scenario worked out in the transaction cost literature – the managerial hierarchy is necessary to monitor and motivate workers because workers pursue their self-interest with guile. They will act as free-riders whenever they can. Furthermore, their employer is possessed of limited knowledge about the lazy, deceitful workers it hires. But transaction cost economists seldom investigate an equally likely scenario in which workers develop systems (unions) of monitoring and motivating employers to perform as expected. In the labour contract, the assumption of self-interest with guile should be applied to the employer as well as the employee. The same holds for the assumption of bounded rationality. (See Dow's chapter in this volume.)

The corporate employer does not fully pay the worker *before* she does the work, as is the usual sequence of actions for a buyer and a seller. Instead, the corporate employer is far more sophisticated and powerful than the usual buyer of a commodity who pays first and takes delivery second, thus giving the second mover advantage to the seller. The sophisticated corporate employer designs the labour contract to ensure that workers receive their full pay only *after* they have been working for some time. Money is handed over after only a week or a month of work, but other forms of compensation are not paid so quickly. Some payments (pensions and health benefits) may be delayed for years. The delay gives the corporate employer a significant second mover advantage. It also creates considerable conflict with employees over pension funding and vesting, and over employment security.

Not only is compensation delayed, giving a second mover advantage to the employer, but the worker usually agrees to work before she really knows the actual conditions of the workplace and the intensity of the work itself. Once the actual conditions and intensity are learned on the job by the new worker, she has often already made a considerable investment in learning the skills needed by the job. What she must learn partakes heavily of employer-specific skills, skills that are not readily transferable to another employer. She makes a significant commitment to her employer before she fully learns the extent of her employer's commitment to her. Does her employer commit itself to providing a safe workplace? Does her employer commit itself to respecting the dignity of the worker? Does her employer expect her to behave in certain ways off the job, to hold certain beliefs and not others?[8] Finding out can be very costly to the employee. Furthermore, skimping on commitments to job safety, pension funding and employment security can be very profitable to the employer. If we assume the pursuit of self-interest with guile and bounded rationality, then we must analyse the extraordinary second mover advantages corporate employers have over their employees.

The disputes over second mover advantages that arise from labour contracts are so intense that centuries of conflict and sovereignty have yet to resolve the issues fully. Neither the inside sovereignty of the corporate state, with its ability to design the workplace and to monitor the worker, nor the outside sovereignty of the nation state, with its ability to establish labour relations boards and to enforce labour laws, have been sufficient to bring harmony to the basic labour contract. Such is the stuff of class conflict and while the Marxian economists have analysed it at length, the class conflict still awaits the full application of transaction cost economics.

In consumer transactions

The simple fact that consumers of finished goods usually pay for the goods before they use the goods usually gives the second mover advantage to the seller. (The same can also apply to sellers of consumer services.) If we assume self-interest with guile and bounded rationality, the basic consumer transaction becomes laden with transaction cost considerations. The disputes that arise in consumer transactions have fuelled the consumer movement, and have also resulted in the intensive and extensive use of sovereignty to settle the disputes. However, consumer transactions remain largely unexplored in the transaction cost literature.

The second mover advantage of the seller is compounded by the fact that the seller knows far more about the good or service being sold than the consumer. Consumers buy a wide range of sophisticated goods and services so they cannot invest the time in becoming technical experts in everything they buy. But the producer and seller are likely to be well-versed in the technical features of their commodity. This asymmetry of information and expertise is inherent to the consumer transaction. It is easier for the sellers to protect themselves against opportunistic buyers claiming harm than it is for the buyers to protect themselves against opportunistic sellers causing harm.

The transaction cost problems inherent in consumer transactions cry out for more adequate theoretical analysis.[9] That analysis has not yet been carried out, in part because most transaction cost analysis has been done with a generally favourable attitude towards the corporation. Consumer transaction problems cry out for the exercise of sovereignty – not the inside sovereignty of the corporate state, because it is an interested party in the transaction, but the outside sovereignty of the nation state, because it is not a party with a direct interest in the transaction. However, this is not the same thing as saying that the corporate state is corrupt and the nation state is above corruption. Neither state is inherently corrupt. But while the corporate state *inherently* has a direct interest in how consumer disputes with it are settled, the nation state has no such inherent interest. Therein lies the important difference between inside and outside sovereignty. Inside sovereignty has an inherent and direct interest in how disputes are settled. Inside sovereignty is a party to the dispute. Outside sovereignty has no inherent and direct interest because it is not a party to the dispute. (However, particularly with regard to labour disputes, the Marxist theory of the state vests the nation state with a direct interest. So in Marxism there is no outside sovereignty that can settle disputes arising from class conflict.)

In financial transactions

Second mover advantages are present in two basic kinds of financial transactions: first, in the sale of securities; second, in the managerial allocation of corporate investment funds.

Let me address the managerial allocation problem first. The separation of ownership from control, emphasized by Adolf A. Berle and Gardiner

C. Means (1968), creates the transaction cost problems involved in managerial allocation of corporate funds. Information impactedness and self-interest with guile rather than second mover advantages are the problems encountered in managerial allocation. Management, being separated from ownership, has far more information than ownership (corporate shareholders) about the profitability of alternative uses of corporate funds. But management, being separated from ownership and being assumed to pursue its self-interest with guile, will not necessarily allocate the corporation's funds to their most profitable uses. Instead, management may use the funds to pay itself or to invest in pet projects that benefit management more than ownership. In the transaction cost literature, most prominently in Oliver E. Williamson's works, this trans-action cost problem is resolved through the evolution of the conglomerate corporation (Williamson, 1975, pp. 40–9). Conglomerate corporations are able to mount successful take-over attacks on corporations beset with managerial misallocation. Once taken over, the miscreant management is subjected to the much more effective monitoring and prioritizing of conglomerate headquarters. Even assuming that conglomerates are successful in this fashion, a serious transaction problem still remains. Conglomerate management can monitor the management of subsidiary corporations, but who can monitor conglomerate management? Surely not the shareholders, for if the shareholders of the previously free-standing corporations could not monitor the managements of the free-standing firms, then the shareholders of the conglomerate will have even more difficulty monitoring the management of the vastly more complicated conglomerate. If the management of the formerly free-standing subsidiaries was not free from guile in pursuing its self-interest *vis-à-vis* the shareholders of the once free-standing subsidiaries, then there is no reason to believe that the management of the conglomerate will be free from guile in pursuing its self-interest *vis-à-vis* the con-glomerate shareholders. Conglomeration does not solve the capital allocation problem of managerial self-interest with guile. It merely shifts the problem up one extra level in the managerial hierarchy (Dugger, 1989c).

In addition to managerial misallocation of capital – largely a problem of the separation of ownership from control rather than of second mover advantage – a serious transaction cost problem arises in the sale of securities. This is a true problem of second mover advantage caused by the simple fact that an investor in securities must pay for the securities and then the seller of the securities delivers them. After the sale, the securities may or may not perform as the buyer was led to believe by the seller. After the seller has the money, performance is the buyer's problem. Assuming self-interest with guile and bounded rationality, the securities transaction becomes fraught with transaction cost implications. But virtually none of them has been explored in the literature of transaction cost economics. A young economist could make a name for herself by doing so.

4 PROVIDING PUBLIC GOODS: MAKE OR BUY?

4.1 Make or Buy in the Transaction Cost Literature

Should a corporation make or buy the various raw materials, components, and services needed in the manufacture and distribution of its products? Led by Oliver E. Williamson, this has been a central question in the transaction cost literature. Since monopoly and concentration are held in general public disfavour, public policy has generally presumed that various combinations and agreements between producers and distributors are not in the public interest. But in the transaction cost literature it is generally argued that such public policy is often in error. Economic integration and even concentration may minimize transaction costs. So integration and concentration should not be condemned out-of-hand as a means of monopolization, but should be reconsidered as a means of cost minimization.

I agree, but insist that the argument should go further. Although the transaction cost literature does not reflect it, the very same argument is true of government ownership of the means of production. Since socialism is held in general public disfavour in many places, public policy has generally presumed that various forms of government ownership and production of goods and services are not in the public interest. But in the transaction cost literature, it should be argued that such a public policy is often in error. The argument should be made, but is not. Particularly in the case of the production and distribution of public goods, government ownership and/or control over the means of production should be reconsidered as a means of minimizing transaction costs. Should the government, the nation state in this case, make public goods (or private goods as well) itself or buy them from outside suppliers? Which method would minimize transaction costs? The make or buy question facing the government is just as important, probably more so, as the make or buy question facing the firm. We err when we dismiss the efficiency possibilities of the government making its own public goods in the same way that we err when we dismiss the efficiency possibilities of the firm making its own components.

Transaction cost considerations in the make or buy question for the firm arise when we assume asset specificity, bounded rationality and self-interest with guile. These considerations can lead the firm to what Williamson refers to as a 'fundamental transformation' from buying to making needed components or services. They can also lead the government to the same 'fundamental transformation' from buying to making needed public goods. Asset specificity is called into play when an independent supplier needs to make a significant, long-term investment in an asset that has little value outside of producing the component or service that would be sold to the other firm. The buying firm might stop buying the component or service and start making the commodity itself. This would leave the supplier with a substantial loss on the specific asset it invested in to produce the component in the first place. Because of bounded rationality and self-interest with guile, getting the buying and supplying firms to agree to a mutually beneficial transaction would involve substantial transaction costs. If other cost considerations are not offsetting, the most efficient thing to do is let the buyer acquire the supplier or let the buyer begin making the component itself. The other cost considerations elaborated in the literature include possibly incurring extra governance costs, and possibly missing economies of scale and scope. Let us focus transaction cost economics on the government's own choice to make or buy goods and services.

4.2   National Defence

The USA has erred in its decision to buy its arms rather then make them. The current procedure apparently originated in the late 1930s when President Franklin Delano Roosevelt decided to contract out the rearmament of the USA.[10] Since then, spurred on by the cold war, defence contracting has become an extraordinarily large, profitable and influential industry. Seymour Melman (1974, 1983) explains that the subsidy-maximizing and cost-maximizing procedures of defence contracting have significantly reduced the productivity of US industry. The defence contract is heavily laden with transaction cost problems. It involves not only the problem of asset-specificity, but also high rewards for corruption. The nation state and its client states, in this case the US government and its allies, are the only customers for the output of the various defence contractors. So the defence contractors, if we assume self-interest with guile and bounded rationality (information impactedness in this case), have very strong motivation to corrupt and confuse their nation state customer. To supply arms to the government, the contractors make large, long-lived investments in assets with low values in alternative uses. So their asset specificity exposure makes it in their self-interest to get as much from the government as possible, before their contract runs out. They are also motivated to hide as much as they can of the technology they learn and the true nature of the costs they incur.

Defence contracting should be reconsidered in light of the principles of transaction cost economics. The reconsideration would change our views about the wisdom of buying national defence from private contractors.

4.3   Health Care

The government of the United Kingdom makes its own health care system. Applying transaction cost considerations to the health care make or buy decision might alter its decision or might reinforce its commitment to a public health system. So far we do not know, since transaction cost economics has largely ignored the health care question. In the United States the matter is far more complex. Except for native American Indians and military personnel and their dependents, the US government neither makes nor buys a health care system. Instead, the US government provides a modicum of health care insurance to select groups of its citizens – the old and the indigent. Provision of health care insurance rather than of health care itself compounds the transaction cost considerations of health care as a public good. Health care insurance involves the tangled problems of third party payment for services rendered to patients by physicians who charge on a fee for service basis. The patient goes to a physician, the physician performs a service and charges a fee, but an insurance company – the third party – pays most of the fee and the patient the rest. The patient is the party of the first part, the physician is the party of the second part, and the insurance fund is the party of the third part. In this tripartite muddle, the patient has little incentive to minimize fees and is hindered by bounded rationality and by information impactedness in choosing a physician. The physician has great incentive to maximize fees and services performed, and when the insurance fund refuses to pay the 'overcharges', the physician can blame the insurance fund for being unfairly parsimonious. Of course, the patient and the physician expect the insurance fund to pay for everything, but the insurance fund's incentives lie in the opposite course of action. So it would like to blame the physician for performing unnecessary or 'experimental' procedures on the hapless patient and then overcharging the fund. The patient does not know what to think. Has she been overcharged by the physician or underpaid by the fund? Were any of the services performed by the physician really needed in the first place? Surely, the muddle cries out for the application of transaction cost economics.

4.4   Education

In the United States, the government makes its own public educational system. At the college and university level, each of the 50 states funds and administers its own group of colleges and universities. Below the college level, each state is traditionally divided up into a large number of independent school districts. Each independent school district funds and administers its own set of schools running from kindergarten to grade 12. Each state also provides partial funding and partial oversight of the districts operating within the state. The federal government provides some partial funding and oversight as well, particularly in matters relating to racial desegregation. Students living in each district attend (school attendance is compulsory) schools in that district free of charge, except for minimal fees for various 'extra' services. Systems of private schools also operate at each level, but are usually not funded by the state and must charge significantly higher fees.[11]

The US educational system is not really a system at all. The different parts are not coordinated into a rational whole. Education in the United States is an immense collage of overlapping public school districts, state higher educational institutions, private schools, colleges and universities. The collage is overlaid with state funding and oversight, and with federal funding and oversight. The educational collage is beset with a number of controversies, including intense conflict over racial desegregation, the quality and content of instruction, and the proper roles of parents, teachers, students and various levels of administrators in the daily operation of the schools. For some years now, many conservatives and most economists have promoted educational vouchers as a way of dealing with the multitide of educational problems in the United States.

The challenges and the opportunities of applying transaction cost economics to the US educational collage are extraordinary. If we assume bounded rationality and self-interest with guile in education transactions, a voucher system will not solve many educational problems. For example, vouchers will not eliminate racism. On the contrary, vouchers may make it worse as the bounded rationality of parents lead them to choose schools that 'protect' their children from their irrational fears of racial 'contamination'. Vouchers will not improve the overall quality of instruction, since the bounded rationality of parents will have to confront directly the self-interest with guile of school teachers and school administrators. Presumably, with vouchers providing parents with the ability to choose which school their children will attend, vouchers would replace the oversight of state and federal educational officials. But then the teachers and administrators of each school will try to induce parents to send the parents' vouchered children to their own school. Schools will advertise and offer inducements to parents. Perhaps each child will be sent home with a free set of dinnerware. Parents will have to deal not only with the inherent information impactedness problem of the educational process itself, but also with the misleading information and irrelevant inducements provided by opportunistic educational entrepreneurs. Without the oversight of state and federal officials, the bounded rationality of the parents and the self-interest with guile of the teachers and administrators will work to the detriment of the educational interests of the students.

The make or buy decision facing the nation state in the provision of public or private goods is overripe for the application of transaction cost analysis. The provision of defence, health and education could all benefit from such an application. I have only scratched the surface and must move on.[12]

5 SOVEREIGHTY: WHAT KIND OF STATE SHOULD EXERCISE IT?

5.1   Sovereignty Defined in the Modern Context

The rise of the powerful multinational corporation has blurred the distinction between the public power of the nation state and the private power of the multinational corporation. Traditionally, the power of the nation state has been referred to as sovereignty, while the power of the corporation or firm has been referred to as something less. But with the corporation's power to form a 'governance structure', its power now rivals that of the nation state itself. So, the concept of sovereignty needs to be enlarged to include the authority exercised by the corporation's governance structure. Sovereignty is here defined as the collective authority to define rights, resolve disputes and monitor performance, whether that authority is exercised by a nation state or a by a corporate state.

5.2   Efficiency and the Sovereignty of the Corporate State

Since transactions of all sorts give rise to serious disputes, the need for sovereignty to resolve such disputes is far wider than the existing literature indicates. With the need for sovereignty so pervasive, the kind of sovereignty relied upon becomes important. Williamson investigates this question at length. He frames the question in terms of the legal centralism of the nation state versus the private orderings of the corporate state, judicial system versus corporate hierarchy (see Williamson, 1985, pp. 9–10, 20–2, 68–84, 164–9, 250–2). That is, he explains that disputes can be resolved either through the judicial system of the nation state or through innovative arrangements worked out by the corporate state disputants themselves. The arrangements worked out by the disputants involve either the use of complex and idiosyncratic forms of contracts between two corporate parties or the use of a corporate hierarchy to resolve the dispute by exercising its authority. Disputes resolved through idiosyncratic contract or through corporate hierarchy can be efficient, particularly when the dispute arises out of the complexities involved in real-life decisions involving the make or buy question. Williamson is displeased that the complex and idiosyncratic forms of contracts developed by the parties themselves are often overthrown by the judicial system as anti-competitive restraints of trade. Williamson argues that the judicial system frequently errs when it overthrows unusual corporate contracts because it suffers from an 'inhospitality tradition'. Following this tradition, the legally centralized courts do not consider the transaction cost efficiencies of unusual contracts. The courts just overthrow them as anti-competitive, even though the 'private' ordering arranged by such contracts may be efficient.

When two corporate disputants themselves resolve make or buy problems by having one buy out the other, the resulting combined corporate hierarchy acts as a governance structure. It resolves the dispute between the parties by exercising its sovereignty over them. Like the 'private' ordering contained in unusual contracts, the 'private' ordering arranged by a merger into one corporate hierarchy may be highly efficient. But again, Williamson points out that court systems frequently break up such governance structures on anti-trust grounds. Recently the US courts have become more open-minded about the 'private' ordering arranged by unusual contracts and about the 'private' ordering arranged by merging corporate hierarchies, but the 'inhospitality tradition' is apparently strongly ingrained in the judicial systems of the English-speaking countries (Williamson, 1985). And Williamson has pointed out quite clearly the potential efficiency losses caused by the tradition.

Williamson's statement of the sovereignty question in terms of legal centralism versus decentralized 'private' ordering is useful, but unduly narrow. It is useful because it demonstrates the potentially efficient nature of 'private' ordering – either the ordering arranged by merging the disputants into one corporate hierarchy or the ordering arranged by drafting unusual contracts. However, examining the sovereignty question in this way unduly narrows the enquiry because far more is involved than the potential efficiency of decentralized 'private' ordering versus the potential inefficiency of centralized legal ordering. First of all, orderings arranged by corporate mergers are not really 'private' in the sense that they do not involve any public costs or public benefits. Corporate mergers are riddled with issues of public cost and public benefit. Orderings arranged by unusual corporate contracts are not really 'private' either because they too are riddled with issues of public cost and public benefit.

Second, Williamson's statement of the sovereignty question is unduly narrow because the sovereignty question also involves the potential inequity of relying on inside sovereignty versus the potential equity of relying on outside sovereignty. Private ordering relies on inside sovereignty to resolve disputes, while legal centralism relies on outside sovereignty. The likelihood that inside sovereignty will resolve disputes equitably for both parties to the dispute is far lower than the likelihood that outside sovereignty will do so. After all, if one of the inside parties to a dispute is powerful enough to exercise sovereignty in the dispute, then that party will use its sovereignty to further its own interests at the expense of the weaker, either by buying out the other party or by writing a complex contract damaging to the other party. After all, we are not assuming the perfect world of general equilibrium theory here. We are assuming self-interest with guile and bounded rationality. These assumptions should make us very sensitive to the equity dimension of inside sovereignty. The interests of the weaker party involved in a private ordering are strongly at risk. And private orderings will always involve a weaker party because, if the parties to a dispute are of equal power, neither one will be able to exercise the sovereignty needed to institutionalize a private ordering. Private orderings inherently involve a stronger and a weaker party.

5.3 Efficiency, Equity and the Outside Sovereignty of the Nation State

Private orderings are products of inside sovereignty. While a particular private ordering may be efficient for the interests that count when the ordering is established, the private ordering may or may not be efficient for the public interest. The public interest will not be considered by the private ordering, unless the public interest is represented by a party to the ordering. This is really another way of saying that a private ordering designed and enforced by inside sovereignty is unlikely to be equitable. But it is also a way of saying that arrangements made to promote efficiency are made to promote the efficient operation of the parties making the arrangements, not to promote the efficient operation of outside parties.

In transaction cost economics, we assume that parties pursue their *own* self-interest, not that of outside parties. A private ordering is efficient, but only to the private interests that count. Which interests should count?

That is a question of equity. But how the equity question is answered also affects the efficiency question. Equity and efficiency are inherently connected. They cannot be separated. Efficiency depends on whose interests are made to count in a particular arrangement. And whose interests are made to count in a particular arrangement is a question of equity.[13] Private orderings, then, are likely to be not only inequitable, but also inefficient when all interests are considered. If the interests of the inside parties to the ordering are in conflict with the interests of the outside parties, the private ordering will be inefficient with respect to the outside parties because their interests did not count in the private ordering.

5.4   The Higher Efficiency

Private orderings posses efficiency potential with respect to the private interests they serve. They serve the *lower efficiency*, efficiency with respect to the private interests of the parties to the ordering. This is efficiency in a local sense. It is the lower efficiency of the Coase theorem (Klein, 1984).[14] But there is also a *higher efficiency*, efficiency with respect to all of the interests in an ordering, whether or not those interests are parties to the agreement that establishes the ordering. This is efficiency in a global sense. The lower efficiency is the efficiency of private interest. But the higher efficiency is the efficiency of all interests affected by an ordering. With external costs and benefits not easily represented by parties to private orderings (who represents unborn generations?), the private orderings of inside sovereignty possess efficiency potential with respect to the lower efficiency only. Inside sovereignty can achieve the lower efficiency. But outside sovereignty is required for the higher efficiency. If the self-interests of parties to a private ordering conflict with the interests of the public, the private ordering possesses efficiency potential only with respect to the private interest, not with respect to the public interest. The logic and the assumptions of trans-action cost economics force us to conclude that the efficiency potentials of private orderings are lower than the efficiency potentials of public orderings. Because we assume that the parties to private orderings pursue their *own* self-interests with guile and with bounded rationality, the agreements they reach cannot be assumed to be efficient with respect to any interests other than their own. Only if we assume that no external costs or benefits are involved in private orderings can we put private orderings on an efficiency par with public orderings. Only if we assume no external costs or benefits does the lower efficiency of private ordering coincide with the higher efficiency of public ordering. Only if we assume no external costs or benefits can we claim that the nation state should not become a party to the private orderings of the corporate state. The discovery and representation of those interests who will bear external costs or who will receive external benefits is an appropriate role for the nation state. In performing that role, the nation state defines, monitors and defends the public interest. Private interests cannot and will not do so.

Realism in assumptions is an important characteristic of transaction cost economics. To be realistic, we must not assume away external costs and benefits. Of course, we must not assume that the nation state can identify the public interest and represent it in private orderings. These are matters for further enquiry. But, on the other hand, we know that the corporate state serves its own self-interest and has no reason to identify and to represent the public interest. Helping the nation state to identify and represent the public interest in private orderings is a major challenge for transaction cost economics.

5.5   Democratic Participation and the Higher Efficiency

Helping the nation state to use its outside sovereignty to identify and represent the public interest in private orderings is an important goal for transaction cost economics. However, an even more important goal is to improve the processes through which private orderings are made. Two issues are involved: (a) including interests in private orderings that are normally excluded; (b) improving the quality of the parties involved in private orderings.

The first issue is a conscious recognition of the cumbersome and formal nature of the nation state's judicial system. The long arm of the nation state can reach into private orderings and improve them, but the arm comes with a heavy fist at the end. Government regulatory agencies and court systems are large bureaucracies. Their relative autonomy from the private interests involved in disputes can give them the needed impartiality, but their general rules and general staffs make it difficult for them to focus on the fine-grained details and nuances of private orderings. Rather than try to sort out the private and the public interests involved in private orderings after they have already been made, the long arm of the nation state would be better used if it ensured that all relevant interests counted in the original establishment of private orderings. A basic shortcoming of private orderings is that they often are based on an incomplete set of rights. Property rights are usually represented in private orderings, but community rights, worker rights, minority rights and environmental rights are frequently not. A basic redefining and enlarging of rights is needed so that the people and groups holding those rights can defend them in private orderings themselves.[15]

To improve the quality of the parties participating in private orderings means to re-examine the assumptions of transaction cost economics. We assume that individuals pursue their self-interest with guile and with bounded rationality. They will shirk and deceive. So, either private or public orderings are needed to minimize the transaction costs that result. But the orderings we create reinforce the original traits that we assume. If we take a long, evolutionary perspective, then individual traits and the orderings designed to control them do not reach a kind of stable, equilibrium balance with one offsetting the other. Instead, in evolutionary time, orderings and individual traits are involved in a process of cumulative causation in which one reinforces the other. So if our current economy began with private orderings designed to control opportunistic self-interest and bounded rationality, those original private orderings (hierarchical institutions) have made individuals more opportunistic and more bounded in their rationality as they adapted to arrangements that assumed individuals to be opportunistic and bounded. If people learn and adapt to the institutions of their culture, and those institutions assume them to be opportunistic and bounded, then as people learn to be more opportunistic and more bounded, the institutions that were originally designed to offset opportunism and bounded rationality must be tightened up. Institutional tightening up leads to further individual learning, which leads to more tightening up, in a cumulative spiral. Hierarchies teach us to shirk and to lie and as we learn, the hierarchies are tightened up, teaching us to become better shirkers and liars in order to avoid the tightening grip of the hierarchies we face.

From an evolutionary perspective, we are caught up in a vicious circle similar to the vicious circles of poverty and racism. In this case, it is a vicious circle of hierarchy. In the vicious circle of poverty, people are poor because they are unproductive and they are unproductive because they are so poor that they cannot invest in their own human capital. Starting out poor, their human capital deteriorates and as their human capital deteriorates, they become poorer. The poor cannot contract out of their poverty. Private physicians will not contract to care for the poor at reduced rates and at convenient locations because doing so is inefficient – to the interests that count. Commercial lenders will not lend to the poor at low interest rates and under favourable terms because doing so is inefficient – to the interests that count. Commercial insurers will not insure the poor at low premiums and under favourable terms because doing so is inefficient – to the interests that count. Corporate employers will not employ the poor at high wages and provide them with expensive on-the-job training because doing so is inefficient – to the interests that count. Private landlords will not rent to the poor at low rates and provide quality housing because doing so is inefficient – to the interests that count. In each case, the interests that count in the private ordering do not include the public interest. The private orderings serve the lower efficiency, not the higher efficiency. Private orderings and private contracts are a part of the poverty problem, so public re-ordering is required. Breaking out of the vicious circle of poverty requires collective action, guided by the nation state and by the search for higher efficiency.

The same thing is true for the vicious circle of racism. In the vicious circle of racism, one race starts out being despised by another race. The despised race will suffer from declining education and declining achievement levels in general. But the lower achievement levels will lead to them being despised even more. The more they are despised the lower their achievements are pushed down, and the lower their achievements are pushed down the more they are despised. The despised race cannot contract out of their predicament. The private orderings in which they are engaged are part of the problem. Given racism, the private orderings of a racist economy and society are efficient to the interests that count so there is no reason for those interests to change their arrangements. Racist orderings serve the lower efficiency and will be protected by inside sovereignty. But racist orderings do not serve the higher efficiency, so they must be changed by outside sovereignty.

Public policy exercised by the outside sovereignty of the nation state is needed to address not only the vicious circles of poverty and racism, but also the vicious circle of hierarchy. If, as workers, we start out in corporate hierarchies because we are assumed to be lazy and dishonest, then as we are monitored and bossed by those hierarchies, we learn passivity and irresponsibility. To avoid hierarchical manipulation – the speed up – we become lazy and dishonest. As we become truly lazy and dishonest, corporate hierarchies monitor and boss us even more rigidly. For the corporation, it is efficient to do so. And pursuit of that lower efficiency pushes us to resist even more resolutely with laziness and dishonesty. Hierarchy serves the lower efficiency. It is expedient to the interests that count. But it is not in the public interest for us to become irresponsible, grudgingly to yield control over our work lives to a private hierarchy and cumulatively to lose our capacity to participate in the decisions that shape our lives. After all, the fascists really could make the trains run on time. But they could not develop democratic societies. Neither can corporate hierarchies.

6 CONCLUSION

A wide gap exists in transaction cost economics. The state is a transaction cost minimizer, but its role lies largely unexplored. The following areas need attention. The sovereignty of the state is needed to institutionalize markets. Markets would not even exist without the property rights that are defined and protected by the state. Furthermore, the market is not spontaneous. The market is institutionalized. The transaction cost minimizing features that the market institutionalizes require the sovereignty of the state. Transaction costs are ubiquitous because disputes are ubiquitous, particularly those arising from second mover advantage. The sovereignty of the state is needed to resolve the disputes that arise from most transaction, not from just a few transactions. Transaction cost economics should be applied to the make or buy decisions of the nation state, as well as to the make or buy decisions of the corporate state, for both states are transaction cost minimizers. Neither the inhospitality tradition's aversion to unusual contracts and to corporate mergers nor the ideological aversion to socialism should blind us to this truth.

Although both the corporate state and the nation state are cost minimizers and therefore serve efficiency, the inside sovereignty of the corporate state serves the lower efficiency while the outside sovereignty of the nation state serves the higher efficiency. Which state we rely upon to minimize transaction costs makes a difference to efficiency, and to equity. It also makes a big difference to the direction in which our societies evolve in the future.

NOTES

1 Further discussion is in Dugger (1983, 1987, 1990).
2 The firm as a 'governance structure' is a theme that runs throughout Williamson (1985).
3 Further discussion is in Lindblom (1977).
4 My definition of a market is based on the actual practices of European city states as they struggled to create markets within the disintegration of feudalism. See Dugger (1992).
5 Further discussion is in Dugger (1980).
6 Further discussion of the market in economic theory is in Davis (1989) and Sawyer (this volume).
7 See Braverman (1974) and Marglin (1974). Williamson (1975) discusses the issues raised by Marglin.
8 For an analysis of the effects corporate employment has on employee beliefs, values and meanings, see Dugger (1989c).
9 An interesting early essay is Mitchell (1937).
10 A short description of the period is in Manchester (1974).
11 Further discussion of US education is in Bowles and Gintis (1976) and Katznelson and Weir (1985).
12 Transaction cost analysis also needs to be applied to a number of additional public goods, including the medium of exchange. For example, in a simple

market system that used a precious metal as its medium of exchange, the nation state typically bought gold or silver and minted it into coins for general use. The nation state frequently earned a small seigniorage for making the coins from bullion and for ensuring their purity and weight. In such simple systems, the nation state made the medium of exchange, thereby providing its market system with a valuable public good – a reliable medium of exchange. The make or buy decision of simple times has been transformed by the complexity of modern banking, finance and international relations. Now the question is whether to tie one's currency to a key currency or to let it float. Transaction cost considerations could be very important in such a decision, particularly since the danger of a dirty float is very real in a world of bounded rationality and self-interest with guile.

13 These issues are discussed at length by Samuels (1981).
14 Klein is an institutionalist and approaches the problem through the contrast between the 'lower' and the 'higher' efficiency. The neoclassical economist approaches the problem through the 'Coase theorem'. See Coase (1960) and also Liebhafsky (1973).
15 Further discussion is in Brown (1992).

REFERENCES

Berle, A. A. and Means, G. C. (1968) *The Modern Corporation and Private Property*, revised edn. New York: Harcourt, Brace and World.

Bowles, S. and Gintis, H. (1976) *Schooling in Capitalist America*. New York: Basic Books.

Braverman, H. (1974) *Labor and Monopoly Capital*. New York: Monthly Review Press.

Brown, D. (1992) The capitalist state as a terrain of rights: a radical institutionalist and post-Marxist convergence. In W. M. Dugger and W. T. Waller, Jr (eds), *The Stratified State*. Armonk, NY: M. E. Sharpe.

Coase, R. H. (1960) The problem of social cost. *Journal of Law and Economics*, 3, 1–44.

Commons, J. R. (1924) *Legal Foundations of Capitalism*. Madison: University of Wisconsin Press (1968).

Commons, J. R. (1934) *Institutional Economics*. Madison: University of Wisconsin Press (1961).

Commons, J. R. (1950) *The Economics of Collective Action*, edited by K. H. Parsons. Madison: University of Wisconsin Press.

Davis, J. B. (1989) Axiomatic general equilibrium theory and referentiality. *Journal of Post Keynesian Economics*, 11, 424–38.

Dugger, W. M. (1980) Property rights, law, and John R. Commons. *Review of Social Economy*, 38, 41–53.

Dugger, W. M. (1983) The transaction cost analysis of Oliver E. Williamson: a new synthesis? *Journal of Economic Issues*, 17, 95–114.

Dugger, W. M. (1987) Review of *The Economic Institutions of Capitalism*, by Oliver E. Williamson. *Journal of Economic Issues*, 21, 528–30.

Dugger, W. M. (1989a) Instituted process and enabling myth: the two faces of the market. *Journal of Economic Issues*, 23, 607–15.

Dugger, W. M. (ed.) (1989b) *Radical Institutionalism*. New York: Greenwood Press.

Dugger, W. M. (1989c) *Corporate Hegemony*. New York: Greenwood Press.

Dugger, W. M. (1990) The new institutionalism: new but not institutionalist. *Journal of Economic Issues*, 24, 423–31.

Dugger, W. M. (1992) An evolutionary theory of the state and the market. In W. M. Dugger and W. T. Waller, Jr (eds), *The Stratified State*. New York: M. E. Sharpe.

Dugger, W. M. and Waller, W. T. Jr (eds) (1992) *The Stratified State*. New York: M. E. Sharpe.

Katznelson, I. and Weir, M. (1985) *Schooling for All*. New York: Basic Books.

Klein, P. A. (1984) Institutionalist reflections on the role of the public sector. *Journal of Economic Issues*, 18, 45–68.

Liebhafsky, H. H. (1973) 'The problem of social cost' – an alternative approach. *Natural Resources Journal*, 13, 715–76.

Lindblom, C. E. (1977) *Politics and Markets*. New York: Basic Books.

Manchester, W. (1974) *The Glory and the Dream*. Boston and Toronto: Little, Brown and Company.

Marglin, S. (1974) What do bosses do? The origins and functions of hierarchy in capitalist production. *Review of Radical Political Economics*, 6, 33–60.

Melman, S. (1974) *The Permanent War Economy*. New York: Simon and Schuster.

Melman, S. (1983) *Profits without Production*. New York: Alfred A. Knopf.

Mitchell, W. C. (1950) The backward art of spending money. In *The Backward Art of Spending Money and Other Essays*. New York: Augustus M. Kelley, 3–19.

Samuels, W. J. (1981) Commentary: an economic perspective on the compensation problem. In W. J. Samuels and A. A. Schmid (eds), *Law and Economics: an Institutional Perspective*. London: Martinus Nijhoff, 188–209.

Samuels, W. J. and Schmid, A. A. (eds) (1981) *Law and Economics: an Institutional Perspective*. London: Martinus Nijhoff.

Tool, M. R. (1979) *The Discretionary Economy*. Santa Monica, CA: Goodyear.

Tool, M. R. (1986) *Essays in Social Value Theory*. Armonk, NY: M. E. Sharpe.

Veblen, T. (1904) *The Theory of Business Enterprise*. Clifton, NJ: Augustus M. Kelley (1975).

Weber, M. (1946) *From Max Weber*, translated and edited by H. H. Gerth and C. Wright Mills. New York: Oxford University Press.

Williamson, O. E. (1975) *Markets and Hierarchies*. New York: The Free Press.

Williamson, O. E. (1985) *The Economic Institutions of Capitalism*. New York: The Free Press.

10

Markets, Hierarchies and Markets Again

STEVE THOMPSON AND MIKE WRIGHT

1 INTRODUCTION

Since the publication of Williamson's *Markets and Hierarchies* in 1975, considerable attention has been devoted to the internalization of activities previously carried out by market transactions. The markets and hierarchies approach and subsequent work by Williamson on governance structures (Williamson, 1979) has attempted to establish a framework for organizational choice. Much of the discussion in this literature has focused on the appropriate degree of decentralization within the given boundaries of the firm. The underlying assumption has essentially been that the development of a firm is uni-directional from markets to hierarchies. The reverse process of dismantling hierarchies and returning to some form of market relationship is either not considered at all or is assumed to take place in a symmetrical fashion to internalization. This is curious given that divisionalization should make divestment easier than would be the case in a firm organized as a U-form. Williamson (1985, 1986, 1987) touches on the divestment process but does not develop its implications. Recent developments in the market in corporate assets show that divestment has become a widespread international phenomenon. Such divestment may involve both deconglomerization and vertical or horizontal disintegration. Moreover, empirical evidence from a variety of approaches indicates that many firms find it difficult to adopt, and maintain over long periods, an organizational form appropriate to their changing opportunity sets. This means that internal markets in capital and labour and internal trading relationships may not operate satisfactorily. This chapter analyses the problems of internalization and considers when divestment (externalization) may be appropriate and the factors that influence whether or not it will occur.

The chapter is structured as follows. Section 2 analyses problems with internalization that may provide the rationale for divestment and deals in turn with problems in internal capital and labour markets and in internal trading relationships. Section 3 analyses whether or not managers will divest when circumstances indicate that they should. Section 4 considers the extent, direction and nature of divestment, and particularly the relative merits of sale to inside (a management buy-out) or outside purchasers. Section 5 covers the impact of divestment on both the selling firm and on the firm that is divested.

2 INTERNALIZATION PROBLEMS AND THE RATIONALE FOR DIVESTMENT[1]

The internal structure of the firm plays an important role in checking opportunistic behaviour by managers (e.g. Williamson, 1975). The creation of a multi-divisional form of organization, characterized by a decomposition of the firm into a strategic headquarters and profit accountable divisions, may be an important hierarchical means of dealing with internal control problems. The operation of a multi-divisional firm ought to reduce the propensity for managerial pursuit of non-profit goals. The headquarters staff constitute a relatively small part of the whole firm, while divisional managers, whose promotions and remuneration depend on divisional performance, have lower incentives to misdirect resources. Internal capital and labour markets are integral elements of the multi-divisional firm. In the strict multi-divisional form of organization, divisions compete for investment funds, with the head office overseeing this process. The existence of an internal labour market ought to permit better-informed recruitment to senior positions, and the possibility of internal promotion and enhanced job security ought to encourage employee commitment to the organization.

A substantial number of studies have tended to support the argument that large complex firms organized into the multi-divisional form have greater efficiency and higher performance than those which are not organized in this way (see Cable, 1988, for a review of the studies). However, there is also strong evidence that many firms apparently organized on a strict multi-divisional basis do not meet the necessary conditions on resource allocation and incentives (Williamson and Bhargava, 1972; Hill, 1985). Moreover, it is also clear that many firms which are not organized along strict multi-divisional lines fail to move in this direction even though it may appear appropriate to do so.

2.1 Problems with Internal Capital and Labour Markets

Even in those firms with a semblance of a multi-divisional structure, investment funds may not be allocated on the basis of rates of return but as a result of relative internal power relations or strategic planning based on non-profit maximizing objectives (Hill, 1984). The problem may be exacerbated by a shortage of internal investment funds provoked by profit crises. With capital rationing, some units may be designated as cash cows and deliberately starved of investment funds even though they have profitable investment opportunities. A further problem is that it is becoming clear that even in firms apparently organized on an M-form basis, investment appraisal is an important internal political process (see Thompson and Stephen, 1988, for a review). Investment proposals may be initiated at divisional level but require considerable central support if they are to be implemented. Correspondingly, if investments subsequently appear to have been unsuccessful, responsibility may be diffused throughout several levels of the organization. As such, the internal capital market of the conglomerate organization may be too forgiving in dealing with poor decisions.[2]

The functioning of an internal capital market may be hindered by the need to monitor an increasing number and diversity of operating divisions. The more, and more varied, the operating divisions that have to be overseen, the less able are head office staff to make use of specific knowledge for monitoring purposes (Wright, 1988). As a result, increased reliance may need to be placed upon standardized performance targets. With limited central office resources, it may not be possible to intervene directly to raise divisional performance when performance targets are not met.

Internal labour markets may also be problematical. The corollary of increased job security may be decreased responsibility and free-riding. The inability to write complete employment contracts raises the possibility of opportunism on the part of employees (Willman, 1982). Incomplete employment contracts give rise to the need for a monitoring function, a task which is made more difficult where inseparable input contributions are involved (Alchian and Demsetz, 1972). Senior management may not carry out this function satisfactorily. As Dugger (1983) has pointed out, the divisionalized form of organization may prevent opportunism in subsidiaries/divisions but the gains may be appropriated to the head office managers in the form of increased salaries rather than being passed on to shareholders. This is closely related to the whole problem of the divorce between ownership and control and introduces the notion of the agency costs of control (e.g. Fama and Jensen, 1983).

Divisional management, especially in the UK, has traditionally been salaried employees with little incentive to engage in profit-oriented activities. The spread of executive stock option schemes and of profit-related remuneration packages might have gone some way to reversing this problem (e.g. Bruce et al., 1990). However, there are key issues concerning the proportion of the total remuneration package that needs to be performance-related in order to motivate managers, the ability to reward individual performance, the danger of encouraging short-term performance to the detriment of longer-term prospects, and the exploitation by divisional managers of an advantage of informational asymmetry, which need to be dealt with. Large numbers of divisions give rise to a potential free-rider problem. Hence, although the incentive effects of equity-based remuneration packages may be significant for head office managers (Jensen and Murphy, 1990), this may be less true in respect of divisional managers.

The problem of adequately remunerating divisional management in order to encourage motivation may be most severe where managers are required to undertake non-routine tasks involving delicate judgements in an uncertain environment. It is unlikely that employees on fixed salaries or with inadequate performance-related remuneration will voluntarily make judgements that meet the interests of senior managers and shareholders. These problems may be particularly severe in respect of support services, such as computer services, market research, internal consultancy, etc. Such operations rely heavily upon the skills and expertise of incumbent employees. The conditions needed to exercise these skills properly and the remuneration required to give sufficient incentives to such employees may be at variance with the rest of the organization. This issue raises the problem of cultural differences between the different parts of a large firm.

Organizations tend to be governed by a specific set of codes and ways of adapting, which may transcend changes in personalities (Arrow, 1974). The existence of an informal distribution of organizational power that does not correspond to the formal organization chart may also heavily influence the way in which control takes place and how different skills are remunerated. This problem extends from potential difficulties in providing sufficient incentives for certain employees to the integration of new acquisitions. Notwithstanding the claims of Williamson (1990) that the M-form increases the ability of firms to digest acquisitions, the assimilation of a new acquisition may be difficult if not impossible where the corporate culture of the acquirer is incompatible with that of the acquired firm (Jones, 1985; Hunt et al., 1987). The nature of incompatibilities may become apparent only when the deal is consummated.

Demsetz (1988) also points out that the transaction cost approach of Williamson ignores important aspects of the capabilities of firms; that is, the problem that all firms can do things equally well. Merged firms, for example, may not be able to duplicate the sum of what independently standing firms can accomplish, not least because of the specific attributes of each firm, which cannot be altered or imitated easily. Prahalad and Hamel (1990) and Teece et al. (1990) provide further insights into the problems of internalization and why many firms which may meet the theoretical conditions for a multi-divisional form of organization do not move in this direction. The reasoning lies in the notion of the firm as a specific bundle of resources and mechanisms for adaptation and learning. The boundaries of the firm are not arrived at in a deterministic manner but rather are influenced by their different competences and capabilities. Hence, the learning systems in some firms may prevent them from adapting adequately. The problems may be exacerbated in dynamic markets by external pressures relating to new legislation, new suppliers, new products, technological change, new competitors, market growth and development, and threats to ownership from the market for corporate control. The difficulties are further compounded in dynamic markets as the 'value' of the firm's specific bundle of capabilities and competences becomes uncertain. Where a given firm adjusts to such new developments through either internal growth or acquisition, appropriate control systems and integration may not be achieved. Firms in any uncertain environment may be conceived as being engaged in constant process of search for a set of assets that fits their given competences (Cable, 1977). Success in such experimentation is a function of external factors and the firm's learning processes. Organizational change can thus be understood in part as a process of experimentation with various forms of management structures. As part of this process, subsidiaries may be acquired which are subsequently found not to fit with the parent firm's overall objectives. Poor fit may mean unsatisfactory performance, but it may also relate to mistakes in acquiring an entity that cannot economically be integrated into the group as a whole, partly because of cultural factors but also because of the relative size of the subsidiary, which impacts on control costs. It may, for example, require almost as much senior management time to control a relatively small subsidiary as it does a relatively large one. Hence, senior management may not consider it worthwhile to invest a disproportionate amount of effort in dealing with problems in smaller divisions (Duhaime and Baird, 1987). Williamson (1990) has also recently pointed out that divestment of an earlier acquisition does not necessarily signal failure, but rather that initial net gains have been exhausted.

2.2   Problems in Internal Trading Relationships

Following Williamson (1979) and Ouchi (1980), the degree of asset specificity and the frequency of transacting determine the broad characteristics of contracting arrangements or governance structures, and hence provide guidance as to whether a trading relationship might most appropriately be carried on within the boundaries of the firm or not. Idiosyncratic investments in physical or human capital and infrequent trading raise the hazards of becoming involved in an exchange relationship. A spot market transaction may be efficient where investments are non-specific and where there are large numbers of potential suppliers. Where recurrent transacting and specific assets are present, the parties may have a continuing relationship. Internal organization may be most appropriate for very idiosyncratic assets and knowledge, while recurrent transactions involving lesser degrees of asset specificity may be handled by bilateral governance or a managed market if a recognition of mutual dependence is sufficient to curb opportunism. Trilateral governance concerns an agreement to use third party arbitration in the event of a dispute involving infrequent but specific investments. These categorizations produce a range of contractual trading forms, from pure market to pure internalization via intermediate types. However, in themselves they may not be wholly efficient. For example, where a managed market is deemed appropriate because of the degree of specificity and frequency of transactions, managers in large organizations may not be motivated fully to behave in an efficient manner, nor may a firm finding itself 'wrongly' positioned, for historical reasons or owing to changed market circumstances, automatically shift to the 'correct' one. In a vertically integrated process, with intermediate activities protected from outside competition by ownership, more 'powerful' parts may be able to exploit others. Hence, although organization theory would suggest that control systems ought to be redesigned to reflect interdependencies, such relationships may be asymmetrical with consequent control problems. The problem may be further exacerbated as poor performance may be maintained as the parent acts as 'lender of last resort'.

It is important not to forget that the decision as to whether to trade internally or externally does not depend exclusively on transactions costs. The decision depends on a comparison of all the gains and losses that relate to internal versus external production (Demsetz, 1988). Demsetz also argues that, where asset specificity is high, the loss associated with contract failure is likely to be more important than the problems associated with increased costs of transacting. The key issue again becomes, as discussed in the previous section, how and whether organizations can select incentive systems that moderate incentive incompatibilities and alleviate monitoring problems, and so retain internal production, or whether production is better externalized.

The discussion can be extended to include multinational enterprises. The rationale for the internalization of transactions by firms operating in several countries is well known (e.g. Buckley and Casson, 1976; Teece,

1983). Foreign operations of multinational enterprises may relate to contracted-out production of final or intermediate goods or the distribution of goods and services manufactured by the parent in its home country. The control problems inherent in large complex organizations may be exacerbated in firms that are spread across several continents. Moreover, cultural differences between countries may create greater control problems in areas where trading relationships exist than is the case within one country. Geographic and cultural differences may exacerbate the difficulties faced by the parent in obtaining informational transparency in relation to foreign subsidiaries' true behaviour. Hence, in dynamic environments the costs of control from a great distance may be too high. Parent firms may decide to exit completely from a particular geographic area or may divest ownership but continue to trade.

3 WILL MANAGEMENT DIVEST?

While changes in an organization's environment may put pressures on management to correct mismatches in control systems or to adopt new ones, the adjustment process may be imperfect. A key issue relates to whether and when management will adopt divestment policies.

On a straightforward financial appraisal, externalization should occur when the present value of the proceeds from selling a division exceed the present value of the returns from retaining ownership. This calculation should include transactions costs arising from the transfer of ownership, imputed costs arising from the risk of loss of supply if the division is sold (in the case of a continued trading relationship) and the costs arising from the disruption to and the need for adaptation in the internal control system when the division is sold.

In the absence of congruence between managerial and owners' interests, managers cannot be relied upon to behave efficiently in their adoption of flexibility. As Mueller (1972) and Marris and Mueller (1980) have pointed out, managerially controlled firms may not divest as readily as those which are owner-controlled. Managers may be aware that the company's activities could be re-organized profitably, but they may be reluctant to make changes where they would bear the effort-costs but reap few rewards and hence have no incentive to undertake the changes.

Where a divorce exists between ownership and control, corporate management may resist sell-offs where they are perceived as an erosion of empire and where there is an absence of outside pressures to change through divestment. Miller (1982) has drawn a distinction between evolutionary and quantum changes and has suggested that organizational processes lead to the absorption of inefficiencies and that adaptation will be delayed until crisis conditions force change to occur. The common incrementalist approach to strategy may limit the extent of flexibility by the divestment route (Johnson, 1988). That is, in the absence of both pressures and incentives, managers may rely on notions of a traditional way of doing things.

Even under a managerialist regime, divestment may provide a basis for subsequent growth and senior management may wish to trade off the benefits of empire building against the problem of controlling large organizations. Evidence from buy-outs and hostile take-over bids suggests that there is a subset of firms with non-optimal modes of organization where, following a change in ownership, it is possible to remove over-large head offices without efficiency losses (e.g. Bhagat et al., 1990). The introduction of greater managerial equity shares, which closes the gap between principal and agent (i.e. the divorce between ownership and control), through for example stock option schemes, may be one means by which managers have greater incentives to divest. A second incentive may be provided by the increased threat of hostile take-over, including newer forms of acquisition such as leveraged buy-outs. The risk that under-performing managers may be removed after a hostile take-over may encourage them to attempt to maximize shareholder wealth in order to minimize the risks of being taken over (Jensen, 1986). Part of this process may involve firms selling off or spinning off unwanted subsidiaries and/or engaging in various forms of capital restructuring. The growth of an active secondary market in corporate assets is thus a crucial element of this process.[3] Moreover, the knowledge among incumbent management that a buy-out possibility exists may mean that the initiative comes from lower down the hierarchy than from senior management (e.g. Wright et al., 1992).

These arguments link closely to the managerial entrenchment hypothesis of Shleifer and Vishny (1989), who consider that managers divest assets in order to raise the distance between themselves and potential replacements. Managers will sell when a set of assets destroys shareholder wealth without increasing entrenchment. The model of managerial entrenchment proposed by Shleifer and Vishny (1989) indicates that firms divesting assets almost always raise their market value and so there is no loss of shareholder value. However, much seems to depend on what the managers actually do with the cash derived from the transaction. There are added complications of information asymmetry and conflicts of interest once the acquirer of a divested subsidiary has manager-shareholders who are currently employed by the target, as in a management buy-out. Leveraged buy-outs themselves may be followed by divestment as the new owners refocus the firm's spread of activities and use the proceeds of disposals to pay down the often substantial amount of borrowings required to fund the buy-out. While such divestments may mean the reversal of previous attempts at conglomeration, there is evidence to suggest that the buyers of such activities are frequently within closely related sectors, which raises questions about the eventual anti-trust impact of divestment actions (Bhagat et al., 1990).

4 THE EXTENT, DIRECTION AND NATURE OF DIVESTMENT

The ability of firms to adapt to changed circumstances may be constrained by various barriers to exit from existing activities (Harrigan and Porter, 1983). The strengthening of the secondary market in divested divisions and subsidiaries facilitates exit where ability to change the use to which specific assets may be put may be limited. A developed divestiture market both reduces the risks attached to making acquisitions among diversified companies, and hence ought to augment search processes, and enables internal control problems to be resolved.

The past decade has been marked, in the USA and UK at least, by an unprecedented level of divestment of subsidiaries and divisions by their parent groups. In the USA, studies by Duhaime and Grant (1984) and Ravenscraft and Scherer (1986), which addressed the strategic rationale behind divestments in the form of sell-offs, concluded that they were likely to involve more peripheral businesses and that it was unusual for divested units to have had a vertically integrated relationship with their parent group. Evidence from UK divestments by sell-off (Wright, 1988) indicates that about one-third had a horizontal relationship with the former parent, a fifth were unrelated, a tenth were related in a vertical manner, and the remainder were divestments by financial companies, breweries, hotels, etc. These figures are broadly supported by a subsequent study covering a later period and using the same methodology by Lye and Silbertson (1981). In respect of the financial services sector, recent evidence suggests extensive undoing of earlier diversification, partly as a result of the market's inability to sustain the level of new entry that took place and partly because of the control problems resulting from entry into new areas with different cultures and requiring different incentives and managerial styles (Wright et al., 1991a).[4] This point highlights the notion of search and the dynamic nature of firm's asset portfolios. US evidence by Porter (1987) shows that in the long term, on average, corporations divested more than half of their acquisitions in new fields, more than three-fifths of their acquisitions in entirely new fields and almost three-quarters of their acquisitions in unrelated areas. In respect of buy-outs, Wright (1988) showed that the majority had been owned for a small proportion of their lives by the divesting parent and that in a significant minority of cases parents also made acquisitions while undertaking divestment. There is thus some support for the view that buy-outs are unwanted parts of acquisitions, but also indications that they have arisen as a result of strategic shifts and control problems. Wright et al. (1991a) show that redefinition of core activities of the group was clearly the most important reason for sale, and that the main reasons why managers wished to buy related to desires to control one's own business and the benefits to be derived from removing head office restraints.

Given a decision to divest, vendor management needs to decide between various options as to who the purchaser might be. The possibilities include management buy-outs, management buy-ins, sell-offs to another group, spin-offs with significant retained ownership, asset swaps or equity carve-outs (Wright and Thompson, 1992). Some of these forms, particularly buy-outs and buy-ins, may only be possible with innovations in financial instruments, such as junk bonds and privately placed mezzanine finance, as well as various forms of quasi-equity to fund the transaction. These instruments introduce important new devices for controlling management behaviour. They introduce significant equity stakes to managers to give a positive incentive to perform and enhance control through the bonding function of debt, institutional board representation and the linking of managerial equity stakes to the meeting of predefined performance targets, so-called equity ratchets (Thompson and Wright, 1991; Jensen, 1989). Williamson (1988), using a transactions cost analysis, has also suggested that debt, equity and new forms of financing instruments, such as 'dequity', may be introduced as control devices (corporate governance), with the balance of debt and equity in the control instrument being influenced by the level of asset specificity. The more redeployable (non-specific) are assets the more financing should involve debt and corporate governance be rule-based; the more non-redeployable (specific) are assets the more financing should involve equity and corporate governance be open to discretion.[5]

The threat not to cooperate with an external purchaser may reinforce management's hand, as may its ability to control information relating to the subsidiary. Where there is a rationale for divesting activities with a trading relationship, a buy-out may offer attractions to the vendor in preference to sale to a competitor or to a supplier, especially where the former subsidiary is heavily dependent on its erstwhile parent (Wright, 1986). The evidence from two surveys covering the first half of the 1980s (Wright, 1986, Wright et al., 1991b), shows that almost two-fifths of buy-outs of divisions or subsidiaries sold their products and services to the former parent. Around one-quarter of buy-outs were found to purchase goods from their former parent. For the most part, these links accounted for a relatively small share of the buy-out's sales and purchases. In at least 10 per cent of cases in the earlier study and in 15 per cent of buy-outs in the later one, the parent accounted for at least 10 per cent of sales, with some buy-outs being very heavily dependent upon their former parent.

An element of retained ownership may enable the former parent as trading partner to influence post buy-out behaviour. Bought-out firms tend subsequently to reduce their dependence upon their former parents in order to avoid being squeezed by their more powerful trading partners (see below). The new relationship may not necessarily involve a pure spot market but may be some kind of managed-market relationship or network where there is a degree of asset specificity in the transaction (Starkey et al., 1991).

Assuming that a buy-out attempt possesses the basic characteristics required for viability, the position of management may be strengthened when the vendor has important non-financial objectives to satisfy. For example, a vendor may prefer sale to management when a local reputation could be damaged by sale to a potentially hostile third party; or the vendor may wish a speedy no-fuss sale. The position of incumbent management may be further strengthened when it is a significant part of the value of the entity (for example, in a service industry), and when there is an asymmetric distribution of information such that local management possesses information that is not available to either an outside party or to the vendor. In the former instance, the threat of a management walk-out or refusal to cooperate fully with a trade purchaser may reduce the price a vendor may expect to receive for the subsidiary as outside buyers, if they remain interested, think they will incur significant costs of replacement of executives and exerting control. In some cases managers may be able to use their market- or product-specific skills in establishing or joining a rival. Even where managers are apparently locked in by highly idiosyncratic and firm-specific skills, an implicit threat of mutually damaging exit may still be credible, since the potential external buyer cannot rule out non-pecuniary motives in human behaviour (Thompson and Wright, 1987). Of course, management needs to assess carefully the bargaining strength that its specific skills give it and, where the advantage is not great, to be wary of pursuing a buy-out attempt against an external bidder, since if it fails it may quickly be replaced. Evidence does lend support to the importance of human capital investments in influencing the insider/outsider sale outcome. For example, buy-outs are more likely to occur in profitable specialist niche sectors of otherwise declining sectors or in service areas where individual specific skills are important. In addition, managers involved in buy-outs, at least in the UK, tend to have spent a considerable proportion of their working lives with the firm they buy out (Wright and Coyne, 1985; Wright et al., 1992).

In the latter case, differences in information levels give rise to different subjective valuations that may benefit managers at the expense of both vendors and external bidders. Various price escalation and clawback mechanisms, such as equity retentions, tying final price to be paid to a future exit value or trading profits, may be used to protect the vendor's interests.

Where there are trading relationships between the vendor and the subsidiary, care may need to be taken in selling a subsidiary to either a competitor or a major supplier or customer. The attractions of reducing control costs and possibly gaining benefits from economies of scale and scope, which sale to a specialist producer might provide, may be offset by the possibility of a dominant supplier exploiting his position to charge a higher price. Sale to a management buy-out avoids these problems, as long as the bought-out company is more reliant upon the vendor than the vendor is upon its former subsidiary. That is, alternative suppliers must be available. Where a managed-market or quasi-vertical integration relationship is required by the relatively specialized nature of the product, managers who have bought out the entity have a stronger incentive to cooperate than may a potential trade buyer. The vendor may also exert pressure by requiring management to bid initially and at subsequent intervals for contracts separately from buying the assets of the business. Control may also be closely monitored through some form of a franchise contract, which replaces internal hierarchical management.[6] To these benefits may be added those which arise when former managers have a greater ownership incentive to perform, the greater pressure upon them to perform because of an increased bankruptcy threat, and the greater control likely to be exerted by the institutions that finance the buy-out.

5   POST-DIVESTMENT EFFECTS

This section examines the impact of divestment on both the vendor and the acquirer. The focus of attention is on cases where divestment involves sale to another group (a sell-off) and where it involves sale to a management buy-out. The section also provides evidence on the extent to which management and leveraged buy-outs of whole firms result in divestment and re-organization, which had not occurred under the previous ownership and management regime, and the effects on performance.

5.1 Sell-offs

Evidence in respect of sell-offs has focused mainly on event studies. Different reasons for divestment may be expected to produce varying impacts on shareholder wealth. Voluntary sell-offs or indeed spin-offs might be expected to result in an upward movement in the share price of the divestor as the action should have an expected positive net present value in comparison with retaining the activity. These results may be expected given the evidence that divested entities are often poor performers and peripheral to core interests (Harrigan, 1908; Duhaime and Grant, 1984). Studies of voluntary sell-offs generally show a positive effect on announcement. Montgomery et al. (1984) found that the reason for sale was more important than the act of sale itself. Sell-offs linked to clearly defined strategic decisions were valued positively by the market, while those that apparently involved the sale of unwanted assets without clear strategic goals were valued negatively. Divestments arising as a response to liquidity problems did not give rise to significant announcement effects. Sell-offs are thus seen as firm-specific events. Denning (1988) also shows that the effect of divestment is significantly related to the motivation behind it. Where loss-making operations are divested, management may achieve significantly positive effects on shareholder wealth. Where units are sold to managers, as a means of dealing with agency cost problems, positive but insignificant shareholder wealth improvements occur. Jain (1985), while confirming the positive effects, found that gains to buyers were smaller than those accruing to sellers. Although the buyer must expect to be able to manage the acquired entity better than the vendor, there is an element of asymmetric information which affects the buyer's perception of how much better he can do and which the market is taking account of. Analysis by Sicherman and Pettway (1987) found significant positive announcement effects for acquirers of divested assets that had product line relatedness and negative effects for the acquisition of unrelated divested assets. In addition, this latter group of firms had smaller proportions of inside equity ownership than firms acquiring related divested assets, suggesting that an economically significant agency conflict exists in decisions to purchase unrelated divested assets. Purchases of related assets from strong sellers resulted in significant positive changes in shareholder wealth.

5.2 Management Buy-outs

Buy-outs and factor supply

Detailed evidence concerning buy-outs and factor supply is given in Thompson and Wright (1987). As regards capital, interest focuses upon changes in capital structure and the effect on cash flow and performance, the size of managerial equity stakes, the link with performance and the relationships with, and control influenced by, institutions. In respect of labour, the issues concern union recognition, manning levels, renegotiation of labour contracts and employee shareholdings.

The need to increase control of financial resources in order to meet external finance commitments is evidenced by a high incidence of tightening working capital control, either through reducing debtor days (43 per cent of UK buy-outs) or extending creditor days (31 per cent of UK buy-outs) (Wright et al., 1992). About one-third of buy-outs which arose on divestment experienced cash flow problems after the buy-out, with pre-buy-out difficulties caused by central control of cash flow often being replaced by problems relating to the servicing of highly leveraged financial structures (Thompson and Wright, 1987).

Management in UK buy-outs typically obtains a majority of the equity, although in larger transactions this falls to little more than a third. Institutions in UK buy-outs typically have a closer involvement in the running of the business than might be expected from a traditional provider of finance, with the relationship between buy-out team and financier resembling what might be termed a quasi-internal capital market (Wright et al., 1992). Among the control devices most frequently used are monthly financial reports, nomination of directors, equity ratchets (contingent contracts by which management's equity stake could be increased or decreased depending upon whether predetermined performance targets were met) and various rules relating to the need to obtain financiers' approval for certain actions. In the USA, the leveraged buy-out (LBO) associations which effect buy-outs may be argued to perform a more effective monitoring role than conglomerate organizations, with the partners of the LBO firm having an incentive to control the business through their direct equity stake (Jensen, 1989).

Divestment buy-outs may be used as a means of controlling labour and reducing trade union power. Buy-outs may to some extent be considered as an attempt by senior managers to deal with control problems by externalizing, either completely or partially, certain activities. Where the break is complete, the control problem is simply passed on. Where a trading relationship exists, control may be reasserted through a market relationship. The break from the parent created by a buy-out may enable conditions of employment to be renegotiated to reflect the specific market conditions of that entity, which may not have been possible under the central bargaining arrangements of the parent (Frank, 1984). The extent of direct market control may be limited because of the generally low level of trading between buy-out and former parent (Wright et al., 1991b). But the managers who buy out the company now have the incentive and the ability to make changes. Managers may take a more indirect route to changing employment conditions by deciding to close certain activities and obtain supplies from contractors or from former employees who establish themselves in a self-employed capacity. Although there are incidences of this kind of action, there is as yet no systematic evidence of its extent. In any case, evidence suggests that industrial relations improve substantially after a buy-out from what were generally satisfactory conditions beforehand (Thompson and Wright, 1987; Wright et al., 1991b). There may be some selection bias in the sense that firms without satisfactory industrial relations may have difficulty in obtaining funding. However, the extent of industrial relations disputes in buy-outs is not out of line with levels found for non-buy-outs of similar sizes and industries. The ending of trade union recognition was unusual, and does not demonstrate a major and explicit attempt by management to remove unions. Rather, there appears to be general acceptance of the need for a formal communication structure for all employees, which trade unions can provide.

A controversial performance issue concerns the impact of buy-outs on employment. In the USA, where the highly leveraged deals might be expected to create redundancy, the evidence is unclear. The prevalence of buy-outs of whole companies means that in most studies the samples comprise few divestments. While there are some indications that following an initial shake-out employment subsequently rises, more robust studies (e.g. Jensen, 1989; Kaplan, 1989) indicate either that employment falls after allowing for industry factors or that buy-outs re-hire at a lower rate than comparable non-buy-outs (Smith, 1990). Yago (1989) reports that LBO firms have a slightly lower incidence of closure than other manufacturing plants.

In the UK, where most buy-outs arise on divestment, there appears to have been a marked reduction in the proportion of buy-outs shedding labour, which is related to a shift away from distress sales to management and to the general recovery in profitability in the mid to late 1980s. In an early survey by Wright and Coyne (1985), 44 per cent of firms reduced employment whereas in a later study carried out on buy-outs completed in the mid-1980s this had fallen to 25 per cent (Wright et al., 1991b). With respect to the amount of job losses, the later survey also shows an improved position. In the earlier survey, 18 per cent of pre-buy-out jobs were found to have been lost on the transfer of ownership, whereas in the later study only 6 per cent of jobs disappeared. The Wright and Coyne survey also found, however, that after buy-out there had been some recovery in employment levels, but that this had not reached the levels prevailing prior to the transfer of ownership. At the time of the later survey, total employment was some 4.5 per cent below pre-buy-outs levels, and 2 per cent above the level immediately after buy-out. The UK firms, being generally smaller than their US counterparts, are less affected by sell-offs of assets. However, when considering comparative employment effects it is important to bear in mind what might have happened in the absence of buy-out. There is some indication in the literature reviewed above that buy-outs occur in relatively weaker sectors. To the extent that this is true, the effects of buying out may be to prevent further adverse changes in employment.

Employee shareholdings may be a means of improving incentives for the wider body of employees and may be associated with changing remuneration contracts to be more performance related. Two particular devices involve the offer of equity purchase at the time of the buy-out and the introduction of stock option schemes. Evidence in the UK suggests that in less than 15 per cent of cases does the wider body of employees participate in equity ownership, amounting on average to only 5 per cent of the equity. In only a tenth of cases are employee stock option schemes likely to be in place (Wright et al., 1992).

Buy-out–former parent trading dependence

It is common to regard the separation between parent and subsidiary which occurs on a buy-out to be immediate and complete. While this is usually the case where the former subsidiary had no trading relationship with its parent, some form of continuing link may exist in other cases. The link may be through trading and /or by means of a retained ownership stake by the former parent.

Where an asymmetry of dependence exists between the parties to a transaction such that the former parent is in a more powerful position, its ability to make the supplier fulfil its contracts and the incentives for the supplier to do so are enhanced. Indeed, as seen above, this reasoning was an important element in the decision to externalize the transaction. In addition, interdependence between the trading partners may be enhanced through collaboration in the design of new products and in the use of long-term contracts.

Bought-out firms may make attempts subsequently to reduce their dependence upon their former parents in order to avoid being squeezed by their more powerful trading partners. While financing institutions may wish to see vendors agreeing to maintain purchases or supplies at a certain level, at least initially, so that the viability of the buy-out is not placed in jeopardy, they may put high pressure on management to reduce dependencies as soon as possible. Evidence strongly suggests that buy-outs attempt to spread their base of trading partners and reduce parental dependence soon after the buy-out has been completed. Buy-outs from non-UK parents are more inclined to reduce their dependence on former parents than is the case for those acquired from domestic parents.

The second element of post-buy-out dependence is where the vendor retains an equity stake. An element of retained ownership may enable the former parent as trading partner to influence post-buy-out behaviour. However, if the stake is so large that the vendor can still effectively block managerial decisions, the incentive for the managers who have under-taken the buy-out may be significantly reduced. In the private sector in the UK, retention of equity stakes is not common, even where trading relationships are to continue. All parties to the transaction have tended to want a complete separation. There may, however, be requirements that the vendor guarantees to maintain a certain level of trading for a specified period of time after the buy-out in order to ensure its viability. Con-versely, there may also be cases where the bought-out company agrees to take a certain level of supplies from the ex-parent in order to protect the latter's interests.

Vendors may be reluctant to leave an equity stake in a buy-out, even though it offers some insurance against having sold the subsidiary too cheaply, as it may be difficult to sell it quickly if the need arises. The retention of such a stake does reduce the need for management to raise outside finance, which would need to be serviced from cash flows. The ability of vendors to liquidate their holding may be much greater in larger transactions than in smaller ones as they more readily meet the require-ments for flotation on a stock market. Indeed, the financing is usually structured with the aim of flotation or sale within a given time period.

In respect of those buy-outs with trading relationships with the vendor, evidence indicates that both product development and customer bases are enhanced by separation from the restrictions imposed by a parent (Wright, 1986), despite the efforts to reduce trading dependence noted above. Moreover, the general state of trading relationships between customers and suppliers is found to improve significantly after buy-out whether or not these relationships are with the former parent.

Management and organizational control

Evidence suggests that about half of buy-outs on divestment made managerial adjustments after the transfer of ownership, roughly in line with buy-outs generally, with changes in the management team, the appointment of new managers and changes in the number of management tiers each occurring in about one-tenth of transactions (Wright et al., 1992). A more detailed study of the short-term changes in accounting control systems following a buy-out provides evidence that the remarriage of ownership and control involved enables more appropriate systems to be introduced, especially at the more stategic level (Jones, 1992). There is also evidence of a perpetuation of standard performance reports, influenced to a great extent by the requirements of financial backers who wish to ensure that buy-outs are effectively controlled in order to meet their finance servicing costs. In addition, there is a weak association between environmental factors and changes to accounting systems after the buy-out. There is a strong influence of managerial choice as to the most appropriate techniques to make best use of the human and capital resources available. There is clear evidence that while management is freed from group constraints, and has the ownership incentive to make improvements, the bonding to meet financial targets is also a key influence on the action it takes. Case study evidence from the USA (Scherer, 1986) shows benefits from the removal of delays and distortions in decision-making and the draining away of resources to other parts of a larger organization.

5.3   LBOs of Whole Firms

We noted earlier the importance of LBOs of whole firms in placing pressure on management to divest where it otherwise may not have done so. Such LBOs may thus, in principle, perform a more effective monitoring and governance role than the Williamsonian head office of a conglomerate organization. Bhagat et al. (1990) show that some 43 per cent of the assets of firms involved in hostile LBOs are sold within a three-year period. In contrast, Kaplan (1991), using a larger sample, shows that 34 per cent of assets are sold within six years after buy-out.

There is, however, considerable debate as to the effectiveness of LBOs as alternatives to conglomerate organizations. Evidence of the initial effects of buy-outs of whole companies, which mainly relates to the USA, has been touched upon already. In addition, important studies by, for example, Smith (1990) show significant improvements in operating profit and reductions in resources tied up in working capital.[7] However, Rappaport (1990) has argued that the LBO is merely a transitory form of organization that is in any case appropriate in only limited circumstances and the effects of which can be produced with the necessity of ownership transfer. There is evidence from both the UK and the USA that a substantial proportion of buy-outs either return to a stock market or are sold to another group (Kaplan, 1991; Wright et al., 1992), which provides some support for the Rappaport hypothesis. However, these changes on average occur several years after the buy-out and may be considered as part of the normal life-cycle of firms. Most buy-outs keep their original ownership form for considerable periods. What is as yet less clear is the extent to which buy-outs do represent a 'better' form of organization in the long term, the relative newness of the phenomenon and their preva-lence, until recently, in buoyant economic conditions hitherto precluding rigorous analysis. There are some indications of problem cases, which may partly be the result of an 'overshoot' in the market (Jensen, 1991) or partly the result of inappropriate forms of what Williamson (1988, 1990) has considered as financing and governance structures resulting from errors in the analysis of the nature of the assets involved in paticular transactions.

6 CONCLUSIONS

This chapter has addressed the limits to internal organization, the con-ditions under which divestment might be expected to occur, to whom a divested entity may be sold and the impact of the divestment decision. Divestment of the parts of a larger group needs to be seen within the context of the wider decision as to the boundaries of the firm. The chapter extends the work of Williamson in that it has analysed the nature of internal versus external organization of production in a dynamic framework. It has directly addressed reasons why the strict M-form structure may not be achievable and has analysed the factors that in-fluence whether externalization of activities previously carried out internally will actually occur and the form that externalization might take. A key element of the analysis is emphasis on the notion that the optimal location of asset ownership is where individuals have the greatest incen-tive to maximize value. Where it is not possible to achieve the appropriate level of incentives inside the firm, divestment may be an appropriate course of action. Not only may divestment be appropriate for peripheral activities, but sale by means of a buy-out may have attractions for the parent where trading relationships exist, especially where an asymmetry of dependence exists in the relationship such that the former subsidiary is more dependent on the former parent than vice versa. The kind of devices embodied in buy-outs in particular have been argued to provide incentive and control attributes that may not be achievable in an M-form organization.

NOTES

1 Other perspectives may influence the divestment decision. The first addresses the relation between phases of the product life-cycle and the appropriate extent of vertical integration. Stigler (1951) argued that vertical disintegration might be expected during a market's expansionary phase through the spinning-

off of decreasing cost activities so as to allow for maximum scale economies. However, Silver (1984) argues that as a market develops, the incremental learning economies associated with the introduction of new ideas will eventually disappear and increasing familiarity with an innovation is likely to lower information-transmission costs. These changes tend to encourage market transactions and hence vertical disintegration through divestment. Harrigan (1980) has pointed to the importance of divesting product areas in the declining phase of their life-cycle, and Pashley and Philippatos (1990) show that divestment may occur at any one of four life-cycle stages but that its nature varies according to the stage. Pashley and Philippatos (1990) find different patterns of divestiture according to whether a firm was in one of four life-cycle groups: late expansion/early maturity, regenerating maturity, late maturity/early decline and decline. For firms in the late expansion/early maturity stage, divestment was found to be associated with reducing debt from the high levels incurred during expansionary phases. Late maturity/early decline firms were found to use divestment primarily to improve profitability by selling off poorly performing units, and this was also the case for those firms in the regenerating maturity group. For the decline group, divestment was mostly associated with improving liquidity. The second approach concerns the existence of economies of scale and scope and the effects on them of technical change. Failure to achieve economies of scale and scope through internal growth or merger activity, coupled with the impact of technical change, is likely to influence the appropriate configuration of assets for the firm. Technical change may both erode natural monopoly type arguments for economies of scale and modify views about joint production of certain goods and services (Chiplin, 1986; Hunt and Lynk, 1990). Hence, divestment may become economically efficient, leading to production by two or more separate entities. The question of separation may, however, involve a trade-off between some loss in economies of scale and scope and greater benefits from a new organizational structure.

2 For example, many recent diversification moves in the financial services sector appear to have been unsuccessful and to have been made without adequate examination of the prospective financial returns, yet few executives seem to have lost their jobs (see Wright et al., 1991a, for discussion).

3 Evidence suggests that there is a strong correlation between entry and exit (see Geroski and Schwalbach, 1991).

4 For example, several financial institutions moved into estate agency, which requires much greater entrepreneurial skills and performance-related remuneration than traditional banking and insurance activities.

5 It may be argued that such devices as those involved in management and leveraged buy-outs can be introduced for the firm as a whole to improve control without necessarily incurring divestment or indeed a buy-out (e.g. Rappaport, 1990). While undoubtedly this is true in appropriate cases it is not a generally applicable argument. For example, the kind of cultural and other organizational complexities described earlier may still suggest divestment, particularly where it is difficult to design management remuneration schemes at the divisional level that avoid free-riding.

6 Although monitoring is still required in a franchise relationship to ensure that the contract is adhered to, the residual claimant status of the franchisee reduces the coverage of such monitoring so that a single monitor may be able to oversee a larger number of outlets than may be possible under conventional internalization. A key issue in franchising, however, is ensuring that the franchisee maintains quality rather than free-rides on the reputation of others. By giving the franchisor the right of termination where quality is deficient and bonding the franchisee by causing him to make specific investments which must be sold on termination, franchising arrangements aim to deal with these monitoring issues. Evidence suggests that franchising is more likely to be positively associated with geographically dispersed units, where repeat customer business is prevalent and information incentives concerning the value of brand name capital is present (Brickley and Dark, 1987).

7 See also Palepu (1990) for a review of US studies.

REFERENCES

Alchian, A. and Demsetz, H. (1972) Production, information costs and economic organization. *American Economic Review*, 62, 777–95.

Arrow, K. (1974) *The Limits of Organization*. New York: Norton.

Baker, G. and Wruck, K. (1989) Organisational changes and value creation in LBOs: the case of O M Scott & Sons. *Journal of Financial Economics*, 25, 163–190.

Bhagat, S., Shleifer, A. and Vishny, R. (1990) Hostile takeovers in the 1980s: the return to corporate specialisation. *Brookings Papers on Economic Activity, Microeconomics*, 1990, 1–73.

Brickley, J. and Dark, F. (1987) The choice of organisational form: the case of franchising. *Journal of Financial Economics*, 18, 401–20.

Bruce, A. et al. (1990) Incentives for senior managers: share options and buy-outs. In G. Jenkins and M. Poole (eds), *New Forms of Ownership*. London: Routledge.

Buckley, P. and Casson, M. (1976) *The Future of the Multinational Company*. London: Macmillan.

Cable, J. (1977) A search theory of diversifying merger. *Recherches Economique de Louvain*, 43, 225–43.

Cable, J. (1988) Organisational form and economic performance. In S. Thompson and M. Wright (eds), *Internal Organisation, Efficiency and Profit*. Oxford: Philip Allan.

Chiplin, B. (1986) Information technology. In R. L. Carter et al. (eds), *Personal Financial Markets*. Oxford: Philip Allan.

Coase, R. (1937) The nature of the firm. *Economica*, 4, 386–405.

Demsetz, H. (1988) The theory of the firm revisited. In *Ownership, Control and the Firm*. Oxford: Blackwell.

Denning, K. (1988) Spin-offs, and sales of assets: an examination of security returns and divestment motivations. *Accounting and Business Research*, no. 73, 32–42.

Donaldson, G. (1990) Voluntary restructuring: the case of General Mills. *Journal of Financial Economics*, 27, 117–42.

Dugger, W. (1983) The transactions cost analysis of Oliver E. Williamson: a new synthesis? *Journal of Economic Issues*, 17, 95–114.

Duhaime, I. and Grant, J. (1984) Factors influencing divestment decision making: evidence from a field study. *Strategic Management Journal*, 5, 301–18.

Duhaime, I. and Baird, I. (1987) The role of business unit size in divestment decision-making. *Journal of Management*, 13, 95–114.

Fama, E. and Jensen, M. (1983) The separation of ownership and control. *Journal of Law and Economics*, 26, 301–26.

Frank, R. (1984) Are workers paid their marginal products? *American Economic Review*, 74, 549–71.

Geroski, P. and Schwalbach, J. (1991) *Entry and Market Contestability*. Oxford: Blackwell.

Harrigan, K. (1980) *Strategies for Declining Businesses*. Lexington, MA: Lexington Books.

Harrigan, K. and Porter, M. (1983) End-game strategies for declining businesses. *Harvard Business Review*, July/August, 61, 111–20.

Hill, C. W. L. (1984) Organisational structure, the development of the firm and business behaviour. In J. Pickering and T. Cockerill (eds), *The Economic Management of the Firm*. Oxford: Philip Allan.

Hill, C. W. L. (1985) Internal organisation and enterprise performance: some UK evidence. *Managerial and Decision Economics*, 6, 210–16.

Hunt, L. C. and Lynk, E. L. (1990) Divestiture of telecommunications in the UK: a time series analysis. *Oxford Bulletin of Economics and Statistics*, 52, 229–52.

Hunt, L. C. et al. (1987) *Acquisitions – the Human Factor*. London: London Business School.

Jain, P. (1985) The effects of voluntary sell-off announcements on shareholder wealth. *Journal of Finance*, 40, 209–24.

Jensen, M. C. (1986) Agency costs of free cash flow, corporate finance and takeovers. *American Economic Review*, May, 326–9.

Jensen, M. C. (1989) Eclipse of the public corporation. *Harvard Business Review*, 67, 61–74.

Jensen, M. C. (1991) Corporate control and the politics of finance. *Journal of Applied Corporate Finance*, 4(2), 13–33.

Jensen, M. C. and Murphy, K. (1990) CEO incentives – it's not how much you pay, but how. *Harvard Business Review*, May/June, 138–49.

Johnson, G. (1988) Rethinking incrementalism. *Strategic Management Journal*, 9, 75–91.

Jones, C. S. (1985) An empirical investigation of the role of management accounting systems following takeover or merger. *Accounting, Organisations and Society*, 10, 177–200.

Jones, C. S. (1992) Management buy-outs and accounting control systems. *Accounting, Organisations and Society*, 17(1), 151–68.

Kaplan, S. (1989) The effects of management buy-outs on operating performance and value. *Journal of Financial Economics*, 24, 217–54.

Kaplan, S. (1991) The staying power of LBOs. *Journal of Financial Economics*, 29, 287–314.

Lye, S. and Silbertson, A. (1981) The sale of subsidiaries between company groups. *Oxford Economic Bulletin*, 43, 257–72.

Marris, R. and Mueller, D. C. (1980) The corporation, competition, and the invisible hand. *Journal of Economic Literature*, 18, 32–63.

Miller, D. (1982) Evolution and revolution: a quantum view of structural change in organisations. *Journal of Management Studies*, 19, 131–52.

Montgomery, C. et al. (1984) Divestiture, market valuation and strategy. *Academy of Management Journal*, 27, 830–40.

Mueller, D. C. (1972) A life-cycle theory of the firm. *Journal of Industrial Economics*, 20, 199–219.

Ouchi, W. G. (1980) Markets, bureaucracies and clans. *Administrative Science Quarterly*, 25, 129–41.

Palepu, K. (1990) Consequences of LBOs. *Journal of Financial Economics*, 27(1), 247–62.

Pashley, M. and Philippatos, G. (1990) Voluntary divestitures and corporate life-cycle: some empirical evidence. *Applied Economics*, 22, 1181–96.

Porter, M. (1987) From competitive advantage to corporate strategy. *Harvard Business Review*, 65, 43–59.

Prahalad, C. and Hamel, G. (1990) The core competence of the corporation. *Harvard Business Review*, May/June, 79–91.

Rappaport, A. (1990) The staying power of the public corporation. *Harvard Business Review*, 68, 96–104.

Ravenscraft, D. and Scherer, F. M. (1986) *Mergers, Sell-offs and Economic Efficiency*. Washington, DC: Brookings Institute.

Scherer, F. M. (1986) Mergers, sell-offs and managerial behavior. In L. G. Thomas (ed.), *The Economics of Strategic Planning*. Lexington, MA: Heath.

Scherer, F. M. and Ross, D. (1990) *Industrial Market Structure and Performance*, 3rd edn. Boston: Houghton Mifflin.

Sicherman, N. and Pettway, R. (1987) Acquisition of divested assets and shareholder wealth. *Journal of Finance*, 42, 1261–74.

Shleifer, A. and Vishny, R. (1989) Management entrenchment: the case of manager specific investment. *Journal of Financial Economics*, 25(1), 123–40.

Silver, M. (1984) *The Economics and Scope of Firms.* Oxford: Basil Blackwell.

Smith, A. (1990) Corporate ownership, structure and performance: the case of MBOs. *Journal of Financial Economics*, 27(1), 143–64.

Starkey, K., Thompson, S. and Wright, M. (1991) Flexibility, markets, hierarchies. *British Journal of Management*, 2(3), 165–76.

Stigler, G. (1951) The division of labor is limited by the extent of the market. *Journal of Political Economy*, 59, 189–200.

Teece, D. (1980) Economies of scope and the scope of the enterprise. *Journal of Economic Behavior and Organization*, 1, 223–48.

Teece, D. (1983) Technological and organisational factors in the theory of the multinational enterprise. In M. Casson (ed.), *The Growth of International Business*. London: George Allen and Unwin.

Teece, D., Pisano, G. and Shuen, A. (1990) Firm capabilities, resources and the concept of strategy. CCC Working Paper No. 90–8.

Thompson, S. and Stephen, F. (1988) Internal organisation and investment. In S. Thompson and M. Wright (eds), *Internal Organisation, Efficiency and Profit*. Oxford: Philip Allan.

Thompson, S. and Wright, M. (1987) Markets to hierarchies and back again: the implications of management buy-outs for factor supply. *Journal of Economic Studies*, 14(3), 1–23.

Thompson, S. and Wright, M. (eds) (1988) *Internal Organisation, Efficiency and Profit*. Oxford: Philip Allan.

Thompson, S. and Wright, M. (1991) UK management buy-outs: debt, equity and agency cost implications. *Managerial and Decision Economics*, 12(1), 15–26.

Vickers, J. and Yarrow, G. (1988) *Privatization: an Economic Analysis.* Cambridge, MA: MIT Press.

Williamson, O. E. and Bhargava, N. (1972) Assessing and classifying the internal structure and control apparatus of the modern corporation. In K. G. Cowling (ed.), *Market Structure and Corporate Behaviour*. London: Gray-Mills.

Williamson, O. E. (1975) *Markets and Hierarchies: Analysis and Antitrust Implications*. New York: Free Press.

Williamson, O. E. (1979) Transaction cost economics: the governance of contractual relations. *Journal of Law and Economics*, 22, 233–62.

Williamson, O. E. (1985) *The Economic Institutions of Capitalism: Firms, Markets and Relational Contracting*. New York: Free Press.

Williamson, O. E. (1986) *Economic Organisation: Firms, Markets and Policy Control*. Brighton: Wheatsheaf Books.

Williamson, O. E. (1987) *Anti-trust Economics: Mergers, Contracting and Strategic Behavior*. Oxford: Basil Blackwell.

Williamson, O. E. (1988) Corporate finance and corporate governance.

Journal of Finance, 43, 567–92.

Williamson, O. E. (1990) Mergers, acquisitions and leveraged buy-outs: an efficiency assessment. In L. A. Bebchuk (ed.), *Corporate Law and Economic Analysis*. Cambridge: Cambridge University Press.

Willman, P. (1982) Opportunism in labor contracting: an application of the organisational failures framework. *Journal of Economic Behavior and Organizattion*, 3, 83–98.

Wright, M. and Coyne, J. (1985) *Management Buy-outs*. Beckenham: Croom-Helm.

Wright, M. (1986) The make–buy decision and managing markets: the case of management buy-outs. *Journal of Management Studies*, 23, 434–53.

Wright, M. (1988) Redrawing the boundaries of the firm. In S. Thompson and M. Wright (eds), *Internal Organisation, Efficiency and Profit*. Oxford: Philip Allan.

Wright, M. and Thompson, S. (1992) Divestments and sell-offs. In P. Newman et al. (eds), *The New Palgrave Dictionary of Money and Finance*. London: Macmillan.

Wright, M., Thompson, S., Chiplin, B. and Robbie, K. (1991b) *Buy-ins and Buy-outs: New Strategies in Corporate Management*. London: Graham & Trotman.

Wright, M., Thompson, S. and Robbie, K. (1992) Venture capital and management-led leveraged buy-outs: European evidence. *Journal of Business Venturing*, 7, 47–72.

Wright, M., Ennew, C. and Wong, P. (1991a) Deregulation, strategic change and divestment in the financial services sector. *National Westminster Bank Review*, November, 51–64.

Yago, G. (1989) Leveraged buy-outs in focus: empirical findings and policy issues. Senate Revenue and Taxation Committee State of California, 7 April.

11

Markets, False Hierarchies and the Role of Asset Specificity

NEIL M. KAY

1 INTRODUCTION

Transaction cost economics, or the markets and hierarchies approach, has developed in recent years as a comparative institutional framework for analysing a large number of issues in industrial organization. The development of Coase's early work in this area was largely due to Oliver Williamson, whose approach is represented in three texts. The initial statement, *Markets and Hierarchies* (1975; henceforth MH) extended Coase's insights into areas such as internal labour markets, vertical integration, conglomerates, and the economics of internal organization. The most recent work, *Economic Institutions of Capitalism* (1985; henceforth EIC) has further developed transaction cost economics. *Economic Organisation* (1986; henceforth EO) is a set of essays selected from Williamson's work in recent years. Here I regard EIC as a definitive statement of his approach to economics, with both of the other works developing the analysis in different areas.

Williamson has made a major contribution in this area and this is acknowledged here. His work has stimulated a great deal of recent and current research activity on the strategy and structure of the modern enterprise. However, I argue below that there are critical problems in Williamson's version of transaction cost economics. It is argued that transaction cost economics as represented in his approach has defects that may critically inhibit his objective of developing transaction cost economics.

In section 2 Williamson's transaction cost approach is briefly described; section 3 looks at difficulties arising from the contractual foundations of Williamson's framework, and then conceptual limitations and implications are analysed in section 4. In section 5, I look at Williamson's analysis of the strategy and structure of the modern corporation.

2 THE TRANSACTION COST APPROACH

The foundations of Williamson's approach are simple and build on three concepts: bounded rationality (cognitive and language limits on individuals' abilities to process and act on information), asset specificity (specialization of assets with respect to use or users), and opportunism (self-interest seeking with guile). If bounded rationality, asset specificity and opportunism coexist together in any transactional situation, the effective operation of the market mechanism may be impeded. However, according to Williamson, if any of the three conditions is absent, then the market mechanism will still operate effectively.

First, if bounded rationality does not exist, all future contingencies may be anticipated and included in contractual agreements. Unbounded rationality excludes the possibility of surprises not recognized in the contract, and so all problems may be dealt with in advance. Contract may settle problems arising from opportunism or asset specificity. Second, if asset specificity is absent, then bounded rationality and opportunism can be dealt with relatively simply. If assets can be easily switched between alternatives, then mistakes can be easily corrected and opportunism does not have major consequences. Finally, if opportunism is not a problem then asset specificity and bounded rationality do not seriously impede the working of the market mechanism. If transactions are conducted by honest individuals, promises to resolve future unexpected problems and surprises in a mutually fair and equitable manner should be sufficient to maintain an effective market mechanism (EIC, pp. 30–2).

Consequently, if any one of these conditions – bounded rationality, asset specificity, opportunism – is absent in a given situation, contract can deal with resource allocation problems efficaciously. This would appear to constitute a strong defence of the market mechanism as a resource-allocating device. However, Williamson argues that situations in which all of these conditions are present are commonly observed in economic behaviour. In such cases the market imperative is replaced by a broader imperative to: '*Organize transactions so as to economize on bounded rationality while simultaneously safeguarding them against the hazards of opportunism*' (EIC, p. 32, italics in original).

This sets the context for subsequent comparative analysis of alternative governance structures for the allocation of resources. For any specific transaction there exists in principle at least a wide range of potential forms of economic organization within which it can be conducted, ranging from centralized control to market exchange with mixed or hybrid modes in between. The problem then reduces to which institutional form is the most efficient with respect to conducting the respective transaction.

It is recognized that all forms of economic organization may involve information problems if all these conditions of bounded rationality, asset specificity and opportunism are present. For example, market transactions may involve bargaining and monitoring costs, which constitute transaction costs. It may be more efficient to internalize the activity and reduce transaction costs by using internal monitors who may be better informed than external assessors and auditors, and who may have available a more immediate direct range of rewards and penalties than would be possible in market transactions. Consequently, internal organization of the transaction may be more efficient than market solutions to the extent it reduces bounded rationality problems and curbs opportunism. Therefore, the existence of transaction costs may encourage expansion of corporate boundaries and the substitution of market exchange possibilities.

Such internalization is also likely to involve costs. Replacing markets with hierarchies is likely to lead to impairment of incentives (EIC, pp. 131–62). Markets involve what Williamson calls high-powered incentives, such as profits and losses. These incentives may be dulled or eliminated inside the firm. Promises to act responsibly made by internal actors are not costlessly enforceable. Internal management may be softer on inefficiency than is the impersonal world of the market. Williamson argues that efficiency criteria will tend to encourage the development and maintenance of the least-cost alternative in respective cases.

These are the basic foundations of Williamson's version of transaction cost economics. In the next three sections I shall discuss difficulties with Williamson's approach, beginning with the transactional nature of hierarchy in his framework.

3 TRANSACTION AND HIERARCHY IN WILLIAMSON'S APPROACH

'In the beginning there were markets' (EIC, p. 87). Williamson starts from this perspective to analyse the problem of individuals and institutions, 'designing governance structures related to their contracting needs'. Only when transaction costs derived from the problems discussed above create pressures for internalization do circumstances arise in which the transaction might be removed from the market place (EIC, p. 87). Thus, 'one of the attractive attributes of the transaction-cost approach is that it reduces, essentially, to a study of contracting' (EO, p. 97). This interpretation is carried to the extent of analysing hierarchy in contractual terms: 'if one or a few agents are responsible for negotiating all contracts, the contractual hierarchy is great. If instead each agent negotiates each interface separately, the contractual hierarchy is weak' (EIC, p. 221).

While Williamson concedes that hierarchy may also be analysed in decision-making terms, he uses the contractual analysis of hierarchy in most of his work.

A difficulty with using *contracting* as a basic building block for the analysis of hierarchy is that it extends exchange-based perspectives for analysis of economic organization from external markets into internal organization. For our purposes this leads to two major problems: inconsistencies in the interpretation of transaction and a distorted view of hierarchy. I shall look first at the analysis of the concept of transaction.

Williamson does not define transaction in either MH or EIC. However, he does refer to John R. Commons's argument that the transaction should be regarded as the basic unit of analysis, though what Commons considered a transaction is not clear (MH, pp. 3, 254; EIC, pp. 3, 6). Williamson does define transaction in EO, but this definition is split into two parts. The two parts are not necessarily mutually consistent with each other:

> The costs of running the economic system to which Arrow refers can be usefully thought of in contractual terms. Each feasible mode of conducting relations between technologically-separable entities can be examined with respect to the *ex ante* costs of negotiating and writing, as well as the *ex post* costs of executing, policing, and when disputes arise, remedying the (explicit or implicit) contract that joins them.
>
> A transaction may thus be said to occur when a good or service is transferred across a technologically-separable interface. One stage of processing or assembly activity terminates and another begins. (EO, p. 139)

Arrow's costs of running the economic system are transaction costs (EO, p. 136), and the first concept of transaction introduced in the first paragraph above is a contractual or exchange-based interpretation. This version of transaction costs is consistent with Commons's definition: '*actual* transactions occur, of course, between those who actually exchange products. The *potential* transactions are those which *may* or *may not* occur, since the parties are on the market and ready to exchange but do not' (Commons, 1968, p. 65, italics in original).

The second definition of transaction as transference across a technologically separable interface is a quite different interpretation of transaction. We can illustrate this with examples, and I start with the simple Robinson Crusoe type example.

Crusoe needs to have farming tools made to help him cultivate crops. Tool manufacture and crop cultivation are obviously technologically separable activities. Transference of tools from the fabrication stage to use in cultivation is therefore a transaction according to Williamson's second definition.

Crusoe's stay on the island passes through three stages. During the first stage he makes all his own tools and farms his own crops. In the second stage Man Friday arrives, and Crusoe instructs him to make tools to assist Crusoe in his farming. At the start of the third stage, Man Friday rebels and refuses to work unless Crusoe teaches him to read. In the third stage Man Friday gets English lessons and Crusoe gets tools. The three stages can be described as representing autonomy, authority and exchange respectively. In each stage transactions in the sense of transference (tools) across technologically separable interfaces (from manufacture to use in agriculture) takes place. However, only in the third stage is there any hint of Williamson's first definition of transaction as a contract-based phenomenon.

To take a second example, suppose we have three farmers whose farms are administered by professional farm managers. The three farmers share property rights in the use of a tractor. We assume that the only contracts that need concern us here are the employment contracts for the respective farm managers and the terms and conditions under which each farmer can use the tractor.

The farmers turn out to be rampantly opportunistic, however, and the tractor contract proves highly expensive to negotiate, police and enforce. One farmer decides to buy out the other two; the net effect is the switching of farm ownership and farm managers' employment contracts to the farmer and the tearing up of the tractor cooperative agreement. The tractor is physically allocated to farms in much the same fashion as before, but there are no longer any contracts specifying conditions under which such allocation takes place.

The net effect in the case of the tractor contract is therefore the *elimination* of the transaction in the contractual sense and the *preservation* of the transaction in the physical transference sense. As in the first two stages of the Robinson Crusoe example, the transference interpretation of transaction need not involve contracts. Unfortunately, situations of this type are common. Mergers to reduce transaction costs involved in licensing, joint ventures and vertical relationships may be designed to eliminate the transaction in the contractual sense, but to maintain it in the physical sense. It may be the case that some of these may be analysable in internal market terms, such as transfer pricing, but to assume that they will be inevitably managed in such terms is to reduce the markets and hierarchies issue to external markets versus internal markets. In practice, autonomy and authority (fiat) may represent more common solutions to both external markets and internal markets.

Williamson usually invokes the contractual interpretation of transaction. This distorts subsequent analysis. Both external markets and hierarchies are treated as exchange-based systems characterized by opportunistic contracting parties. This is first developed in MH, in which the transaction costs of external markets and internal markets in labour, capital and intermediate products are compared. The idea of the firm as hierarchically organized is in fact attended to when the multi-divisional form is analysed in chapter 8 of MH but here the comparative basis of the analysis is limited to alternative hierarchies (U-form and M-form). Therefore the comparative foundation of Williamson's analysis is essentially internal markets versus external markets, or hierarchy versus hierarchy in the case of the M-form analysis, not market versus hierarchy. Even hierarchy is reduced to a question of markets when Williamson argues that the superior efficiency of the M-form is based on its ability to create an internal capital market. Thus, MH is really about markets, not markets and hierarchies, and consistent with this, EIC analyses hierarchy itself in contractual, exchange-based, terms (p. 221).

Williamson (1992) has argued that the Crusoe and tractor examples above are confused, but does not satisfactorily explain the sources of apparent confusion. If it is still felt necessary to demonstrate further that the physical and contractual definitions of transaction given by Williamson are different, pick up a pen and stick it in your pocket. You have conducted a transaction in the physical transference sense, but not in the contractual sense.

Thus, the view in this chapter is that Williamson's markets and hierarchies approach may be more appropriately described as involving false hierarchies. The training of economists naturally emphasizes prices, markets and exchange. However, using these perspectives in an analysis of hierarchy leads to the misconception that hierarchical relations may be adequately dealt with in exchange-based terms. This results in the misspecification of organizational relations discussed above.

Williamson (1992) argues against this characterization of his hierarchies as 'false' by pointing out that he identifies fiat as a distinguishing feature of hierarchies. However, the essential point here is that in looking at the efficiency of organizational relations, Williamson focuses on only one narrow form of human action – exchange. This may be sufficient in dealing with the market place, but not with complex organizations.

4   SOME CONCEPTUAL LIMITATIONS OF WILLIAMSON'S TRANSACTION COST ECONOMICS

As discussed in section 2, Williamson's approach is built on the proposition that the existence of non-trivial transactional problems requires the simultaneous presence of the three phenomena: bounded rationality, opportunism and asset specificity (EIC, pp. 30–2). Williamson's treatment of opportunism and bounded rationality is questioned here. In particular, opportunism is too limited a motivational basis for adequate treatment of economic activity, while asset specificity is neither necessary nor sufficient for problems of economic coordination to arise, even in the presence of bounded rationality and opportunism.

Williamson's use of opportunism extends the distorting bias of his contract-based framework into the motivational arena. For example, in the case of Japan, Williamson argues that 'the hazards of trading are less severe in Japan than in the United States because of cultural and institutional checks on opportunism' (EIC, p. 122). This interpretation of Japanese economic behaviour implicitly assumes, first, that individual opportunism is the definitive behavioural characteristic and, second, that the role of culture is only as a constraint in this process. This contrasts with Patrick and Rosovsky's (1976) observation of Japan's emphasis on 'group rather than individual, on cooperation and conciliation aimed at harmony, on national rather than personal welfare' (p. 53). Williamson does appear to note such effects in his description of the Japanese system (EIC, pp. 120–3), but he still argues that 'the same principles that inform make or buy decisions in the United States and in other Western countries also apply in Japan' (EIC, p. 122), with opportunism retaining its central role.

Williamson links 'obedience' with utopian literature and social engineering, and argues that it involves the unjustified assumption of 'mechanistic orderliness' (EIC, pp. 49–50). However, the case of Japan appears more consistent with description of group harmony rather than individualistic self-interest, suggesting that obedience would be a more reasonable behavioural building block than would be opportunism. This is inconsistent with Williamson's analysis, since replacing opportunism with obedience would make Williamson's whole transaction cost framework inapplicable in view of his treatment of opportunism as a necessary condition for transactional problems to exist.

Further, despite Williamson's claims, the existence of asset specificity is not precondition for the existence of transactional problems. Indeed, there is evidence that asset specificity can actually maintain market exchanges. For example, Blois (1972) analysed cases where dependence of suppliers on dominant customers allowed the buyers to use their buying power to extract special arrangements and concessions from suppliers. The resulting economies bore comparison to those achievable under vertical integration.[1] Blois also found evidence that some areas, such as high technology, exhibited transactional protection for producers if their firm-specific expertise created mutual dependency between themselves and customers (pp. 165–6). The idea that *mutual* dependency created by specificity of transactional relationship may help create orderly and well-behaved markets is obvious and reasonable. Joint specificity of transactional relationships may reduce or eliminate opportunistic behaviour. If both parties are sitting in the same rowing boat, a threat to pull out the bung will be unconvincing.

Asset specificity may indeed create transaction costs,[2] but the actual effects may be more complex than in Williamson's analysis. However, more serious is the neglect of recognition that transactional difficulties may be generated by asset *non*-specificity rather than specificity of transactional relations.

This issue arises because Williamson (EIC, pp. 31–2) argues that if asset specificity is absent in contractual situations, then discrete market contracting is unproblematic, given markets with full contestability,[3] due to ease of entry and exit between markets resulting from asset non-specificity. However, this neglects the fact that *non*-specificity of assets may generate property right problems. If knowledge leaks from firm A to firm B, and firm B uses this knowledge to bolster its competitive position, these problems for firm A are a consequence of the fact that this asset is *not* specialized by use or user. Patenting may be ineffective in protecting the intellectual property rights of an innovation. Consequently the licensing contract may potentially incur significant transaction costs for the licensor due to the *absence* of asset specificity expressed as appropriability problems. Non-specificity of assets expressed as property right problems may create rather than resolve transactional problems.[4] A common solution for such appropriability problems is internalization of the transaction, as research in the area of multinational enterprise has demonstrated. I shall discuss this further in the next section.

Opportunism and asset specificity may indeed influence transactions but Williamson's interpretation is likely to lead to problems of analysis. In section 5 I shall consider how such problems arise in Williamson's analysis of three major issues: conglomerate diversification, the evolution of the M-form and the rationale for multinational enterprise.

5 THE CONGLOMERATE, THE M-FORM AND MULTINATIONAL ENTERPRISE

In this section we look at the application of Williamson's approach to three particular microeconomic phenomena, the conglomerate, the M-form structure and multinational enterprise respectively.

5.1 Conglomerates and Transaction Costs

Williamson (MH, pp. 155–75; EO, pp. 154–8) provides an explanation for conglomerate existence based on failures in the external capital market. It is offered as an explanation for the apparently paradoxical existence of firms diversifying into unrelated product-markets with no synergy benefits.

Williamson argues that the conglomerate may create a miniature capital market that mitigates transaction costs in the external capital market. First, *internalization* of the capital market might improve information available to financial monitors and give more direct control over incentives to reward or penalize performance. These advantages were discussed in section 2. Second, *divisionalization* encourages profit centre creation in an M-form (multi-division) organization. Divisionalized profit centres allow the creation of an internal capital market within the firm. Divisions can be monitored in terms of the uniform, measurable standard of profit, facilitating divisional comparability with concomitant incentive effects. Therefore, Williamson's explanation for the conglomerate is that the combination of internalization and divisionalization advantages allows it to operate as a miniature capital market with enhanced efficiency compared to the external capital market.

In fact, this explanation is quite satisfactory when used to explain why the conglomerate may be more efficient than the external capital market, and, consistent with the general internal markets versus external markets perspective of MH, this is how the argument is presented. The argument that capital market failure may encourage internalization and divisionalization is convincing. The difficulties arise when this is offered as an explanation for the conglomerate. In this context, Williamson is not making the appropriate comparisons. Rather than explain why the conglomerate may be more efficient than the external capital market, transaction cost economics has to explain why it may be more efficient than the specialized firm. By Williamson's own chosen criterion of efficiency, conglomerateness must have some advantage over specialization that favours this strategy over the specialized firm. However, the internalization/divisionalization argument contains no such advantage and this can be illustrated with a simple example.

Assume a grouping of nine specialized firms: three petroleum, three drug and three aerospace. The firms have each been facing external capital market problems. The firms may be characterized in terms of managerial teams deploying existing resources inefficiently and being unable to attract new funds, consistent with Williamson's analysis of the growth of specialized U-form (unitary form) firms (MH, pp. 133–6). We assume for simplicity that the firms are identical in terms of size, profitability and all other relevant financial characteristics.

Creation of a miniature capital market could mitigate these effects, and Williamson's internalization/divisionalization argument helps explain how this might be achieved. Merger or take-over are obvious devices by which the necessary restructuring could be achieved. Critically, however, Williamson's internalization/divisionalization explanation does not favour conglomerate internalization over internalization through specialization. Assume that one internalization strategy would involve the merger and divisionalization of the three aerospace firms, while a second internalization strategy would involve an amalgamation of three firms, one from each sector. Both strategies result in internal capital markets with independent profit centres drawn around the former corporate boundaries. Both the specialized aerospace-based strategy and the conglomerate strategy could exploit internal capital market advantages. In these respects they are able to extract similar advantages.

This superficial neutrality of effect disappears when the specialization/ conglomerate choice is examined more closely. There are transaction cost reasons why the specialized strategy is in fact superior to the conglomerate when analysed in internalization/divisionalization terms.

First, in the specialized aerospace strategy, similar markets and technologies between divisions facilitate profit comparison between divisions and may improve the profit centre operation of the internal capital market, as Williamson in fact recognizes (EIC, p. 140). It is easier in practice to infer efficiency from performance within sectors than it is between sectors, and the specialized strategy scores over the conglomerate in this respect.

Second, complementary markets or technologies between divisions resulting from specialization may facilitate internal trades or deals to exploit complementarities. Quasi-independent profit centres may be monitored by senior management mediators, reducing internal transaction costs of such deals compared to external strategies such as leasing, joint venture or licensing. The same transaction cost arguments that justify the internal capital market can also justify other internal markets involving inter-divisional resource transfers, exploiting potential market or technological linkages. Consequently, Williamson's internalization/ divisionalization argument explains specialization, not conglomerateness. There is no efficiency gain that could be generated by the conglomerate in Williamson's analysis that could not also be generated by specialized strategies, and specialization may also provide further efficiency gains over conglomerates. Thus, Williamson does not explain why conglomerateness should evolve in preference to specialization.

The conglomerate is in fact an unusual strategy even among large firms (Channon, 1973; Rumelt, 1974; Dyas and Thanheiser, 1976). Even highly diversified firms typically exploit economics of scope in the form of market and technological linkages between product-markets. Williamson's analysis does not provide sound reasons for conglomerateness rather then specialization in the cases where it does evolve. One such explanation is developed separately in Kay (1982, 1984) in terms of potential costs of specialization: specialization may provide vulnerability to external surprises in turbulent, dynamic environments, and the conglomerate strategy is one possible option in such circumstances. Management moves away from market and technological linkages, because it wishes to avoid dependence on a given set of market and technological opportunities.

Williamson (1992) does not really defend his internal capital market explanation for the conglomerate, but instead brings in auxiliary explanations based on history and anti-trust legislation without really attending to the points I make here. His 1992 reply tends to misquote me by replacing 'alternative corporate strategies' with 'horizontal or vertical mergers'. As I make clear above, alternative corporate strategies include related diversification and it should also include internal expansion.

Beyond dealing with the special case of conglomerate, Williamson neglects diversification. There is no treatment of related diversification in Williamson's analysis, a curious neglect considering such diversification is far more common than is the conglomerate. Most diversification exploits some economies of scope, such as shared marketing or technology.

In fact, Williamson's theory does not extend to the multi-product firm in general, not just the specific case of the conglomerate in particular. By definition, related diversification internalizes assets that may be *shared* in different product markets, the opposite of Williamson's explanation of internalization, which depends entirely on asset specificity, or *specialized* use or user. If Williamson's theory is applicable, then its dependence on asset specificity suggests that it can only be with respect to the special case of the single product firm and vertical market relations.

Williamson (1992) claims that I ignore the need for a comparative institutional approach when in fact arguments such as the above not only depend on a comparative institutional approach but are predicated on the incompleteness of Williamson's own identification of institutional alternatives.

5.2 The Evolution of the M-form Corporation

The development of the M-form corporation has been a major issue in Williamson's transaction cost economics (MH, pp. 132–54; EO, pp. 65–77; EIC, pp. 279–94). However, there are problems with Williamson's M-form explanation. According to Williamson, U-form firms (those organized by functional specialism) eventually encounter control loss and strategy formulating problems as they grow, with diversification exacerbating these problems. Centralization of decisions results in significant organization costs in these circumstances. Information has to pass through various levels before it is acted on, leading to control loss problems. Short-run problems may dominate at the expense of long-run strategic decision-making. Attempts to alleviate decision-making/capacity problems at this level by involving functional heads in strategic decision-making may distort the profit orientation of the corporation by facilitating pursuit of functional goals. Consequently there may be major organizational costs as a result of the growth and expansion of the U-form.

Williamson argues that the M-form, divisionalized corporation alleviates these problems. Divisional responsibility for inter-functional operating problems means that control loss problems are reduced. Top management now has the opportunity to concentrate on long-run strategic problems, and the creation of divisional profit centres may provide the building blocks of an internal capital market.

In themselves these arguments are quite reasonable. The problems arise when they are applied by Williamson to the origins of the M-form. He argues that, with corporate expansion, 'the ability of the management (in the U-form) to handle the volume and complexity of the demands placed upon it becomes strained and even collapsed . . . the U-form laboured under a communication overload while the pursuit of sub-goals by the functional parts (sales, engineering, production) was partly a manifestation of opportunism' (EIC, pp. 280–1). Consequently, 'faced with the need either to retrench or to develop a new set of internal contracting relationships, organizational innovators devised the M-form structure' (EIC, p. 295).

Williamson is therefore arguing that U-form expansion leads to crisis and the subsequent development of the M-form to solve critical problems: 'eventually the U-form structure defeats itself and results in the M-form structure to solve these problems' (Williamson, 1971, p. 350). The evolution of the M-form is interpreted as an evolutionary process involving natural selection criteria (EIC, p. 296), and indeed Williamson interprets transaction cost reasoning in general as depending on the competitive process to select the most efficient forms over the long run through natural selection (EIC, pp. 22–3, including footnote).

These arguments are simply not sustainable. To argue that the U-form somehow 'defeats itself' through over-expansion, resulting in system collapse and the M-form innovation to deal with crises, is to reverse natural selection. In natural selection it would be the superior M-form innovation that would compete out the (inferior) U-form, rather than U-form collapse generating the M-form innovation. Natural selection selects from what actually exists. It does not generate new forms but selects out inferior forms as a consequence of competition from superior forms *after* the appearance of the latter, not before such appearance.

As Alchian (1950) points out, 'even in a world of stupid men there would still be profits' (p. 213) and the same could be said of economies populated by U-form corporations before the introduction of the M-form innovation. However, this leaves us with an unanswered question: if the M-form was not around to create systemic crises among the U-form population, what did cause such problems?

My main point here is that natural selection arguments have not been applied properly by Williamson. But it may be helpful to consider how natural selection arguments should be developed here. Before the M-form innovation, the only competition U-forms faced was from other U-forms or smaller more specialized firms.

If a given U-form is losing out in competition against other U-forms the selection process should lead to appropriate switches in the U-form population in favour of winners. If the U-form is losing out in competition against smaller, more specialized firms (which may or may not be U-forms), the selection mechanism should impose limits to growth in favour of the smaller, more specialized firms. This is what one would expect with Williamson's weak-form selection mechanisms in which the relatively fitter survive (EIC, p. 23, footnote).

Dow (1987) points out that there are problems associated with Williamson's use of selection concepts in the context of diffusion of organization forms, but as we have been there are severe problems when he attempts to explain the development of organization forms. In Elster's (1983, pp. 49–50) terms, evolutionary or natural selection theories are classified as providing functional explanation and are contrasted with theories of intentional explanation. Theories of intentional explanation involve either optimizing or satisficing decision-making criteria if rationality is assumed (Elster, 1983, p. 69). Williamson's approach is atypical of modern microeconomics in that it does not draw upon either decision-making process. Consequently there are no criteria by which intentional explanation could be pursued and Williamson (1992) does not take the opportunity to clarify this point. Such a neglect could be justified if functionalist natural selection explanations were reasonable, but as we have seen they are not properly applied. Consequently there are no acceptable theoretical foundations on which to base Williamson's argument that efficient forms will evolve.[5]

Williamson (1992) challenges me to produce a rival hypothesis to the M-form hypothesis. In fact refutation of the M-form hypothesis as stated by Williamson would be an event as earth shattering as the discovery that large industrial enterprises would be more efficiently run by four chief executives rather than one. To argue against the M-form hypothesis as stated would effectively imply that virtually all chief executives of large corporations are making the same fundamental error. It is beyond reasonable doubt that 'the organization and operation of the large enterprise along the lines of the M-form [more closely approximates] neoclassical profit maximization than does the U-form organizational alternative' (MH, p. 150).

The *ex post* revelation of the preference of large enterprises for the M-form does not in itself legitimate any of the specific claims Williamson makes as to *why* the M-form is more efficient in this context. Nor – and this is the point I am dealing with here – does it legitimate Williamson's explanation as to *why* the M-form evolved in the first place. This reinforces the point that Williamson does not have any theory of decision-making or selection.

5.3   The Nature of Multinational Enterprise

Williamson argues that his transaction cost framework can be extended to multinational enterprise and analysis of choice of technological transfer mechanisms, such as licensing (market) versus multinationalism (hierarchy).

In this context, Williamson again argues that asset specificity represents a necessary consideration for internalization and replacement of markets with corporate hierarchy.

> A more harmonious and efficient exchange relation – better disclosure, easier reconciliation of differences, more complete cross-cultural adaptation, more effective team organization and reconfiguration – predictably results from the substitution of an internal governance relation for bilateral trading under those recurrent trading circumstances where assets, of which complex technology transfer is an example, have a highly specific character. (EIC, p. 294)

However, Contractor's (1981) licensing strategies do not support this argument. Indeed Contractor's study provides evidence that *specificity* of transactional relationships may encourage the market exchange option of licensing in some cases, consistent with the discussion in section 4. Contractor reviewed the empirical evidence and argued that 'the disadvantages of licensing arising from licensee independence are often removed if the licensee is kept dependent on trademarks, foreign market access, technical improvements, etc.' (p. 78). Contractor also points out that licensing may be adopted if *non*-specificity of assets in the form of appropriability problems is not likely to be problematic, either because of product life-cycle characteristics or because rapid technological change means that potential competitors would find it difficult to catch up in any case.

Consistent with Contractor's analysis of licensing, it is *non*-specificity of assets and problems of protection of property rights that are frequently identified as a major transactional problem stimulating the adoption of multinational strategies through internalization (Casson, 1974; Dunning, 1981; Caves, 1982). Coombs et al. (1987, p. 161) emphasize the role of internalization in preventing information leakages to other firms, while Casson (1987) argues that 'because knowledge has the characteristics of a "public good" the firm with privileged knowledge tends to become multinational' (p. 29). These transactional non-specificities are not treated by Williamson and indeed pure public goods may be thought of as polar opposite cases from asset specificity.

In fact, the technological transfer is likely to be influenced by the specific forms in which both asset specificity and asset non-specificity are expressed. Galbraith and Kay (1986) argue that analysis of multinational enterprise must build on recognition that technology transfer processes a bundle of specific and non-specific assets and that this interpretation is based on empirical and theoretical studies of multinational enterprise neglected by Williamson. Unfortunately, Williamson's interpretation of transaction cost economics does not provide an adequate basis for analysing the evolution of the modern multinational enterprise, reflecting his general neglect of the links between technology, transaction costs and institutional arrangements, as noted by Englander (1988).

Williamson (1992) argues that all of the multinational practices referred to above are areas to which transaction cost economics can be brought to bear, and on this we agree. However, the *Williamson* version is not applicable here, because it builds on asset *specificity*, as his 1985 text makes clear.

6   CONCLUSION

Coase's original (1937) article stated that 'the distinguishing mark of the firm is the supersession of the price mechanism' (p. 389) and emphasizes that this means the replacement of outside market relationships with internal organization and hierarchy. 'If a workman moves from department Y to department X, he does not go because of a change in relative prices, but because he is ordered to do so' (Coase, 1937, p. 387).

By contrast, Williamson represents the comparative institutional foundations of transaction cost economics as internal markets versus external markets, whether capital markets, labour markets or intermediate product markets. However, to represent the firm as a series of internal markets is to create a distorted representation of hierarchy. Internal markets and internal prices certainly exist in practice, but a market, internal or external, is a very rare and unusual device. As with Coase's workman moving from department to department under instruction, methods of allocating resources other than market exchange are likely to be important within hierarchies.

The development of false hierarchies in Williamson's framework leads to problems of analysis. His explanations for the evolution of the conglomerate and the M-form corporation are unsustainable even within the frame of reference of his own approach, given the flaws in his capital market failure and natural selection arguments. His treatment of multinational enterprise is inconsistent with the theoretical and empirical analysis, which indicates that non-specificity rather than specificity of assets determines the choice of hierarchy over market arrangements in this area.

It is also important to note that, contrary to Williamson's (1992) suggestion, I nowhere suggest that transaction cost economics is underdeveloped in property right respects. In section 5.3 I clearly identify property rights as a major transactional problem contributing to the creation of multinational enterprise through drives towards internalization. I refer to Casson's work and my own with Galbraith in this context, all of which may be regarded as transaction cost writings. I consequently reject Williamson's (1992) inference that I believe that property right weaknesses are beyond the reach of transaction cost reasoning – they are in fact central to analysis of transaction costs. As Williamson effectively concedes in his discussion of table 1.1 from page 31 of *Economic Institutions of Capitalism*, it is his own approach that neglects property right issues. Crucially, Williamson cannot admit property right issues (and asset *non*-specificity) without negating the central tenet of this approach: the existence of asset specificity as a necessary indication for transactional problems. Thus my criticisms here are directed at Williamson's approach and remain unmodified.

One way of moving forward from these problems is provided by Coase's original article: 'within the firm . . . in place of the complicated market structure with exchange transactions is substituted the entrepreneur-coordinator, who directs production. It is clear that these are alternative methods of coordinating production' (Coase, 1937, p. 388). If the term transaction was used for exchange relationships, and comparative institutional economics was seen as being concerned with costs of coordination, not just transaction costs however defined, then this would be sympathetic to Coase's original analysis, as well as resolving the ambiguities over the word 'transaction' as used by Williamson.[6] Coordination cost economics would then genuinely encompass costs of organization as well as exchange costs, and help set a truly general framework for a comparative institutional research programme.

Coordination cost economics in the Coasean tradition would extend beyond opportunism and asset specificity and include perspectives from the behaviour and property rights literatures. As far as the problems discussed here are concerned, some alternative approaches have been suggested.

Williamson (1992) has argued that the above arguments ignore recent developments in transaction cost economics, but it must be emphasized that Williamson's approach builds on the central concepts of contract and asset specificity, which he presents as *the* transaction cost approach, set out in the *Economic Institutions of Capitalism*.

In a recently published work, Williamson retains this narrow interpretation of transaction cost economics:

> The principal dimensions on which transaction cost economics presently lies for purposes of describing transactions are (1) the frequency with which they recur, (2) the degree and type of uncertainty to which they are subject, and (3) the condition of asset specificity. *Although all are important, many of the refutable implications of transaction cost economics turn presently on this last.* (Williamson, 1988, cited in Williamson, 1992, italics added)

The 1988 article is a straightforward restatement of 'the transaction cost approach' as set out in the *Economic Institutions of Capitalism*.

It is not possible to have it both ways. Williamson (1992) cannot claim that I have ignored the fact that the 'purported shortcomings of transaction cost economics already have been or can be dealt with by an extension or refinement of transaction cost reasoning' *and* still retain the narrow version of transaction cost economics as presented in his 1985 work and restated in his 1988 article above. In support of this it is pertinent that the 1988 article is largely concerned with vertical integration; as I point out above, extending his approach beyond intermediate product markets to deal with the diversified firm and the multinational enterprise is difficult or even impossible.

If Williamson now is restating *the* transaction cost economics approach to encompass cases involving asset *non*-specificity, such as appropriability problems and economies of scope, then this is one route forward. Indeed, unless he does so, his approach is limited by default to the special case of vertical integration and the single-product firm, and, as we have seen, is problematic even in this context. However, this is quite different from the narrow frame of what he has defined as transaction cost economics up to and including the 1988 article. To reinterpret his own phrase, it would mean a fundamental transformation in what he would define as transaction cost economics. It would negate the essential and fundamental role accorded to asset *specificity* in his work to date, including the 1988 article.

Williamson's acceptance of this point would facilitate the integration of his work with the wider body of coordination cost economics. Rejection of it would restrict his contribution to special and limit cases.

NOTES

This chapter is based on ideas in a paper 'Markets, false hierarchies and the evolution of the modern corporation', which appeared in the *Journal of Economic Behaviour and Organisation* (JEBO) in 1992. A response by Williamson (1992) was invited and published in the same issue. At the invitation of the editor a short rejoinder was submitted by myself and my advice to the editor to publish Williamson's response as it stood was based on my assumption that my reply would also be published. However, this reply was not published by the journal. As a matter of academic record this is now available as a discussion paper of the Economics Department, University of Strathclyde. No changes of substance or presentation have been made since no editorial criticisms relating to any specific points discussed in the reply were made by JEBO. The following builds on the original JEBO paper by drawing on my reply to Williamson's (1992) defence.

1 Blois notes that frequently the only significant difference between quasi and full vertical integration is that large customers can exercise dominance through buying power while the vertically integrated firm extracts compliance through legal power.
2 Williamson (EIC, p. 104) discusses the empirical literature relevant to his analysis of the role of asset specificity, while Englander (1988) interprets asset specificity as a refined version of Williamson's earlier concept of information impactedness.
3 Contestability theory assumes that asset specificity is insignificant. On this, see Baumol et al. (1982), Baumol (1986) and Williamson's discussion (EIC, p. 31, footnote).
4 Williamson only briefly recognizes the property rights literature in EIC (pp. 27 and 29).
5 In fact, Williamson's analysis of the M-form innovation can be interpreted as Lamarckian rather than Darwinian. Lamarck argued that life climbs a ladder of complexity, motivated by a 'force that tends incessantly to complicate organization', operating through the creative response of organisms to 'felt needs' (Gould, 1982, p. 77). Gould in fact recognizes that human cultural evolution may be interpreted in Lamarckian rather than Darwinian terms (1982, pp. 83–4). However, model organizational evolution in a Lamarckian fashion would require specification of 'creative responses' and 'felt needs', and Williamson does not specify decision criteria for such intentionality in his evolutionary approach. For an approach that does so, see Nelson and Winter (1982).
6 However, this ambiguity is not resolved in Coase's original paper either.

REFERENCES

Alchian, A. (1950) Uncertainty, evolution and economic theory. *Journal of Political Economy*, 58, 211–22.

Baumol, W. J., Panzer, J. and Willig, R. (1982) *Contestable Markets and the Theory of Industrial Structure*. New York: Harcourt Brace Jovanovich.

Baumol, W. J. (1986) Williamson's The economic institutions of capitalism. *Rank Journal of Economics*, 17, 279–86.

Blois, K. (1972) Vertical quasi-integration. *Journal of Industrial Economics*, 20, 253–72.

Casson, M. (1979) *Alternatives to the Multinational Enterprise*. London: Macmillan.

Casson, M. (1987) *The Firm and the Market*. Oxford: Blackwell.

Caves, R. E. (1982) *Multinational Enterprise and Economic Analysis*. Cambridge: Cambridge University Press.

Channon, D. F. (1973) *The Strategy and Structure of British Enterprise*. Boston: Harvard University Press.

Coase, R. H. (1937) The nature of the firm. *Economica*, 4, 386–405.

Commons, J. R. (1968) *Legal Foundations of Capitalism*. Madison: University of Wisconsin Press.

Contractor, F. (1981) The role of licensing in international strategy. *Columbia Journal of World Business*, 16, 73–83.

Coombs, R., Saviotti, P. and Walsh, V. (1987) *Economics and Technological Change*. London: Macmillan.

Dow, G. K. (1987) The function of authority in transaction cost economics. *Journal of Economic Behavior and Organization*, 8, 13–38.

Dunning, J. H. (1981) *International Production and the Multinational Enterprise*. London: Allen & Unwin.

Dyas, G. R. and Thanheiser, H. T. (1976) *The Emerging European Enterprise: Strategy and Structure in French and German Industry*. London: Macmillan.

Elster, J. (1983) *Explaining Technical Change*. Cambridge: Cambridge University Press.

Englander, E. J. (1988) Technology and Oliver Williamson's transaction cost economics. *Journal of Economic Behavior and Organization*, 10, 339–53.

Galbraith, C. and Kay, N. M. (1986) Towards a theory of multinational enterprise. *Journal of Economic Behavior and Organization*, 7, 1–19.

Gould, S. J. (1982) *The Panda's Thumb: More Reflections in Natural History*. New York: Norton.

Kay, N. M. (1982) *The Evolving Firm: Strategy and Structure in Industrial Organisation*. London: Macmillan.

Kay, N. M. (1984) *The Emerging Firm: Knowledge, Ignorance and Surprise in Economic Organisation*. London: Macmillan.

Kay, N. M. (1992) Markets, false hierarchies and the evolution of the modern corporation. *Journal of Economic Behavior and Organization*, 17, 315–33.

Kuran, T. (1988) The tenacious past: theories of personal and collective conservatism. *Journal of Economic Behavior and Organization*, 10, 143–71.

Nelson, R. R. and Winter, S. G. (1982) *An Evolutionary Theory of Economic Change*. Cambridge: Cambridge University Press.

Patrick, H. and Rosovsky, H. (1976) *Asia's New Giant: How the Japanese Economy Works*. Washington, DC: Brookings Institution.

Rumelt, R. P. (1974) *Strategy, Structure and Economic Performance*. Boston: Harvard University Press.

Williamson, O. E. (1971) Managerial discretion, organization form, and the multi-division hypothesis. In R. Marris and A. Wood (eds), *The Corporate Economy*. Cambridge, MA: Harvard University Press.

Williamson, O. E. (1975) *Markets and Hierarchies: Analysis and Antitrust Implications*. New York: Free Press.

Williamson, O. E. (1985) *The Economic Institutions of Capitalism: Firms, Markets, Relational Contracting*. New York: Free Press.

Williamson, O. E. (1986) *Economic Organisation: Firms, Markets and Policy Control*. Brighton: Wheatsheaf.

Williamson, O. E. (1988) The logic of economic organization. *Journal of Law, Economics, and Organization*, 4, 65–93.

Williamson, O. E. (1992) Markets, hierarchies and the modern corporation: an unfolding perspective. *Journal of Economic Behavior and Organization*, 17, 335–52.

12

On Transactions (Costs) and Markets and (as) Hierarchies

CHRISTOS PITELIS

1 INTRODUCTION

The analysis of the emergence, evolution, failures and interrelationships of social, economic and political institutions and organizations for the coordination of human activity is currently transforming social science in general and economics in particular. Theories on the nature and role of market exchange, the firm (including the transnational), the state, but also of networks, the family, religion, customs, norms, traditions and ideology, are currently the central focus of a thriving literature, broadly referred to here as new institutionalism. Instrumental in the emergence of this new research programme has been Ronald Coase, the winner of the 1991 Nobel Prize in economics, whose two papers on 'the nature of the firm' (1937) and 'the problem of social cost' (1960) have, for the first time in mainstream economics, provided an answer as to the very reason for the existence of the firm and the law, in the two papers respectively. In both cases, the answer was market transaction costs, namely costs incurred when voluntary exchanges take place exclusively on the basis of relative price changes (the market or price mechanism). In the absence of such market transaction costs, it was claimed, there would be no reason for either the firm or the law.

Coase's 'fundamental insight' has been used and extended particularly by Oliver Williamson (1981) in order to provide an explanation of the emergence of hierarchies (firms) from markets, in particular the 'employment relation', vertical integration and changes in the internal organization of firms, notably the M-form organization and also conglomerate diversification and the transnational corporation. The emergent transaction costs, markets and hierarchies (TCMH) perspective is now the focus of an ongoing debate, complete with critiques and alternative theories.

An aim of this chapter is to establish two related propositions. The first is that from all the institutional-organizational developments mentioned above, it is only the (reason for the) 'employment relation' that has a potentially legitimate claim in explaining or defining the multi-person hierarchy (Coasean firm) from assumed pre-existing markets. All the others already involve hierarchies-firms, so they just represent a change in hierarchical relationships. Second, I wish to establish here that all employment relations are hierarchical (Coasean) firms. Taken together, the two propositions suggest that the fundamental issue addressed and answered by Coase is: why does *the employment relation* emerge from pre-existing non-hierarchical market type relations?

Another aim of this chapter is to assess the adequacy of Coase's answer. My main claim is that Coase's approach remains fully at the level of exchange, assuming pre-existing production as well as pre-existing market exchanges of this production. However, exchange involves the existence of what is being exchanged, i.e. 'goods'. It is the *production and* (for) *exchange* of these products, I claim, that should be seen as the ultimate reason for the emergence of both the market and the employment relation. That is, it is claimed that production and exchange are inseparable and so are markets and employment relations (Coasean firms). Production and exchange exist for the same fundamental reasons, which are benefits from specialization and the division of labour and (which are only realized through/as) the benefits from trade (exchange). The employment relation helps to enhance such benefits for production-*and* exchange-related reasons, so it cannot be fully explained with an exclusive focus on the exchange side.

The observation of the need to consider production and exchange factors to explain the employment relationship raises the important issue of the agents who bring about the process of change, the related issue of the aims and objectives of these agents, the question of whether the agents' objectives and the existence of Coasean firms can be separated, and the issue of the efficiency or otherwise aspects of the emergent changes. Furthermore, provided that production in general pre-exists production through hierarchies (Coasean firms), it follows that such firms are *historically* specific. Given this, the important question emerges of whether Coasean firms can be fully explained on purely conceptual grounds, i.e. without a full historical analysis of the emergent institutional changes in hand. These issues are raised in section 5, which also concludes this chapter. Section 2 briefly summarizes the Coase–Williamson perspective, with some critiques and alternatives. Section 3 discusses the two propositions raised earlier in this introduction and section 4 tries to explain why there are markets, firms and the employment relation, within a production cum exchange framework.

2 TRANSACTION COSTS, MARKETS AND HIERARCHIES

In Coase's classic 1937 paper, the existence of the firm is explained in terms of market failure due to 'marketing costs', i.e. the 'costs of using the price mechanism' (p. 403). The logic is simple. If markets pre-exist (or are a legitimate starting point) then resource allocation could take place efficiently through the price mechanism, i.e. changes in relative prices. However, in real life, resources are also allocated through an authority-entrepreneur, who directs other factors of production. This direction or authority separates firms from markets, which instead are based on voluntary exchanges. In this sense, firms and markets are different means of resource allocation, the very existence of the former representing the supersession of the latter. Given pre-existing markets, firms should not exist in the absence of some sort of market failure. The very existence of firms implies the existence of such market failure, the reason for which is the existence of 'marketing costs'. Some such costs are saved when an authority-entrepreneur is 'allowed' to direct resources. In this sense firms are efficient solutions to market failures. The 'marketing costs' mentioned by Coase are costs of discovering the relevant prices and negotiating and concluding separate contracts for each exchange-transaction. Contracting costs in particular are reduced if a long-term contract, in which one factor of production agrees to obey the directions of another factor of production, replaces short-term contracting between those two factors.

Following a long period of indifference to Coase's paper, the past twenty years in particular have experienced a dramatic surge of interest in his analysis, and have led to many extensions, critiques and alternatives. First, the term 'marketing costs' has now been replaced by the term 'transaction costs' and these costs have been argued to include costs of measurement, and policing and enforcing agreements (see Eggertson, 1991, for a survey). Second, the reasons for the existence of high transaction costs *vis-à-vis* firms have been analysed by, in particular, Williamson (1975, 1986). In brief, Williamson believes that the coexistence of bounded rationality (limits to obtaining and processing information), opportunism (self-interest seeking with guile) and asset specificity (the existence of dedicated assets, which implies sunk costs) will tend to generate organization failures in general and market failures in particular. The replacement of the *market* by a *hierarchy* (firm) could alleviate such failures. Reasons for this include a presumed emergence of convergent expectations and a feeling of community between firm members, but also that the (threat of the) use of authority can help to attenuate opportunism and stop prolonged bargaining (arising from asset specificity). The problems from bounded rationality are alleviated through the use of adaptive, sequential decision-making.

Coase and Williamson do not claim that firms (hierarchies) eliminate transaction costs. When further supersession of the market does not help to reduce transaction costs incurred by these same transactions being carried out by the market or within another firm, such supersession will simply not occur. Accordingly the boundaries of the firm are *also* defined in the Coase–Williamson perspective. A reason for transaction costs within firms for Williamson is the high-power incentives of market prices, which are blunted or even lost by hierarchies, giving rise to a trade-off between high powered incentives of markets and the adaptability of hierarchies. Once the boundaries of the firm have been defined we also have a reason for the *persistence* of the market, given the assumption of its pre-existence! Finally, the transaction costs, markets and hierarchies framework can be used to explain the vertical integration of firms, changes in the internal organization of firms, such as the M-form organization, conglomerate diversification and the transnational corporation (Williamson, 1981). All these are efficiency enhancing (transaction costs reducing), which provides a revolutionary new insight on industrial and competition policies, traditionally guided by the 'inhospitality tradition', which regards oligopoly as the cause of (structural) market failures, rather than the solution to it.

The revolutionary implications of the TCMH framework, in particular the observation of the self-correcting, efficiency enhancing tendencies of the market system as a whole, for the problem of pervasive 'natural' (transaction costs related) market failure have generated a thriving (and healthy) debate on a multitude of issues relating either to the programme in general or to particular applications of it, primarily Oliver Williamson's. On the general level, for example, concerns have been voiced over: the exact definition of firms, markets and transaction costs; whether transaction costs are operationalizable; their necessity for the existence of firms; the pre-existence of markets assumption; the claims that failure of markets will lead to efficient hierarchies; that such hierarchies will be (Pareto) efficiency enhancing rather than sectional interest enhancing; the role of power considerations in explaining the firm and the relation between transaction costs and (market) power; the view that markets and hierarchies are substitutes rather than complements; the slight treatment given by the TCMH programme to production in general and production costs in particular; and the neoclassical underpinning of the whole approach, in particular its focus on methodological individualism, the rational choice model and comparative statics. Concerning Williamson's specific contributions, criticism has focused primarily on the importance of asset specificity. Much of this criticism is reflected in the contributions to (and indeed has been the motivation of) this volume. Reviews can be found in the Introduction to this volume and in Pitelis (1991), so they will not be given further consideration here. Moreover, the list is indicative but not exhaustive.

Alternatives to the TCMH scenario have also been proposed, albeit largely independently from it. A notable contribution is Alchian and Demsetz (1972). According to them, firms are essentially a market, a nexus of contracts involving no more or less hierarchy than any other (external) market-type relationship. The distinguishing feature of the firm is the existence of a centralized contractual agent in a team production process. Given metering problems associated with team production, a monitor is required to reduce 'shirking' by team members. Giving the right to a residual claimant of any surplus derived from team production ensures that the monitor is being self-monitored. It follows that the firm-like (team) organization can be more productive, if it survives the greater shirking costs it faces (Demsetz, 1988). This analysis has been extended to more general agency problems by Jensen and Meckling (1976).

The perspective adopted by Marglin (1974) is apparently different. For Marglin the reason for the emergence of the 'factory system' from its *historical* predecessor, the putting-out system, was the benefits this transition conferred on its orchestrators (capitalists) in terms of a sub-stitution of capitalists' for workers' control over the production process. In the putting-out system a merchant-manufacturer would put out raw materials to dispersed cottage labour, to be worked up into (part) finished products, usually by the cottagers' own equipment. Then materials would be moved from home to home in batches under the direction of the merchant-manufacturer. In the factory system, on the other hand, workers would agree to work as a team under the merchant-manu-facturer's authority. This involved sacrificing (part of) their control over the production process for a longer-term employment contract in a team production. For Marglin it was this 'sacrifice' (which was involuntary, orchestrated by capitalists and for their exclusive benefit) that gave rise to the factory system.

If we disregard at the moment the agency issue (is the process con-tractual or predatory?) the Williamson and Marglin perspectives agree on one issue: that more hierarchy allows better supervision, thus poten-tially higher productivity of labour, thus *ceteris paribus* profits. This point in recognized by Williamson, who sees merit in Marglin's views, but chooses to focus on the transactional efficiency gains of increased super-vision, rather than on distributional ('rent-seeking') factors, for he considers transaction costs issues more operationizable. On the other hand, following criticisms to the effect that team work need not always result in productivity gains, Demsetz (1988) more recently concedes this point: thus the failure of Alchian and Demsetz (and Jensen and Meckling) to explain why there are firms: 'Abating the costs of shirking helps explain the firm's inner organization but provides no rationale for the firm's existence' (Demsetz, 1988, p. 154).[1]

We can conclude this section by stressing the emerged consensus (see note 1) that *direction* is a key factor explaining the firm in all existing theories. Differences emerge as to the issue of who directs what and what for.

3 MARKETS AS HIERARCHIES

Coase's introductory sentence in his 1937 classic was a plea for clear assumptions by economic theorists. Interestingly, his own assumptions were less than clear. Particularly interesting for the purposes of this section is Coase's definition of the firm. This is in terms of direction or authority of one factor of production (entrepreneur) over another (labour), and it downplays the case of a factor of production *directing* other resources, and/or his or her own work. Accordingly Coase's definition in effect excludes the *unitary* (or single-person) firm (unlike, for example, McNulty, 1984; Demsetz, 1988; Fourie, this volume), and refers almost exclusively to the *employment relation*.[2] In his more recent writings Coase (1991) acknowledges this point and indeed expresses regret for this early exclusive focus of his. In his words, 'I consider that one of the main weaknesses of my article stems from the use of the employer–employee relationship as the archetype of the firm' (p. 64). Although this relationship for Coase approaches the firm relationship, one can only have the full firm relationship when several such contracts are made with people and for things which cooperate with one another. Focus on the employment relationship alone generates a neglect of the 'main activity of a firm, running a business' (p. 65) and it submerges the key idea of the 1937 article, 'the comparison of the costs of coordinating the activities of factors of production within the firm with the costs of bringing about the same result by market transactions or by means of operations undertaken within some other firm' (p. 65).

The claim in this section, however, is that it is indeed only the employment relation that has a potentially legitimate claim in explaining or defining *the existence of multi-person hierarchies (Coasean firms)*. The employment and direction of other factors of production is already there in 'unitary firms' or single-person producers, and involves no authority of one person over another. On the other hand, vertical integration, the M-form, conglomerate diversification and transnational firms, among others, only refer to changes in existing Coasean firms (hierarchies).

Furthermore, I claim here that all employment relationships are forms of Coasean firms.

The case of vertical integration, the M-form, conglomerates and transnationals is straightforward. To the extent that an *existing* Coasean firm integrates vertically, becomes M-form, conglomerate or transnational we do not observe the emergence of a hierarchy (Coasean firm) from a market, but rather the extension of the activities of an existing hierarchy (Coasean firm). The same applies to other types of firms' activities, for example licensing, franchising, joint ventures, subcontracting, strategic alliances, networks of firms, etc. Such strategies by existing Coasean firms cannot be legitimately claimed to supply an explanation of the *emergence* of Coasean firms, by definition. Evidently, depending on one's perspective, definitions and approach, such relationships between Coasean firms can be claimed to be more or less market- or firm-type, a point of contention and debate in the literature, as reflected in this volume.[3] This leaves only the employment relation as a *potentially* legitimate explanatory factor of Coasean firms' existence (for a more detailed discussion of this point see Pitelis, 1991).

Similar considerations apply to Coase's concern with the fact that the employment relationship does not account for the full essence of the firm: running a business, which includes direction of other factors of production than labour, including direction of one's own faculties and activities. The reason for this is that any single producer already directs other than labour factors, including the 'entrepreneur's' own work. What distinguishes Coasean firms from single-person producers (unitary firms) is the existence of an employment relation, or authority of *people* (e.g. capital) over other *people* (labour). Improvements in the direction of other resources etc. due to the emergence of Coasean firms are just that: improvements in existing functions. The *employment relation* is the *differentia specifica* of the Coasean firm.[4] To summarize, my discussion so far has intended to establish the following:

Proposition 1 It is only the employment relation that has a potentially legitimate claim in explaining the *existence* of multi-person hierarchies (Coasean firms) from pre-existing market-type relationships. Interrelationships and integration strategies between (Coasean) firms already involve hierarchies, even when using market-type transactions.

The second proposition I wish to establish here is that any employment relationship is a Coasean firm. This would be a tautology, were it not for the interesting historical example of the putting-out system. As we have seen in the previous section, this was the starting point of Marglin's attempt to explain the factory system and is a point of contention between him and Williamson. Interesting about the putting-out system is that this incorporates relationships between single producers (unitary firms) where these single producers work *for* a merchant-manufacturer (entrepreneur). Accordingly, the putting-out system already involves an *early form* of the employment relation; therefore of a Coasean firm. This point is supported by Landes (1966) among others (see also Pitelis, 1991). Its interest for our purposes here lies in that it shows that Marglin too was not concerned with the emergence of the Coasean (let alone the unitary) firm, but rather with the transition from a Coasean firm (putting-out) to another Coasean firm (factory system). Marglin's problematic, accordingly, is also hierarchy versus hierarchy. This raises the question of what explains the putting-out (or any employment relation) in the first place, a point Marglin does not explicitly address.

From the above discussion there follows:

Proposition 2 All employment relations are hierarchies, i.e. Coasean firms. Market-type relationships between such firms are relations between existing hierarchies. From the point of view of production (the employment relation) the market itself involves hierarchy.

Given propositions 1 and 2, the questions that emerge are: what explains the emergence of the Coasean firm – the employment relation – and to what extent are existing explanations an adequate characterization of the existence and functions of the employment relation (Coasean firms) in particular and firms (including the unitary firm) in general?

4 WHY THE EMPLOYMENT RELATION, THE MARKET AND THE FIRM?

Conceptually we can approach the issue of the emergence of the employment relationship by starting from an imaginatory situation where no employment relation exists. In this scenario individuals can exchange (semi-finished or finished) goods that they have access to with other goods to which others but not them have access and for which they have a need. With the only (and rather uninteresting) exception of *free* goods, the above individuals would be involved in exchanging *produced* goods, i.e. goods in the generation of which human activity – time – has been involved.[5] Hunting, fishing and ironmonging can all qualify as such activities. In this sense, what is involved here is exchange between *single producers*.

Assume now, for the sake of the argument, that five individual producers involved in a particular activity decide that it will be beneficial to them if one of them is allocated the role of a supervisor (an undertaker), which involves the right to direct the activities of the others. They all agree that for their contribution to the production of the goods they will receive a compensation (in terms of the product, if in a barter situation, or money if such is available) and the remainder of the product will be the undertaker's. This arrangement is arrived at given the mutual understanding that access to the residual would motivate the undertaker to work (more) 'diligently', in terms of directing the activities of others and also his or her own. What has emerged now is an employment relationship.

The first question that arises from the discussion so far is why these individuals would want to exchange the status of single producers for that of employer–employee, the employment relation. A possible answer is that they perceive that they will all be better off under the new arrangement, let us say in terms of all of them receiving more output (or money) than in the previous arrangement. If so, one has to explain the source of this increased output. One possibility is through increased productivity of labour, of the employees, the employers or both: the former, for example, because they now have to obey orders (or face disciplinary action) and are subject to better supervision; the latter because of the incentive for a high residual. A second possibility is the better direction and use of raw materials, including the process of their acquisition. This can arise by virtue of the possibility that the employer's organizational abilities were a reason why he or she was originally allocated the task. A third possibility is through reductions in the costs of exchanging (transaction costs). Under the previous arrangement each single producer had to get involved in exchanging his or her product for other needed products. Now this is done by the undertaker, which (under the realistic assumption of possible bulk exchanges) could reduce the costs of exchange substantially. When these possible advantages are realized the original perceptions of the coalition members have also been satisfied, and all are better off than in the previous arrangement.

The description so far is intended to be fully within the logic of the Coasean perspective but an important limitation of this perspective has emerged: its disregard of production costs. The very essence of supervision and hierarchy is intended to lead to labour productivity increases, as both Marglin and Williamson recognize. Accordingly, production costs cannot be usefully separated from the analysis for an exclusive focus on costs of exchange (see also Demsetz, 1988). If we relax the assumption of the four employees-to-be being single producers, but allow for the possibility that they were not producing for exchange before (self-sufficient), then any gains from the employment relationship would be gains from production, while gains from exchange might even be negative, given the larger output to be exchanged! It follows that the Coasean perspective has serious limitations even when examined with its own framework, in that transaction costs need not necessarily be the most important, let alone the exclusive, source of gains emerging from the 'employment relationship'.

To keep within the Coasean perspective we have so far assumed exchange and (thus) markets.[6] However, this begs the question: why exchange, and (thus) why markets? The essence of the Coasean perspective is the existence of costs of exchange (transaction costs), which means that exchange is *not* costless. An alternative to exchange does exist – self-sufficiency. Given this and the costs of exchange, one has to address the question of why exchange and (thus) markets. A related issue is that exchange (and self-sufficiency) presupposes the existence of what is being exchanged (or consumed) – normally produced goods. Whether one wishes to define the producers of such goods as (unitary) firms or not, the issue remains that exchange (or consumption) presupposes production. This again raises the question: why production for exchange rather than production for self-sufficiency (personal consumption)? I believe that this is the starting point from which one can potentially explain (rather than assume) markets, exchange *and* firms (including the employment relationship).

Given that exchange and (thus) production for exchange are costly, an individual's state of nature is self-sufficiency. For this situation to be 'exchanged' for one where positive costs of exchange emerge, there should be some benefits associated with production *for* exchange, sufficient to offset the costs of exchange. Such benefits exist and are those of specialization and the division of labour. As analysed extensively by Adam Smith, Karl Marx and scores of other economists since, specialization and the division of labour allow one to raise oneself from the state of self-sufficiency through the generation of substantial savings in time, in turn expressed as increased productivity and total output. Once self-sufficiency is abandoned, however, production assumes the role of production for exchange, and thus for the market. From the above, it follows that the reason for the existence of the market is the benefits from specialization and the division of labour. It also follows that production (for exchange) and exchange itself become inseparable in that the very realization of the benefits of the division of labour occurs through exchange (markets), while production for the market without exchange forfeits the reason for this production. It follows that the *raison d'être* of exchange, of the market and of production for exchange is the same: *the exploitation of the benefits from the division of labour*. If one is willing to define the single producer who produces for exchange in the market as a (unitary) firm (McNulty, 1984) then the (unitary) firm is also the result of the benefits from division of labour.

It is worth noting that whatever its strengths, or weaknesses, the above argument attempts to explain the existence of markets, exchange (and thus transaction costs) and the (unitary) firm, rather than simply assuming such existence. Moreover, if the argument here is accepted, interesting implications follow for the Coasean perspective. As already suggested, the emergence of the employment relation from the unitary firm can result in production and (perhaps) transaction costs reduction. Given, however, that the origin of production for exchange has been argued to be the division of labour, it follows that any benefits of the employment relationship could also be attributed to furthering the benefits from the division of labour, in the sense of improvements in the existing division and/or in terms of better exploitation of the existing division (through, for example, increased supervision, and/or benefits – if any – from team work, in the workplace).

This is not to deny the possibility of other benefits arising from improved direction of other resources through firm-like coordination, as Coase (1991) observes. However, such benefits need to be shown and in any case do not deny the *possibility* of the *employment relation*, in particular, emerging for its effects on the division of labour.

The theme of the 'division of labour' as a reason for the firm has been given some consideration by Coase (1937) himself. Coase criticized Maurice Dobb's view that the firm is the result of increasing complexity of the division of labour and represents an integrating force in the absence of which the growth of economic differentiation would lead to chaos. For Coase the answer to Dobb is obvious, that the integrating force is there in terms of the price mechanism, so that the question is why there is one integrating mechanism (the entrepreneur) rather than the other (the price mechanism). However, Coase's treatment is too cavalier and (thus) simply inadmissible. He directs attention away from the issue of the division of labour and towards that of chaos in the absence of firms! Even so, an obvious answer to his own question is that the 'entrepreneur' could simply achieve a more 'efficient' exploitation of (the division of) labour than the price mechanism; my argument here.[7]

To summarize, exchange, the market, the unitary firm and the Coasean firm can all be explained in terms of the benefits from the division of labour. The transition from single producers exchanging in markets to the employment relation (historically putting-out first, factory system afterwards), has been because of their efficiency properties (in terms of transaction and/or production costs) in allowing a better exploitation of (the division of) labour (and for the case of the factory system possible benefits from team work). In this sense, the Coasean perspective also fails to explain the reason for the *existence* of the firm (unitary or employment relation). It only contributes towards our understanding of the changes in the organizational forms of firms, arising from possible benefits in terms of transaction costs, of organizing certain activities by one type of organizational form, rather than organizing these same activities by another. Considering the pre-Coasean indifference of economists to these issues, the quantitative importance of transaction costs (estimated to be around 50 per cent of total costs is the US economy; see Eggertson, 1991) and the emergent exciting literature on the economic (and other) institutions of capitalism, this is no small contribution. Similarly, it is not what its proponents want to make from it: a general theory where all institutions emerge for their *transactional efficiency* properties. Even accepting the efficiency logic of the Coasean perspective, as I have done here, production and production costs need to be considered. Demsetz (1988) makes this point too and goes on to conclude that despite its undoubted successes, the Coasean perspective (and the focus on monitoring costs) might also have served as a barrier to the development of new ideas. This is a view I share.

5 FURTHER ISSUES AND CONCLUSIONS

The previous analysis (and the Coasean perspective as a whole) is based on a number of assumptions, currently the subject of much debate, as in part reflected in this volume. One such assumption is that the transition from single producers to the employment relation is a contractual (not predatory) process. This is not a foregone conclusion, given the possibility of one agent (e.g. the undertaker) perceiving benefits for himself or herself from this transition and bribing and/or coercing (on his or her own or with the assistance of the state) the single producers to accept the employment contract. Even when employees-to-be perceive positive gains from accepting this contract (for stability of employment or access to more products or money *vis-à-vis* the previous situation), the issues of *agency* and the post-transition distribution of benefits have to be addressed.

An analysis of these issues also has implications for whether the emergent situation will be Pareto-efficient (in terms of tangible and/or intangible costs and benefits), and for whether one can separate the issue of the *existence* of institutions from the underlying *objectives* of the agents whose actions bring them about. Furthermore, despite the purely conceptual analysis here (and of the Coasean perspective in general) the emergence of the Coasean firm (the employment relation) is an *actual historic* phenomenon. This raises the question of whether a historical analysis would also have something to offer to the debate. As history involves time, such analysis would also be evolutionary and dynamic. Thus, even if all these issues are analysable on purely conceptual grounds, the introduction of history and dynamics might have something to offer to the debate.

The above are some of the issues one has to address for a comprehensive analysis. There are many others too, many of them discussed by the other contributors here. An attempt to address such issues within a conceptual *cum* historical framework by the present author is in Pitelis (1991). There the emergence, evolution and failure of capitalist institutions is explained in terms of the attempt by principals to exploit the fruits from the division of labour (and cooperation and team work). Even without addressing these issues, however, it was seen in this chapter that the Coasean perspective is severely limited in its ability to address the issues of why there are markets, exchange and unitary firms and in its attempt to explain the employment relation from the unitary firm exclusively in terms of costs of exchange.

To summarize and conclude, I have claimed in this chapter that if we accept the Coasean definition of the firm as a multiple person hierarchy, then it is only the employment relation that defines/explains it. All other changes in the organizational forms of firms and/or firm strategies are *hierarchical* to the extent that they already involve Coasean firms. In this sense the Coase–Williamson perspective primarily deals with market exchange, which involves hierarchies. The Coasean firm can be explained conceptually in terms of efficiency gains resulting from transaction and/or production costs reductions, *vis-à-vis* a situation of single producers exchanging in the market. If one goes a step further, however, one should explain the existence of both specializing single producers (production for exchange) and (thus) the market. This I have attempted to do in terms of the benefits from the division of labour, a perspective that also provides an origin from which the Coasean firm can emerge, and the focus on production that is missing from the Coasean perspective.

NOTES

1 Demsetz goes on to observe that the same is true of the TCMH perspective, that firm-like organization involves specialization, continuity of association and direction (thus partly conceding Alchian and Demsetz's other major claim, as Alchian has done before him; see Williamson and Winter, 1991), and that the focus of a more general theory of the firm should be on the economics of acquisition and use of knowledge.
2 Hodgson (this volume) approximates this to the Marxian definition of a capitalist firm.
3 If one focuses on ownership, subcontracting would be seen as a market-type relationship, while focus on control might turn a subcontracting relationship to a firm-type one (see Cowling and Sugden, this volume).

4 Despite his own warning for clear assumptions, Coase has been guilty of excluding single-person producers from his definition of a firm. Whether this is legitimate or not (and the debate on this is still raging), it does have the immediate effect of directing the focus on to the distinctive feature of Coasean firms, namely the employment relation. For this to be avoided, one needs to extend the definition of the firm to encompass the single producer (the unitary firm) and analyse its *raison d'être*, functions and their *differentia specifica* from Coasean firms (see below).

5 Note that many 'free' goods (e.g. water) also require that some time is spent for their acquisition, which renders them products for our purposes here.

6 The very definition of the market is itself not an uncontroversial issue, as reflected in most writings in this volume. Here, I adopt the general definition of any voluntary exchange of products or commodities being a market, as opposed to the price-making market.

7 Note that my argument does not state (or deny the possibility) that a certain development in the social division of labour is required before an improved division of labour can be achieved through the 'entrepreneur', a theme Dobb borrows from Marx (in Putterman, 1986). Hymer (1970) comes nearer to this proposition when, after having observed the importance that both Marx and Marshall attributed to the division of labour, he goes on to regard the 'market' and the 'factory' as 'two different methods of coordinating the division of labour. In the factory entrepreneurs consciously plan and organize cooperation and the relationships are hierarchical and authoritarian, in the market coordination is achieved through a decentralized, unconscious competitive process' (p. 57).

REFERENCES

Alchian, A. and Demsetz, H. (1972) Production, information costs, and economic organization. *American Economic Review*, 62(5), 777–95.

Coase, R. (1937) The nature of the firm. *Economica*, 4, 386–405.

Coase, R. (1960) The problem of social cost. *Journal of Law and Economics*, 3(1), 1–44.

Coase, R. (1991) The nature of the firm: meaning, and The nature of the firm: influence. In O. E. Williamson and S. G. Winter (eds), *The Nature of the Firm: Origins, Evolution and Development*. Oxford: Oxford University Press.

Demsetz, H. (1988) The theory of the firm revisited. In *Ownership, Control and the Firm: the Organization of Economic Activity, Vol. I*. Oxford: Basil Blackwell.

Eggertson, T. (1991) *Economic Behaviour and Institutions*. Cambridge: Cambridge University Press.

Hymer, S. H. (1970) The efficiency (contradictions) of multinational corporations. *American Economic Review, Papers and Proceedings*, 60, 441–8.

Jensen, M. C. and Meckling, W. (1976) Theory of the firm: managerial behaviour, agency costs and ownership structure. *Journal of Financial Economics*, 3, 304–60.

Landes, D. S. (1966) *The Rise of Capitalism*. New York: Macmillan.

McNulty, P. J. (1984) On the nature and theory of economic organization: the role of the firm reconsidered. *History of Political Economy*, 16(2), 233–53.

Marglin, S. (1974) What do bosses do? The origins and functions of hierarchy in capitalist production. *Review of Radical Political Economics*, 6, 60–112.

Pitelis, C. N. (1991) *Market and Non-market Hierarchies*. Oxford: Basil Blackwell.

Putterman, L. (1986) *The Economic Nature of the Firm: a Reader*. Cambridge: Cambridge University Press.

Williamson, O. E. (1975) *Markets and Hierarchies*. New York: Free Press.

Williamson, O. E. (1981) The modern corporation: origins, evolution, attributes. *Journal of Economic Literature*, 19(4), 1537–68.

Williamson, O. E. (1986) *Economic Organisation: Firms, Markets and Policy Control*. Brighton: Wheatsheaf.

Williamson, O. E. and Winter, S. G. (eds) (1991) *The Nature of the Firm: Origins, Evolution and Development*. Oxford: Oxford University Press.

Index